The Social Contract Theorists

D1613313

Critical Essays on the Classics
Series Editor: Steven M. Cahn

The volumes in this new series offer insightful and accessible essays that shed light on the classics of philosophy. Each of the distinguished editors has selected outstanding work in recent scholarship to provide today's readers with a deepened understanding of the most timely issues raised in these important texts.

Descartes's *Meditations*: Critical Essays
   edited by Vere Chappell
Kant's *Groundwork on the Metaphysics of Morals*: Critical Essays
   edited by Paul Guyer
Mill's *On Liberty*: Critical Essays
   edited by Gerald Dworkin
Mill's *Utilitarianism*: Critical Essays
   edited by David Lyons
Plato's *Republic*: Critical Essays
   edited by Richard Kraut
Kant's *Critique of Pure Reason*: Critical Essays
   edited by Patricia Kitcher
The Empiricists: Critical Essays on Locke, Berkeley, and Hume
   edited by Margaret Atherton
Aristotle's *Ethics*: Critical Essays
   edited by Nancy Sherman
The Social Contract Theorists: Critical Essays on Hobbes, Locke, and Rousseau
   edited by Christopher Morris

Forthcoming in the series:

The Rationalists: Critical Essays
   edited by Derk Pereboom

The Social Contract Theorists

Critical Essays on Hobbes, Locke, and Rousseau

Edited by
Christopher W. Morris

ROWMAN & LITTLEFIELD PUBLISHERS, INC.
Lanham • Boulder • New York • Toronto • Oxford

ROWMAN & LITTLEFIELD PUBLISHERS, INC.

Published in the United States of America
by Rowman & Littlefield Publishers, Inc.
A wholly owned subsidary of The Rowman & Littlefield Publishing Group, Inc.
4501 Forbes Boulevard, Suite 200, Lanham, Maryland 20706
www.rowmanlittlefield.com

PO Box 317
Oxford
OX2 9RU, UK

British Library Cataloguing in Publication Information Available

Library of Congress Cataloging-in-Publication Data

The social contract theorists : critical essays on Hobbes, Locke, and
   Rousseau / edited by Christopher W. Morris.
      p.   cm.—(Critical essays on the classics)
   Includes bibliographical references and index.
   ISBN 0-8476-8906-9 (cloth : alk. paper).—ISBN 0-8476-8907-7
(pbk. : alk. paper)
   1. Social contract.   2. Hobbes, Thomas, 1588–1679—Contributions
in political science.   3. Locke, John, 1632–1704—Contributions in
political science.   4. Rousseau, Jean-Jacques, 1712–1778—
Contributions in political science.   I. Morris, Christopher W.
II. Series.
JC336.S526   1998
320′.01′1—dc21   98-37119
                                                         CIP

Printed in the United States of America

♾ ™ The paper used in this publication meets the minimum requirements of
American National Standard for Information Sciences—Permanence of Paper
for Printed Library Materials, ANSI Z39.48–1984.

To the memories of
Jean Hampton
and
Gregory Kavka

Contents

Introduction   ix

Acknowledgments   xiii

1   Hobbes's War of All against All   1
   Gregory S. Kavka

2   Hobbes's "Mortall God": Is There a Fallacy in Hobbes's
   Theory of Sovereignty?   23
   M. M. Goldsmith

3   The Failure of Hobbes's Social Contract Argument   41
   Jean Hampton

4   Hobbes's Social Contract   59
   David Gauthier

5   Why Ought One Obey God? Reflections on Hobbes and
   Locke   73
   David Gauthier

6   Locke's State of Nature   97
   A. John Simmons

7   Political Consent   121
   A. John Simmons

8   Structure, Choice, and Legitimacy: Locke's Theory of the
   State   143
   Joshua Cohen

9   A Possible Explanation of Rousseau's General Will   167
   Patrick Riley

10 Reflections on Rousseau: Autonomy and Democracy   191
        Joshua Cohen

11 Rousseau, the Problem of Sovereignty and the Limits of
        Political Obligation   205
        John Charvet

12 The General Will   219
        Arthur Ripstein

        Bibliography   239

        Authors   243

Introduction

Arguably the three greatest modern political philosophers, Thomas Hobbes (1588–1679), John Locke (1632–1704), and Jean-Jacques Rousseau (1712–1778) inaugurated the modern social contract tradition. Now undergoing a revival, this tradition would have us evaluate political institutions and arrangements in terms of a "social contract": Are these institutions and arrangements ones to which we would agree or to which we have consented? This important idea reappears in the work of many contemporary thinkers as well in the proposals of political actors in different parts of the world.

The classical contractarian thinkers all based their political theories on the idea that humans are, by nature, free and equal. In rejecting the then-influential view that rulers are entitled to govern by virtue of birth, Hobbes, Locke, and Rousseau denied that the powers and privileges of monarchs and aristocrats are natural. All social distinctions and political hierarchies are conventional and in need of justification. If we are by nature free, then what other than agreement could legitimate government?

The powers and privileges of our rulers, on this view, are conditional on their performance of their responsibilities. Rulers need to serve the interests of the governed if they are to elicit their consent. Rulers are, in this sense, the servants of the ruled. The latter cease being *subjects* and become *citizens*. In Rousseau's particular version of this idea, "the people" rule and become "the sovereign"; government is merely their agent.

These influential ideas of original freedom and equality, of basing government on agreement and expecting it to serve the interests of the governed, are developed in different ways in the social contract theories of Hobbes, Locke, and Rousseau. Hobbes and Locke differ especially in their views of the status of the moral law of nature and of our natural rights, the former seeming to deny that natural laws are genuine laws and asserting that our only natural right is essentially a mere liberty to do whatever we think conducive to our survival. Hobbes's apparent skepticism about "right reason" and his view of property rights as conventional set him apart from Locke who premises his contractarian theory on a more traditional understanding of the laws of nature and God's creation. Rousseau's implicit view of morality is harder to ascertain; in his main political work, the *Social Contract*, justice and right are determined by the will of the people, that is, the "general will." From these differing assumptions about justice and our basic rights the classical social contract theorists reach different conclusions about legitimate government and our right to rebel.

Hobbes, Locke, and Rousseau develop their views of government by putting forward conceptions of humans and society. Prior to living in commonwealths or states—in a "state of nature"—we were free and equal. Government is established by a "social contract." An ancient criticism of this account is that it is literally false; we were not in such a state of nature and did not make any such compact. The texts in question are not unambiguous, but it usually seems best to understand these ideas of states of nature and original agreements metaphorically; the point is not so much to explain exactly how our political societies came to be, but to express the conditions for their legitimacy. The social contract is thus to be understood as *hypothetical*: Are our political institutions and arrangements such that we would agree to them? This seems to meet the well-known criticism that the so-called social contract is a fiction, and contemporary contractarian theorists virtually all appeal to hypothetical choice.

There may, however, be some explanatory import to the tales of states of nature and social contracts that should not be overlooked. Even if our particular societies did not result from any actual agreements, and even if we never found ourselves in any pre-political setting, nevertheless our political institutions and arrangements are, in some sense, our creations. They are brought into existence by humans and maintained by our acquiescence and support. Government everywhere depends on the acts of the ruled; it is, in this sense, a creation of convention. The stories of states of nature and social contracts, while not meant to be interpreted literally, seem to express something more than particular conceptions of legitimacy; they remind us that governments and political hierarchies are, in a sense, something we create and sustain.

This collection of critical essays on the classical social contract theorists is intended to assist university students in their studies of the political doctrines of Hobbes, Locke, and Rousseau. My aim has been to assemble a set of excellent articles and extracts from books that would be accessible to students coming to these texts for the first time in courses in philosophy, government, or legal studies. Ideally, these essays will assist students in understanding the texts of these great thinkers as well as stimulate them to reflect on their ideas and their implications for our political societies. My choices, already very difficult given the high quality of much recent scholarship, have also been constrained by these goals. Given limitations of space, I have limited my selections to essays on the political thought of Hobbes, Locke, and Rousseau and especially the contractarian elements thereof. This constraint is especially regrettable in the case of Rousseau whose mature political writings are quite complex and need to be understood in light of many of his other works. I have concentrated on the interpretative works of recent political theorists and not included very much history of ideas. And I have as well limited myself to sources in English, excluding, for instance, some of the excellent French scholarship on Rousseau. Readers will find some guidance for further study in the bibliography.

I am grateful to Daniel Farrell, David Gauthier, Pasquale Pasquino, and John Simmons for useful advice and suggestions, and to Csaba Nyiri for his assistance.

Acknowledgments

"Hobbes's War of All against All" by Gregory Kavka originally appeared in *Ethics* 93 (January 1983), pp. 291–310. Reprinted by permission of the University of Chicago Press.

"Hobbes's 'Mortall God': Is There a Fallacy in Hobbes's Theory of Sovereignty?" by M. M. Goldsmith originally appeared in *History of Political Thought* 1 (1980), pp. 33–44, 49–50. Copyright 1980 Exeter Press. Reprinted by permission of Imprint Academic and the author.

"The Failure of Hobbes's Social Contract Argument" by Jean Hampton originally appeared in her *Hobbes and the Social Contract Tradition* (Cambridge: Cambridge University Press, 1986), pp. 189–190, 197–207. Reprinted by permission of Cambridge University Press.

"Hobbes's Social Contract" by David Gauthier originally appeared in *Nous* 22 (1988), pp. 71–82. Reprinted by permission of Blackwell Publishers and the author.

"Why Ought One Obey God? Reflections on Hobbes and Locke" by David Gauthier originally appeared in the *Canadian Journal of Philosophy* 7, no. 3 (1977), pp. 425–46. Reprinted by permission of the University of Calgary Press and the author.

"Locke's State of Nature" by A. John Simmons originally appeared in *Political Theory* 17, no. 3 (August 1989), pp. 449–70. Copyright 1989 by Sage Publications. Reprinted by permission of Sage Publications and the author.

"Political Consent" by A. John Simmons originally appeared in his *On the Edge of Anarchy: Locke, Consent, and the Limits of Society* (Princeton: Princeton University Press, 1993), pp. 59–79. Reprinted by permission of the publisher and the author.

"Structure, Choice, and Legitimacy: Locke's Theory of the State" by Joshua Cohen originally appeared in *Philosophy & Public Affairs* 15

(Fall 1986), pp. 301–24. Reprinted by permission of Princeton University Press and the author.

"A Possible Explanation of Rousseau's General Will" by Patrick Riley originally appeared in *American Political Science Review* 64, no. 1 (March 1970), 86–97. Reprinted by permission of the American Political Science Association and the author.

"Reflections on Rousseau: Autonomy and Democracy" by Joshua Cohen originally appeared in *Philosophy & Public Affairs* 15 (Summer 1986), pp. 275–88. Reprinted by permission of Princeton University Press and the author.

"Rousseau, the Problem of Sovereignty and the Limits of Political Obligation" by John Charvet originally appeared in *Rousseau and Liberty*, ed. R. Wokler (Manchester: University of Manchester Press, 1995), pp. 139–151. Reprinted by permission of the publisher and the author.

"The General Will" by Arthur Ripstein originally appeared in the *History of Philosophy Quarterly* 9, no. 1 (January 1992), 51–66. Reprinted by permission of North American Philosophical Publications and the author.

1

Hobbes's War of All against All

Gregory S. Kavka

It is surprising that, in the voluminous literature on Hobbes, his most original and important argument rarely receives detailed examination. I refer to the argument, centered in chapter 13 of *Leviathan,* that the state of nature is a state of war of all against all.[1] There seem to be two main reasons why this argument escapes careful scrutiny. Some apparently regard it as so straightforward, and so obviously correct, as to require little analysis or elucidation.[2] Others, who accept the common view that the argument is dependent on Hobbes's egoistic psychology,[3] may doubt it is of substantial interest for those of us not sharing this gloomy view of human nature. I shall argue that these attitudes are not warranted. Hobbes's argument relies only on assumptions about human beings that are much more plausible than psychological egoism, but it is invalid. Yet, despite its invalidity, it makes a significant and lasting contribution to our understanding of certain important problems concerning human interaction.

I shall proceed as follows. After sketching what I take Hobbes's argument to be, . . . a crucial objection to Hobbes's argument is raised, based on the possibility of parties in the state of nature forming defensive coalitions. The most promising line of response to this objection is an argument, in the spirit of Hobbes, that resembles the well-known Hangman Paradox.[4] After developing this argument, I explain why it ultimately fails to vindicate Hobbes. Next, I consider the question of whether Hobbes's argument can be extended to cover relations among groups. This leads to the uncovering of a significant error in his view about how security can best be achieved, and to a reinterpretation of his argument that is more defensible, but less ambitious, than the origi-

1

nal. I conclude by pointing out two important insights that Hobbes's argument contains.

I. The Argument

Hobbes argues that people living in a state of nature, without a common power over them to keep them in awe, are in a state of war of every person against every other. He defines war not in terms of actual fighting, but as a known willingness to fight.[5] So a war of all against all is a state in which each knows that every other is willing to fight him, not one in which each is constantly fighting. But it is more than *just* this, for Hobbes contends that, in the state of war, there is so little security of life and property, that all live in constant fear and productive work is pointless.[6] (And he uses this contention as the ground of a favorable comparison of absolute sovereignty with the state of nature.)[7] But, because people learn by experience, a state of known universal willingness to fight would not long leave its inhabitants feeling so insecure unless acts of violence, coercion, and theft actually occurred with some frequency. Hence, the real conclusion that Hobbes draws (and needs) is that the state of nature is a state of war of all against all, punctuated by frequent violence, in which the participants correctly perceive themselves to be in constant danger. In the sequel, I abbreviate this by the simple phrase "the state of nature is a state of war."

To prove the state of nature is a state of war, Hobbes begins with five assumptions. (The last two are not stated explicitly in the presentation of the argument, but clearly are presupposed.)

1. *Natural equality.* People are roughly equal in their mental and physical powers. Two aspects of this equality are of special importance. First, as relatively brittle organisms, each of us may be destroyed by practically any of the rest of us. The weaker among us are not so weak as to prevent their killing the very strongest using stealth or weight of numbers.[8] Second, the differences in people's natural powers are not so great as to make one an obvious loser to another should they come into conflict.[9]

2. *Conflicting desires.* The desires of different people are frequently at odds. The supply of many commodities is not large enough to satisfy the desires of all who want them. Often two people will want to exclusively possess the same particular object, for example, a spouse or par-

cel of land.[10] Their objectives are bound to clash with those of the people they seek to dominate.

3. *Forward-lookers.* People, if they are at least minimally rational, are concerned with their long-term well-being. They care about the satisfaction of their future, as well as present, desires, and strongly desire to prolong their lives.[12]

4. *Advantage of anticipation.* In cases of conflict between persons, anticipation generally improves one's chances of success. "Anticipation" means either striking first or gathering power so that one will be in a stronger relative position when the battle eventually erupts. Since the primary means of gathering power that Hobbes discusses is conquering others so as to put *their* power at *your* disposal, it is clear that anticipation generally involves the use (or threat) of force.[13]

5. *Limited altruism.* Individuals value their own survival and well-being much more highly than the survival and well-being of others,[14] and act accordingly. Hence, if a person believes a certain course of action best promotes his own security, he is very likely to undertake it, even if it jeopardizes the survival or well-being of others.

From these five quite reasonable and realistic assumptions about human beings, Hobbes constructs an elegant and insightful argument for the state of nature being a state of war. Imagine people in a state of nature, in which there is no common power over them to punish them for robbing, assaulting, and killing one another. As forward-looking creatures vulnerable to death at the hands of virtually any of their fellows, they will rightly be quite concerned about their future security. Lacking a system of law enforcement, they cannot expect potential attackers to be effectively deterred by fear of counterviolence. For due to the rough equality of people's natural powers, and the advantages of striking first, potential attackers will realize that they have a good chance of success.[15] Nor can one expect potential attackers—whose altruism is, at most, limited—to refrain from attack out of concern for their potential victims. Thus, each person in the state of nature must fear violence by others who may attack for any of three reasons.[16] First, glory seekers may attack simply because they enjoy conquest. Second, competitors may attack to remove one as an obstacle to the satisfaction of their desires. Third, and most important, even "moderate" people, who have no desire for power or glory for its own sake and who may have no specific quarrels with one, may, for defensive purposes, engage in *anticipatory* violence against one.[17] That is, they may attack to remove one as a potential future threat to themselves, or to conquer one to use one's power to deter or defend against future attacks by others. In these circumstances, eventual involvement in violent conflict is not unlikely. And since anticipation generally improves one's chances of success, it is the most reasonable course of action for rational persons caring about their future well-being (and caring much less, if at all, about the well-being of others) to follow. In Hobbes's words, "there is no way for any man to secure himself, so reasonable, as anticipation."[18]

At this point, there is a gap in the argument that we must fill in for Hobbes. For a universal state of war to exist, it is not enough that anticipation be the most reasonable strategy, it must also be *believed* so by all who do not wish to fight for other reasons, and most must be aware that others so believe it. For only then is it guaranteed that "the will [of each] to contend by battle is sufficiently known."[19] The gap may be filled in by supposing that each person in the state of nature is aware, perhaps subconsciously and in rudimentary form, of the logic of the argument to this point, and correctly assumes that others will reason similarly and reach the same conclusion about anticipation.[20] And once we establish the existence of a known universal willingness to fight by this general line of argument, the rest of our conclusion—the frequent occurrence of violence and subsequent high degree of insecurity—is assured. For unless nearly all are too inhibited to carry out the hard dictates of reason in these circumstances, there would be much violence undertaken by defensive anticipators, in addition to whatever glory seeking or competitive fighting might take place. Thus, a state of nature is a condition in which the will of each to fight others is known, fighting is not infrequent, and each correctly perceives that his life and well-being are in constant danger. . . .

In *Leviathan,* Hobbes offers a hypothetical contract argument in support of the conclusion that political sovereigns have absolute and unlimited authority over their subjects, and that—save when their survival is immediately at stake—these subjects are morally obligated to obey all of their sovereign's commands. Hobbes, in effect, imagines rational self-interested parties in a state of nature choosing among three alternatives: (1) remaining fully in this state of nature; (2) grouping themselves together under a government with limited, or divided, power and authority; and (3) forming themselves into a civil society, or commonwealth, governed by a sovereign with unlimited power and authority. He contends, however, that the second alternative is basically illusory. Because of the constant danger of factionalism, civil war, and social disintegration in a group governed by a limited or divided power, such a form of social organization does not provide its members with sufficient security to really remove them from the state of nature.[21] Each is forced, in order to protect his long-term well-being, to anticipate—to use force and cunning to increase his power and thus his ability to come out in a favorable position when the inevitable civil strife breaks out into open warfare.[22] The conflict of each person with every other thus goes on, perhaps in muted form, with trickery and deceit being more common forms of aggression than overt violence, but nevertheless leaving each person in a basically insecure, and thus unhappy, position.

Now as the formation of a government with limited or divided powers would not constitute a real escape from the state of nature, the choice of the parties, in Hobbes's hypothetical contract theory, effectively reduces to one between absolute sovereignty and the state of nature. The argument that the state of nature is a state of war of all against all supplies the *crucial* remaining premise that allows Hobbes to conclude that the parties would choose the absolute sovereign as the lesser evil.

This brief synopsis of what Hobbes is up to in *Leviathan,* shows that his main line of argument relies on a very *narrow* conception of what constitutes a civil society, or situation in which a common power exists, and a very *broad* conception of what constitutes a state of nature, or situation in which no common power exists. Hobbes takes the view that only the absolute sovereign is a genuine common power.[23] Otherwise, he could not draw a verdict in favor of absolute sovereignty from the proposition that, in the absence of a common power, people are in a state of war.

III. Is Anticipation Most Reasonable?

The premise concerning mutual awareness by the parties in the state of nature of the reasons for anticipation, which was supplied in Section I to close the gap in Hobbes's argument, is not a very plausible one. But the main weakness in the argument occurs earlier. It is the transition, for which Hobbes offers no explicit justification, from the observation that persons in the state of nature must fear violence from others, to the claim that anticipation is the most reasonable way for such persons to attempt to protect themselves. Despite the fact that this crucial inference has escaped criticism in the literature, it is clear that it is fallacious. For in emphasizing the obvious advantages of anticipatory or preemptive violence, Hobbes utterly ignores three special dangers one would encounter if one were to engage in it. One would expose oneself to the defensive violence of those one attacked. Also, one would identify oneself to other potential anticipators as an especially dangerous person who should be eliminated at the earliest opportunity. Finally, if one succeeds in amassing substantial power by anticipation, one will make oneself a tempting target of glory seekers trying to show how powerful they are. Given these dangers of preemption, it is likely that in some state of nature situations, pursuing a strategy of lying low, staying alert, and fighting only when and if attacked will be more likely to promote one's interests than would anticipation.

Lying low is not, however, the most attractive alternative to anticipation. Joining with others in a defensive coalition promises to yield much greater benefits. Now, of course, Hobbes's own ultimate solution to the state of nature security problem is for the parties to leave the state of nature by forming a defensive coalition of a particular sort, a commonwealth under an absolute sovereign. But less extensive coalition arrangements still within the state of nature are imaginable, the simplest being an exchange, among a number of persons, of promises of mutual aid in case of attack. Admittedly, there are dangers involved in making and adhering to such a pact; one may lose one's life defending the life or property of one's partners. But its advantages—stronger defense against, and deterrence of, attacks on oneself and one's property—would seem to greatly outweigh the disadvantages, and make the coalition strategy clearly preferable to the highly dangerous anticipation strategy.

It is worth noting that to treat the possibility of the formation of defensive coalitions as an objection to Hobbes's argument requires rejecting McNeilly's interpretation of the argument. For, on McNeilly's view, a defense pact enforced by the threat of expelling noncompliers is not an alternative means of defense *within* the state of nature, but instead constitutes the erection of a common power by the parties to the pact, and thus an exit *from* the state of nature. If this were so, the attractiveness of defensive coalitions would not bear on the question of the most rational course of action in the state of nature, or on the conclusion that the state of nature is a state of war. Hobbes, though, clearly would question the correctness of the defensive coalition argument, rather than its relevance. He would, that is, deny that defensive

coalitions consisting of mere promises of aid provide one with any security at all in the state of nature. Such promises are, in his terminology, covenants of mutual trust, and are not binding, essentially because
the party called on to perform first has no assurance that, if he performs, the second party will then do his part.[24] Thus, Hobbes would
argue that it is unreasonable for you to risk your life to save your partner (or his land), since he may well flee when you or your property is
attacked. Further, your coalition partner's awareness that *you* may reason in this way and not keep the pact in the future, makes it even more
likely that he will not come to your aid.

This Hobbesian response is far from convincing, however, as it ignores a crucial motive that rational, forward-looking, self-interested
parties would have for adhering to such a pact. In coming to the aid of
an attacked partner, one encourages others to offer similar aid to one
in the future. While, by not coming to his aid, one would place one's
credibility and one's membership in the coalition in jeopardy. Thus, if
you aid a coalition partner today, you can expect him to aid you tomorrow to increase the chances that you and others will aid him the day
after tomorrow. Or, to put the point in more general terms, the fear of
losing credibility and hence future opportunities for beneficial cooperation can suffice to motivate rational self-interested parties in the state
of nature to keep their agreements with one another. This is a significant point about rational cooperation that Hobbes, to the detriment of
his analysis, overlooked.[25]

IV. Are State of Nature Defense Pacts Viable?

We would not be giving Hobbes's position a full hearing, however, if
we failed to consider a significant objection against founding defensive
coalitions in the state of nature on the parties' hopes or expectations of
benefiting from future cooperation with their partners. This objection
consists of a specific application of a general argument that is interesting in its own right. I shall first outline the general argument, then the
specific version concerning defense pacts in the state of nature. While
these arguments cannot be attributed to Hobbes, the latter is a development of his theme that defense pacts in the state of nature are in
vain because no party can trust his self-interested fellows to come to
his aid.

The general argument concerns the game Prisoner's Dilemma, and applies to all situations having the structure of this game. Prisoner's Dilemma consists of two players, each choosing independently and without knowledge of what the other player is doing, between a cooperative and a noncooperative move. The payoffs to each player are determined by the combination of their moves, and are such that each player orders the four possible outcomes, from most preferred to least preferred, as follows: (1) unilateral noncooperation, (2) mutual cooperation, (3) mutual noncooperation, and (4) unilateral cooperation. The following matrix in which the numerical entries represent payoffs to the players is an instance of Prisoner's Dilemma (see fig. 1).

Prisoner's Dilemma constitutes a "dilemma" in the following sense. Noncooperation seems to be the rational move for each player, for it is a *dominant* move. That is, whatever move the other player makes, one fares better if one does not cooperate than one would have fared if one had cooperated. (This is because unilateral noncooperation is preferred to mutual cooperation, and mutual noncooperation is preferred to unilateral cooperation.) Yes, oddly, if both players make the rational move, they both fare less well than if they had both played the irrational cooperative move. What this seems to show is that, in some situations, there is a genuine divergence between individually rational behavior and collectively rational behavior, and that methods for achieving coordination of parties' behavior in such situations can provide real benefits for all. For present purposes, however, all that we

Player 2 (Payoffs in upper right corner)

	Cooperation	Noncooperation
Cooperation	10 — 10	20 — 0
Noncooperation	0 — 20	5 — 5

Player 1 (Payoffs in lower left corner)

FIG. 1

need assume is that noncooperation is the rational, because dominant, move for an individual to make in a single play of Prisoner's Dilemma.

Suppose now that we *iterate* Prisoner's Dilemma, by supposing the parties know that they will be playing the same game against each other n times in succession. How would this influence the rational strategy of the game? Intuitively, it seems to open up the *possibility* of cooperative moves being rational. For in the iterated game, one has the opportunity to influence one's opponent's moves on later plays by one's moves on earlier plays. Thus, suppose you think playing a cooperative move on a given play will make it more likely your opponent will cooperate on later plays. (Or, to put it somewhat differently, suppose you believe your opponent may "punish" a noncooperative move on your part, by later not cooperating when he otherwise would have cooperated.) Then it may be rational for you to make a cooperative move even though it is dominated on the play in question. And it seems that cooperation *can* make later cooperation by your opponent more probable, by posing an invitation to future cooperation, or by accepting such an invitation that he has offered by cooperating on earlier plays. And, in fact, when iterated Prisoner's Dilemma is actually played in experiments; many pairs of players achieve a rewarding pattern of mutual cooperation on most plays.[26]

Nevertheless, there is a powerful argument designed to show that sufficiently rational and knowledgeable players will make noncooperative moves on every play. The argument begins with the assumption that we have a game of iterated Prisoner's Dilemma of some definite number of moves, n, to be played by two players who are rational and interested solely in maximizing their personal payoffs, and will remain so throughout the game. It is further assumed that this is all *common knowledge* among the players, that is, each knows it, knows the other knows it, knows the other knows he knows it, and so on.[27] Given the assumptions of self-interest and rationality, and the dominance of non-cooperation on a single play, it follows that a player will cooperate on a given play only if he believes so doing may induce his opponent to cooperate on some later play or plays. Since each party, being rational, knows this, each party knows his opponent will not cooperate on the nth (i.e., last) play. For there are no later plays on which cooperation by one's opponent could be induced by a cooperative move on the nth play. But then each party knows that a cooperative move on the n-1st play could not induce future cooperation by his opponent, and being rational, he will not cooperate on the n-1st play. But his opponent, knowing this, will have no reason to cooperate on the n-2d play and will not so cooperate. Thus, by similar reasoning, we work our way back step-by-step (or by mathematical induction) to the very first play, and conclude that each party will make the noncooperative move on every play.

It is important for our purposes to note that this argument can be generalized in two ways. First, it can be extended to cover *multiparty* versions of Prisoner's Dilemma. Let us say that a game with two possible moves on each play is an instance of multiparty Prisoner's Dilemma if *(a)* one move (called the "noncooperative move") is dominant for every player (i.e., each does better playing that move no matter what combination of moves the others make), and *(b)* universal play of the other (i.e., cooperative) move yields higher payoffs to every player than universal play of the dominant move. Assuming that each player knows the conditions of the game, that the others know all this, and so on, we can extend the above argument to apply to iterated multiparty Prisoner's Dilemma. We simply note that each knows that *each* of his opponents will not cooperate on the nth play, and hence will have no reason to himself cooperate on the n-1st play. As this is known to each, each will not cooperate on the n-2d play, or the n-3d play, and so on, and we may conclude that all players will make the noncooperative move on all plays.

Second, we may generalize the argument to cover cases in which the players do not know the exact number of plays there will be, but do know that *(a)* some definite number n is an *upper bound* on the number of plays, and *(b)* how they play the game will have no influence on the number of plays there are. For assuming this is all common knowledge among the players, each knows that if there is an nth play, the others will all make the noncooperative move. Each therefore knows that if there is an n-1st play, each will have no reason to cooperate on that play. For each will know that this play will either turn out to be the last play, or it will be followed by an nth play on which the others will all make noncooperative moves. It follows that each knows his opponents will not cooperate on the n-1st or nth plays, if there are such, and by reasoning similar to the above, we work back to the conclusion that none will cooperate on any play.

Now this argument that rational players will never cooperate in bounded iterated multiparty Prisoner's Dilemma can be applied to try to show that mutual aid pacts will never be kept by rational parties in the state of nature. Briefly stated, the argument as applied to aid pacts, goes as follows. Suppose that we have a number of people who make a mutual aid pact in the state of nature that calls on each to come to the aid of any of their number that are attacked. Each party is rational and purely self-interested, and will remain so as long as he lives and the pact is in effect. The parties will, between them, suffer at most a definite number of attacks, n,[28] with the actual number determined by the propensities of external attackers and not in any way by their own behavior. We suppose that coming to another's aid is dangerous, and that therefore each party will keep his promise to aid an attacked member only if he expects this will make it more likely (than if he did not offer aid) that the present victim and/or other members will aid him if and when he is the victim of future attacks. Finally, we assume that all of this is common knowledge among the pact members.

Given these assumptions, it follows that each knows that if an nth attack occurs, the partners of the victim will not come to his aid, there being, by hypothesis, no future occasions on which they might be victims, and thus benefit from the aid of others. But since each knows the others will not help him if he is the victim of the nth attack, each will have no reason to offer aid on the n-1st attack (if there is one). For the only possible reasons for a self-interested party helping—to decrease the number of future attacks or to encourage reciprocal help later—have been ruled out. Each party will thus realize that none will help another on either the n-1st or the nth attack (if there are such attacks). But this removes all possible reasons for any to help others on the n-2d attack should it occur. And by similar reasoning, we work our way back to the n-3d, n-4th, and eventually the first attack, concluding that no party to the pact has any reason to help the victim of the first or any subsequent attack, and that each knows that no other member will ever help him if he is attacked.

The conclusion of the argument, the hopelessness of aid pacts in the state of nature, is counterintuitive, even paradoxical. It seems that truly rational parties so situated would at least try aiding their fellows a few times in hope of creating a practice of beneficial reciprocal aid. Nevertheless, I am inclined to think that the argument, or some more precisely stated variant of it, is valid. The implausible conclusion derives not from fallacious reasoning, but from other sources: the argument's extremely strong assumptions and, possibly, deep problems with the concept of practical rationality as it is applied to situations in which agents reason reciprocally about one another's reasoning. In the present context, we need consider only the former source of implausibility.

For the argument to go through, the parties must be assumed rational in a sense that guarantees they will replicate the line of reasoning contained in the argument itself. While this assumption may be only somewhat unrealistic, the assumption that each knows each of the others is thus rational, that each knows each of the others knows all are thus rational, and so on, is wildly implausible. Furthermore, the kind of knowledge of the circumstances and the other parties that is required for the argument to work is "certain" knowledge, that is, true beliefs about whose truth the believers have not the slightest doubts. This is because the rational parties' chains of reasoning invoke a large number of (relatively) independent premises, and their degrees of belief in the conclusion of the argument at each stage will not (since they are rational) exceed their degrees of belief in the conjunction of the premises used up to that point.[29] So, if their beginning degrees of belief in the premises about the risks of aiding others, the rationality of their partners, and so on, were significantly less than "certainty," they would not conclude that their partners surely will not cooperate. And they might rationally attempt cooperation on common sense grounds.

In addition, the assumption that the number of attacks by outsiders is independent of the behavior of the coalition members is almost certainly mistaken. The more the parties band together to successfully repel early attacks on members, the less likely they are to be attacked in the future, other things being equal. Common defense acts as a deterrent against potential aggressors. Since it is to the advantage of each partner to minimize the total number of attacks (as he may be among the victims), each thus has an additional self-interested reason for coming to the defense of attacked coalition partners.

We must conclude, then, that the iterated Prisoner's Dilemma argument for the futility of defense pacts fails to close the gap in Hobbes's argument that the state of nature is a state of war, because it requires quite unrealistic assumptions about the people in the state of nature.

V. Groups, Nations, and Security

A supporter of Hobbes might concede the possibility of coalitions in the state of nature, yet contend that the substance of Hobbes's hypothetical contract argument for unlimited and undivided sovereign power remains intact. For Hobbes claims that the logic of anticipation applies among *groups* as well as individuals in the state of nature. Thus, if persons are joined together in families (or other small groups), the destructive war of all individuals against all others will simply be replaced by a war of all groups against all others, that has similar disastrous consequences.[30] According to Hobbes, the only viable solution to the insecurity generated by this war of all groups is the formation of a commonwealth—a political entity governed by a sovereign with undivided and unlimited powers.

To evaluate this new variation on the war of all argument, we must examine the reasons Hobbes offers (in chap. 17 of *Leviathan*) for supposing that no social arrangement short of a commonwealth, as he defines it, can provide its members with sufficient security to eliminate the need to anticipate. In doing so, it is important to keep separate arguments related to two distinct properties of groups, their size and the concentration of power within them.[31] For, as we shall see, some of Hobbes's most plausible remarks concern group size and have only an indirect bearing on his conclusions about the desirability of the concentration of power.

Consider first the question of size. Hobbes observes that security rests on deterrence, which in turn rests on one's group being large enough so that potential attackers cannot be reasonably sure of victory. Contending that a relatively small advantage in numbers is a reliable sign of victory in conflicts between small groups, he concludes that small groups cannot deter attack and provide their members with security. But will this not depend upon the empirical details of the case, in particular on whether there are larger groups in the vicinity? Might not small, but nearly equal-size, groups provide sufficient security for their various members in state of nature situations? Perhaps, but Hobbes could plausibly argue that for reasons of both defense and conquest, people in such circumstances would have strong incentives to increase the size of their groups, for example, by merging one group with another. Hence, an equilibrium among small groups in the state of nature would be highly unstable, and would not provide protection for long.

This line of argument raises an interesting question that Hobbes never addresses. Why should those in the state of nature not opt for a grouping of all persons, worldwide, or at least try and form a group containing the majority of mankind? Why would they settle for a group smaller than this, when doing so would provide others with the incentive and opportunity to form a larger group and defeat them? There are two sorts of reasons. First, for large groups, being the largest is not always necessary for deterrence and defense. So many variables interact to determine victory in conflicts among large groups, that even a substantial advantage in numbers cannot begin to assure one group victory over another. Also, some geographical barriers (e.g., oceans, mountains) will reliably deter a larger group from attacking smaller ones. Second, there are disadvantages associated with increasing group size. It is difficult to coordinate the actions of large numbers of people spread over large distances. The larger the group, the greater the potential for internal conflict, as there is likely to be greater variation in beliefs and values among the members, and less group cohesion based on personal attachments. Given these, and other, inefficiencies of scale, coupled with the fact that deterrence capabilities are not primarily a function of size for large groups, we would not expect rational inhabitants of the state of nature to seek to increase the size of their groups without limit. Rather than the grand (or a majority) coalition of all mankind forming, we would expect rational parties to gather into large groups, with the exact sizes varying in accordance with the particular circumstances.[32]

Suppose the parties in the state of nature coalesced into a number of large groups for security reasons. Would the state of war argument not apply to the relations among these groups as it does to individuals and small groups? Hobbes allowed that it would, claiming that the nations of the world are in a constant state of war of each against the others. But the consequences of war (in Hobbes's sense) among nations are not so bleak as those of war between individuals and small groups. For even while known to be willing to fight each other, nations are able to "uphold . . . the industry of their subjects."[33] The import of this cryptic remark may (charitably) be interpreted as follows.

Nations are large enough and orderly enough to secure a man's life and property against those he is likely to come in direct contact with, and to provide him with enough reliable "partners" to make his productive activities worthwhile. Further, the state of war between his nation and others constitutes a much smaller threat to his life than would a war of all individuals (or small groups). For because of the problems of organizing large groups for combat, the uncertainty of the outcome in battles between states, the geographical barriers between states, and the relatively small number of agents on the international scene, actual fighting between states is relatively infrequent, and directly involves only a small segment of a warring nation's population when it does occur. Hence, there is much less fighting and killing per capita in the war of all nations than there would be in a war of all individuals (or small groups).

This argument, that nations can provide their inhabitants with a tolerable degree of security, depends to a considerable extent on the likelihood and the effects of war being constrained by *(a)* the difficulties of mobilizing and of overcoming geographical barriers, and *(b)* the fact that there are only a small number of international agents whose calculations (or miscalculations) could produce large-scale fighting. This becomes apparent when one imagines an international situation in which these constraints are not present.

Consider what is unfortunately a possible state of the real world eighty years from now. A hundred or so nations are armed with nuclear weapons and long-range missiles or bombers. Enormous destructive power is thus continually mobilized, relatively unconstrained by distance and geographical barriers, and may be set loose by any of a hundred or so government heads (or cabinets, or military councils). These nations, like the individuals in Hobbes's state of nature, are competing for scarce natural resources and for international reputation. Given their unclear arsenals, they are equals in the sense Hobbes stresses: each can kill any other, unilaterally or with the help of confederates. The uncertainty of victory—in the modern form of likelihood of mutual annihilation—would constitute an enormously powerful constraint on any nation attacking another under these circumstances. But with the other aforementioned constraints absent, a citizen of this multinuclear world might rightly feel far from secure. Given the grave conflicts of interest between nations, the apparent advantages of striking first in a nuclear conflict, and the large number of actors whose (mis)calculations could produce an attack, sensible individuals and governments would greatly fear the occurrence of a nuclear attack that could set off a spiral of international nuclear violence.

Two plausible strategies for dealing with the dangers of this sort of international situation are suggested by our earlier discussion of Hobbes's war of all argument. Nations might pursue the defensive coalition strategy by forming alliances, thus attempting to convince even the most irrational adversaries that attack would surely be suicidal, and at the same time reducing the number of independent actors who could start a nuclear war. Or they might follow the strategy of forming a sovereign world government. What would such a world government be like? It might be argued that, to be effective, a world government would need a monopoly on nuclear weapons. But it hardly seems that it would have to have unlimited and undivided power over all the people of the world. Authority over economic and internal security matters, for example, might be left in the hands of national governments. This observation brings us back to the second property of groups that Hobbes discusses, the degree to which power is concentrated within them.

Questions of power concentration and group size are connected, in that the larger a group is, the more it will need specialized organizations, procedures, and functionaries to provide security effectively and efficiently. Thus, Hobbes points out that a large group in which each individual acts in accordance with his own desires and opinions can provide little security. It will be ineffective against external enemies because its members will not agree on and coordinate their defensive efforts. And, because they have conflicting interests, group members will fight among themselves when threats from outside the group are not imminent.[34]

Having already eliminated small groups as an effective form of defense, Hobbes draws a significant political conclusion from these observations. He infers that people can obtain real security only under an absolute sovereign, that is, a single individual or assembly with unlimited authority to act for all members of the group. But this is a non sequitur. The most that follows from the dangers of unbridled individualism in large groups is that *some* concentration of authority in matters of external and internal defense is needed. That is, there must be some arrangement for the performance of police and military functions, and this will inevitably lead to significant inequalities in authority and power among the members of the group in question. That this must be carried to the point of investing *unlimited* authority and power in a *single* body is, however, a more extreme proposal that requires independent grounding. And Hobbes offers none, save for the bare assertion that the limitation or division of sovereign power inevitably leads to civil war, and that civil war will never occur in the absence of such limitation or division.[35]

Now it cannot be denied that limits on, or divisions in, the authority of the governing apparatus of a nation can lead to paralysis in the face of external threats and to damaging internal struggles. But they need not. Whether they will depends on the nature of the divisions or limits, the general historical-political situation, and a variety of other facts about the nation and its environment. In claiming otherwise, Hobbes presents a greatly oversimplified generalization (apparently based on

his view of the English Civil War) as a description of a deep and enduring fact about human societies.

In addition, he systematically overlooks or downplays the imperfec-
tions of the absolute sovereignty solution to the problem of individual
security. He does not mention that an unrestrained sovereign may involve a nation in disastrous wars that a more limited government would
refrain from undertaking. He de-emphasizes the significance of the loss
of individual liberty that citizens must endure as the usual price of a
system of government with a greater (rather than a lesser) concentration of power. And, most important of all, he fails to notice that even
unlimited and undivided sovereign authority is no guarantee against
internal strife. It cannot be a guarantee, because the physical powers
of a monarch or a sovereign assembly are never great enough, in themselves, to deter violent opposition. Thus, all sovereigns depend upon
the cooperation of others for the effective exercise of their authority,
for their power.[36] So serious civil strife—in the form of military coups,
local rebellions, civil wars involving competing factions within a sovereign assembly or the royal family or the military—can and does occur
even under absolute sovereigns. Life within Leviathan is not so tranquil
as Hobbes would have us suppose.

Let us summarize the implications of our discussion of security
within and between groups. We could interpret Hobbes's analysis of
security problems in the state of nature as an insightful and rather plausible argument against anarchy and in support of the state. The first
stage in the argument traces the logic of anticipation in an anarchical
situation. Its conclusion is that anarchy leads inevitably to an insecure
and poor life, and that people must therefore form defensive groups
to have a decent life. The second stage of the argument establishes that
only large groups are safe from external aggression. But to effectively
provide security to a large group, military and law-enforcement organizations, procedures, and specialists are needed. Thus, the third and
final stage of the argument establishes the need for the basic apparatus
of the state.[37]

This revised Hobbesian argument falls short of the conclusion
Hobbes wanted: the justifiability of the *absolute* state. But this is as it
should be. For Hobbes reaches that conclusion only be setting up a
false dichotomy between *(a)* each individual fending for himself and
(b) people reliably protected by unlimited power concentrated in the
hands of a single body. He overlooks all security arrangements in-be-
tween. Or, rather, he assimilates them to the first side of the above

dichotomy, based on his implausible assertion that civil order will break down if, and only if, state power is not fully concentrated. The above three-stage reconstruction of Hobbes's argument leaves out these false moves that he made in order to reach the political conclusions he desired.

VI. The Significance of Hobbes's Argument

I have suggested that Hobbes's discussion of the problem of individual security contains two basic flaws: *(a)* it overlooks the possibility of rational present cooperation based on the expectation of future cooperation, and *(b)* it oversimplifies and inaccurately portrays the relationship between security and the concentration of power within a group. Yet, when adjustments are made in Hobbes's argument to remedy these flaws, we are left with a powerful and plausible justification of the state. And the initial stage in this justification, the argument that the state of nature is a state of war of each individual against every other, contains two elements of substantial and lasting significance.

The first is the focus on *anticipatory* violence as the prime danger of an anarchical situation. Anticipatory violence plays a special role in the argument because such violence is escalatory in a way that competitive and glory-seeking violence need not be. Violence from the latter two sources alone might stay within tolerable limits, but once substantial anticipatory violence *starts,* it makes further anticipation more reasonable as a means of gaining the advantage on others who may reason similarly and anticipate. Thus, belief among the parties that anticipation is, or may be, the rational course of action, feeds an escalatory spiral of violence, and becomes a self-fulfilling prophecy.

Now, in the course of emphasizing anticipatory violence as the source of the war of all, Hobbes claims that even moderate persons, who are not evil and grasping, are forced into violence to preserve themselves. This observation that the dangers of violence can arise even among virtuous parties, provided they are sufficiently vulnerable to and distrustful of one another, is an important one having obvious implications concerning international, as well as domestic, order.[38] It also makes clear that law enforcement has at least a double function: to discourage evil and aggressive persons from violence and fraud by threatening them with sanctions, and to provide all with enough security that they will know that they need not engage in preventive violence and fraud to protect themselves.

A second contribution of Hobbes's analysis of the state of nature as a state of war is the introduction of an idea noted above in our discussion of Prisoner's Dilemma. Namely, that in certain important situations, there is a divergence between individual and collective rationality. That is, if each individual performs the act that is, in fact, in his own *individual* best interest, all—ironically—end up worse off than if they had all acted otherwise. Hobbes, in effect, though not in so many words, points out this problem with respect to attack behavior and promise keeping in the state of nature. Each would be better-off if they all kept their agreements and refrained from attacking one another. But there are apparent unilateral advantages to be gained by violating agreements and by conquest, and one will suffer substantial disadvantages if others do these things and one does not. As a result, agreements are in vain and anticipatory attack is the most reasonable individual strategy. Further, Hobbes proposes a plausible solution to the problem of diverging individual and collective rationality: the creation of a power to impose sanctions that would alter the parties' payoffs so as to synchronize individual and collective rationality.

Now if my criticisms of Hobbes's argument that the state of nature is a state of war are correct, the problem of security in an anarchical situation may not be a genuine instance of diverging individual and collective rationality. It may be *both* individually and collectively rational for the parties to form defensive coalitions by making and keeping mutual aid pacts. But this in no way detracts from the significance of Hobbes's contribution in bringing forth, and proposing a solution for, the general problem of divergent individual and collective rationality. In this, and in his discussion of the anticipation question, Hobbes took critical early steps toward the identification and clarification of central issues in the theory of rational conflict and cooperation. To the considerable extent that such theory contributes to our understanding of moral and political phenomena, we are in debt to Hobbes and his argument that the state of nature is a state of war.

Notes

Earlier versions of this paper were presented at the University of California, Irvine, and the Hobbes Tercentenary Congress at the University of Colorado in

1979. I am grateful to members of both audiences (especially Daniel Lyons, my commentator at the congress), and to a referee for *Ethics* for helpful comments.

1. Earlier (but significantly different) versions of the argument appear in *Elements of Law* and *De Cive*. I here consider only the *Leviathan* version. References to *Leviathan* (originally published in 1651) are to Sir William Molesworth, ed., *The English Works of Thomas Hobbes* (London: John Bohn, 1839), vol. 3 (hereafter cited at *Leviathan*).

2. See, e.g., David Gauthier, *The Logic of Leviathan* (Oxford: Oxford University Press, 1969), pp. 14–18; Richard Peters, *Hobbes* (Harmondsworth: Penguin Books, 1956), pp. 168–72; and D. D. Raphael, *Hobbes* (London: George Allen & Unwin Publishers, 1977), pp. 30–31.

3. The view that the argument rests on egoistic premises may be found, e.g., in Leslie Stephen, *Hobbes* (Ann Arbor: University of Michigan Press, 1961), pp. 136–42, 182–84; and C. B. Macpherson, *The Political Theory of Possessive Individualism* (Oxford: Oxford University Press, 1962), pp. 32–33, 67–69.

4. See, e.g., W. V. Quine, "On a So-called Paradox," *Mind* 62 (1953): 65–67.

5. *Leviathan*, chap. 13, pp. 112–13.

6. Ibid., p. 113.

7. See Sec. II below.

8. *Leviathan*, pp. 110–11.

9. Ibid., p. 111. Cf. chap. 14, p. 129: "In the condition of mere nature the inequality of power is not discerned but by the event of battle."

10. Ibid., chap. 13, p. 111.

11. Ibid., pp. 111–12.

12. Ibid., chap. 11, p. 85.

13. Ibid., chap. 13, pp. 111-12. Hobbes speaks here of mastering people by "wiles" as well as by force, but in his later discussion of conquest (chap. 20), the only method of gaining dominion over another that he mentions (besides parenthood and the original covenant) is the threat of force. Perhaps he is imagining that wiles are used to get another in a position in which a promise of obedience can be obtained by threats of force. Or it may be that he considers wiles a method of attaining mastery over others that is practiced in the "attenuated" state of nature, i.e., under a government of limited power. On this last point, see Sec. II below.

14. Loved ones, generally close relatives, may constitute a class of exceptions. Taking account of this would, at most, require recasting the argument of terms of relations among small family groups, rather than between individuals. Cf. Sec. V below.

15. Hobbes does not mention it, but to the extent that people overestimate their power (i.e., are "vainglorious" in his sense), they will overestimate their chances of success and will be more likely to attack.

16. *Leviathan*, chap. 13, pp. 111–12.

17. Ibid., p. 112, and chap. 11, p. 86.

18. Ibid., chap. 13, p. 111.

19. Ibid., p. 113.

20. Weaker assumptions than this would suffice. These would take account

of the possibility that some people will infer that others are enemies in some other way, e.g., by generalizing from the hostile behavior of those with whom they come into contact.

21. *Leviathan*, chap. 17, p. 155; chap. 18, pp. 169–70; chap. 19, p. 172; chap. 20, p. 195; chap. 30, p. 262. In pointing out that this is Hobbes's view, I am not endorsing it. See Sec. V below.

22. See ibid., chap. 17, p. 154: "If there be no power erected, *or not great enough for our security,* every man will—and may lawfully—rely on his own strength and art for caution against all other men" (italics mine).

23. See ibid., pp. 57–58: "The *only way* to erect such a common power as may be able to defend them . . . is to confer all their power and strength upon one man, or upon one assembly of men that may reduce all their wills . . . unto one will. . . . This done the multitude so united is called a COMMONWEALTH. . . . And he that carries [their power and strength] is called SOVEREIGN" (italics mine). Cf. ibid. chap. 15, p. 131, and chap. 31, p. 343.

24. Ibid., chap. 14, pp. 124–25. I oversimplify Hobbes's view on covenants of mutual trust. The complications I ignore would, if anything, weaken the Hobbesian argument against defensive coalitions. See F. S. McNeilly, *The Anatory of Leviathan* (London: Macmillan, 1968).

25. Hobbes did not entirely overlook it. In his reply to the fool (ibid., chap. 15, pp. 133–34), he claims fear of being left out of a specific future scheme of cooperation, the commonwealth, should motivate rational parties to comply with *some* agreements in the state of nature. Why did he not generalize the point? Apparently, he doubted one party could count on others being rational in this way. And perhaps he was vaguely aware of the problem discussed in Sec. IV below.

26. See Anatol Rapoport and Albert Chammah, *Prisoner's Dilemma* (Ann Arbor: University of Michigan Press, 1965), pp. 63–66. In *Anarchy and Cooperation* (London: John Wiley & Sons, 1976), Michael Taylor analyzes iterated Prisoner's Dilemma games in detail to provide insight into a class of problems similar to the one discussed here. However, two of his assumptions—the infinite number of iterations and the discounting of future payoffs—are not appropriate for representing the security problem for rational parties in the state of nature.

27. See David Lewis, *Convention* (Cambridge, Mass.: Harvard University Press, 1969), pp. 52–58.

28. This is not an unrealistic assumption, as n may be chosen as large as we wish.

29. I borrow this point from Tyler Burge who applies it, in a different context, in "Reasoning about Reasoning," *Philosophia* 8 (December 1978): 651–56.

30. At places in *Leviathan* (see chap. 13, p. 114; chap. 17, p. 154), the war of all is portrayed as being among families rather than individuals.

31. As Hobbes opposes both on the same grounds, I treat the limitation and division of state power together under the single heading of "concentration" of power.

32. Technological advances tend to increase the optimal size of defensive

groups. For they make transportation and communication over long distances, and the organization and direction of large numbers of persons, faster and more efficient.

33. *Leviathan,* chap. 13, p. 115.

34. Ibid., chap. 17, p. 155.

35. See, e.g., ibid., chap. 18, p. 168.

36. Often, one's main reason for cooperating with the sovereign is the expectation that others will cooperate because they expect others to cooperate. Hence, the glue that holds the state together is much like that which holds together the defensive coalitions discussed in Sec. III above. I develop this point in my "Rule by Fear," *Noûs* 17 (1983).

37. The Hobbesian argument against anarchy is not a priori, as McNeilly supposes, but empirical. In special, but relatively unlikely, circumstances (e.g., a rich, geographically isolated environment with low population density), going it alone or in small groups will provide sufficient security.

38. The Surprise Attack Problem is clearly a descendant of this point. For an elegant recent treatment, see Thomas Schelling, *The Strategy of Conflict* (New York: Oxford University Press, 1960), chap. 9.

2

Hobbes's "Mortall God": Is There a Fallacy In Hobbes's Theory of Sovereignty?

M. M. Goldsmith

For Thomas Hobbes, sovereignty was an essential characteristic of the state. By contracts of authorization or of submission, "the Multitude" are "united in one Person" or commonwealth."This is the Generation of that great LEVIATHAN, or rather (to speake more reverently) of that *Mortall God,* to which wee owe under the *Immortall God,* our peace and defence."[1] This uniting of a number of men into a body politic, creating a real union of them all has, in all three versions of Hobbes's political philosophy, similar consequences.[2]

These consequences are the endowing of the commonwealth with sovereign power. By their actions of authorizing or transferring their rights, the subjects have disabled themselves from revoking these powers, from varying the arrangements they have agreed to and from performing the same action again.[3] That upon whom these powers have been conferred, the sovereigner (whether one man or an assembly), is immune from forfeiting authority. (The sovereign can have made no covenant with all collectively since the collectivity did not exist, indeed only exists by virtue of the generating contracts. Covenants with the subjects individually are void, since any pretended breach by the sovereign is an action done by the authorization of all—including the individual claiming that there has been such a breach.)[4] Although the sovereign may act iniquitously toward the subjects, nothing done by the sovereign can be an injury to them. Moreover the sovereign is immune from punishment.[5] Thus once the commonwealth has been constituted, the subjects are disabled from changing the result of that action—the constitution. They cannot revoke the constitution, revise the constitution or make a different constitution. Only the authority constituted can do these things.

In addition to the disabilities which the subjects incur and the immunities which the representative acquires, the act of generating Leviathan results in the state possessing those powers or rights which, Hobbes holds, are required for achieving "the End of this Institution . . . the Peace and Defence of them all."[6] There are a set of things Hobbes calls "powers" or "rights" and which he describes as "annexed to the Sovereignty." They indicate the areas in which the state may act in the pursuit of its goals of internal and external peace, both in deciding that there is a danger—a hindrance or disturbance—and in deciding what is to be done about it. Hobbes therefore attaches to sovereignty the following powers:

1. To judge "what Opinions and Doctrines are averse, and what conducing to Peace" and so to permit or forbid the publication of opinion by speech or writing.[7]
2. To prescribe "the Rules, whereby every man may know, what Goods he may enjoy and what Actions he may doe, without being molested by any of his fellow Subjects." This legislative power thus includes the "Rules of Propriety (or *Meum* and *Tuum*) and of *Good, Evill,* and *Lawfull,* and *Unlawfull* in the actions of subjects," i.e., the civil laws of each state.[8]
3. To judge and decide all controversies concerning law or fact—the judiciary power.[9]
4. To make "Warre and Peace with other Nations." The state's military or defence power includes the rights of deciding what military forces are necessary, of levying taxes to provide for them and of the supreme command, for "whosoever is made Generall of an Army, he that hath the Sovereign Power is alwayes Generallissimo."[10]
5. To choose "all Councellours, Ministers, Magistrates, and Officers, both in Peace, and War"—the appointing power.[11] (I presume that Hobbes intended to include here the power to dismiss officials.)
6. To reward (with riches or honour) and to punish (with corporal or pecuniary punishments, or ignominy) subjects both according

to law and also so as to encourage service and deter disservice to
the commonwealth.[12]
7. To establish and enforce rules of honour, bestow titles and provide rank and precedence among subjects.[13]

"These are the Rights, which make the Essence of Soveraignty" according to Hobbes. Such prerogative sovereign rights of English kings
as the powers "to coyn Mony; to dispose of the estate and persons of
Infant heires; to have praeemption in Markets; and all other Statute
Praerogatives" are dismissed as inessential.[14] The necessity to sovereignty of all the rights mentioned in the discussion in chapter eighteen
of *Leviathan* is reiterated in chapters twenty-one and thirty.[15] From
the way in which Hobbes lists the powers in these other chapters, for
example, prominently mentioning the taxing power, it seems clear that
his concern in chapter eighteen is not to formulate a complete list of
the logically distinguishable rights of sovereignty but rather to justify
these rights by showing that they are necessary means to the performance of the state's functions. For example, the right to levy taxes, mentioned prominently in the later *résumés,* is introduced in chapter eighteen as a consequence of the power of making war and peace although
it is subsequently treated as a distinct right.[16] (In *The Elements of Law*
and *De Cive* Hobbes's discussion connects the powers of sovereignty
with two "swords": the sword of justice and the sword of war.)

But is there anything in Hobbes's discussion of sovereignty which is
startling—or even new? Sir Robert Filmer thought not. In his *Observations Concerning the Originall of Government* he remarked, "With no
small content I read Mr. Hobbes's book *De Cive,* and his *Leviathan,*
about the rights of sovereignty, which no man, that I know, hath so
amply and judiciously handled: I consent with him about the rights of
exercising government, but I cannot agree to his means of acquiring
it."[17] Filmer objected to the generation of a commonwealth from a state
of nature by individuals covenanting together (by institution) or to a
conqueror (by acquisition). He thought that Hobbes's account of these
processes failed to explain how such processes could occur, and he
also held that men had never been in such a state of nature. Indeed he
objected to all theories which asserted original equality and the absence of private property under a law of nature and then derived the
right or power of government from an act of subjection by the people.[18]
He even regretted that Hobbes had used the word "commonwealth"
in *Leviathan*'s subtitle since that form suggested a "popular govern-

ment"; the translator of Bodin's *De Republica* had "carefully observed" the better form, "weal public, or commonweal."[19] Filmer's content with Hobbes's treatment of the rights of sovereignty is explicable, for Filmer, like many seventeenth-century Englishmen, not only had discovered in Bodin a defence of absolute monarchy, but also had derived from him a conception of sovereignty.[20]

Bodin had defined sovereignty as "the most high, absolute, and perpetuall power over the citizens and subjects in a Commonweale."[21] It is "not limited either in power, charge, or time certain"; it is unconditional and supreme—not subject to (civil) law or to another's command. Thus sovereignty is unconditional and irrevocable—indeterminate in time in the sense that for corporate sovereigns there is no time limit and for a natural individual his power cannot be terminated during his lifetime.[22] He identified the "true markes of Soveraigntie" and of a sovereign: (1) "to give lawes to all his subiects in generall, and to everie one of them in particular, (yet is not that enough, but that we must ioyne thereunto) without consent of any other greater, equall, or lesser than himselfe"; (2) to make war and peace; (3) to create and appoint magistrates; (4) to be the last tribunal of appeal; (5) to grant clemency and pardon; (6) to receive liege fealty and homage; (7) to coin money; (8) to appoint weights and measures; (9) to levy taxes and imposts; and there are also a number of minor rights as well as those peculiar to various princes. But the first right of sovereignty, the legislative power, contains all the rest, "So wee see the principall point of sovereign maiestie, and absolute power, to consist principally in giving laws unto the subiects in generall, without their consent."[23]

Hobbes followed Bodin in identifying the central powers of sovereignty; the legislative power, the judicial power, the power to make war and peace and the power to appoint officials are included by both. Of the other marks of sovereignty mentioned by Bodin, the power of being the final tribunal of appeal and of granting pardon are surely possessed by any Hobbesian sovereign. So too the right to fealty and homage is subsumed in the relationship of subject to sovereign. Coining money and presumably setting weights and measures are minor prerogatives, and in any case would be included in the legislative power. The power of levying taxes is definitely and fully included in Hobbes's rights of sovereignty; Bodin does explicitly make this a mark of sovereignty, but other passages in the *République* (at least in some versions) suggest that taxation requires the subjects' consent as well as the sovereign's imposition.[24] Again although Bodin does not explicitly mention the sovereign's powers to reward and punish subjects in Book I chapters 8 or 10, it is discussed in Book V, chapter 4. Bodin too has something to say about opinions, at least about religious opinions, even if it is not what Hobbes says; he suggests that where unanimity of religious opinions exists it should be preserved but that where it does not toleration of private worship is to be allowed. Moreover Bodin goes on to warn of the dangers of "immoderate libertie of speech given to orators" which, sometimes under the guise of religion, has led to sedition.[25] Bodin contemplates the correct ordering of citizens (Book III, chapter 8) but not as Hobbes does in *Leviathan,* making the sovereign the sole fountain of honour. Thus where Hobbes differs from Bodin, the effect of those differences is to emphasize or increase the powers of sovereignty over all aspects of society: property, opinion and honour were all placed within the explicit sphere of sovereignty.

But the importance of the concept of sovereignty for Thomas Hobbes and for his contemporaries was not confined to the specific rights and powers attributed to sovereignty or the sovereign state. At least equally significant was what might be called the logic of the concept of sovereignty. Consider a system of rules, norms, laws or authorities. If one asks "what makes this rule (or authority) valid?" the answer must be that it is validated by being derived from a superior norm or authority. Thus the systematic character of a set of rules or norms or authorities is its hierarchical order: each subordinate rule or authority owes its validity to, is derived from, a superior authority. But to "close" the system, to prevent its being infinitely regressive, a highest or supreme norm or authority is required. This is the sovereign, or Kelsen's "grundnorm," or H.L.A. Hart's ultimate rule of recognition. Its validity is not derived from any superior—as Kelsen says, "the basic norm is presupposed to be valid." Thus rules, norms or authorities form a single system by virtue of their having a single, ultimately validating authority or rule; the system is a closed system by virtue of that rule being ultimate—there being no going behind it.[26]

So the logic of the concept of sovereignty involves two notions: (1) hierarchy and (2) closure. The first is the notion of a chain of norms or authorities, each subordinate to the next higher link and superior to those below it. The notion of closure ensures that the chain does not extend infinitely upward and that the system is independent, i.e., not subordinate to another system of authorities or norms. This implies that there is no appeal outside the system, or, to put it another way, other systems or authorities are external to it.

Even a cursory examination of the principal rights attributed to sovereignty by Jean Bodin and Thomas Hobbes makes it evident that they were using the concept as a device for picturing the state as a closed normative system. The sovereign is the legislator or validator of all laws, the highest military commander, the source of magisterial authority and so on. Moreover each consciously formulated the notion of sovereignty in terms of this logical characteristic. Bodin stresses the absurdity of suggesting that vassals, subordinates or dependents could be sovereign—just "as the great soveraigne God, cannot make another God equall unto himselfe" since there cannot be two infinites, so "he onely is a soveraigne, which hath none his superiour or companion with himself on the same Kingdome."[27] In *Leviathan,* Hobbes frequently emphasizes the supremacy of the sovereign and the subordinate and derivative authority of all other laws and officials; for example, he identifies a commonwealth as a "systeme" which is *"Absolute* and *Independent"* as opposed to those which are subordinate. Anyone who "thinking Soveraign Power too great, will seeke to make it lesse; must subject himselfe, to the Power, that can limit it; that is to say, to a greater."[28] But the most explicit formulation of the logic of the concept occurs in *De Cive:* in every perfect city, there must be supreme right in some one, greater than which cannot by right be conferred by men . . . that right we call absolute. It is as great a right as each had over himself outside of civil society—a supreme and absolute power limited only by the powers of the city and by nothing else. For if this power were limited, that limit must necessarily be from a greater power. For he that prescribes limits has a greater power than he who is confined by these limits. This confining power is either unlimited or is itself limited by a greater. And so eventually we must come to a power which has no other limit, but which is the *terminis ultimus* of all the forces of the citizens. This is called the supreme power *(imperium summum).*[29]

Thus Hobbes explicitly emphasized both hierarchy and closure in explaining his notion of sovereignty. Exactly the same points are given as reasons why the sovereign cannot be subject to the civil laws: it is an error to set the laws above the sovereign, because it "setteth also a Judge above him, and a Power to punish him; which is to make a new Soveraign; and again for the same reason a third, to punish the second; and so continually without end, to the Confusion, and Dissolution of the Commonwealth."[30]

But it was not just the systematic and hierarchical logic of concept of sovereignty which made Bodin's conception of sovereignty congenial to Hobbes. There were several other characteristics of his doctrine which made it particularly useful. (To some extent these aspects of Bodin's and Hobbes's conception of sovereignty have already slipped into this discussion, but they are distinct and separable elements even if absolutists attempted to argue the contrary.) Bodin held not only that every state to be a state must possess sovereignty (that is, have the characteristics of a closed hierarchical system of authority), but also that the powers of sovereignty were indivisible and consequently that they must all be possessed by some identifiable human being or organization of human beings. Thus he supposed that a political society which was independent possessed not only a closed hierarchical system of norms—sovereignty—but also that the highest authority in such a system must be an actual human being or beings—a sovereign. For Bodin thought that there had to be a sovereign, not just sovereignty, in every state.[31]

These were views also adopted by Hobbes. In one of the very few times Hobbes approvingly mentions a previous political writer, he cites Bodin on the indivisibility of sovereign powers: "and if there were a commonwealth, wherein the rights of sovereignty were divided, we must confess with Bodin, Lib. II. chap. 1 *De Republica,* that they are not rightly to be called commonwealths, but the corruption of commonwealths."[32] For both Hobbes and Bodin there were only three possible kinds of commonwealth, for sovereignty had to be held by one man or an assembly of either some part or all: "for either One, or More, or All must have the Sovereign Power (which I have shown to be indivisible) entire."[33] Like Bodin, Hobbes held that there must be a sovereign, not just sovereignty.

Thus the conception of sovereignty which Hobbes deployed in the *Elements of Law* and *De Cive* as well as in *Leviathan* contained not only the assertion that states were sovereign but also the assertion that sovereignty was indivisible and so must be held by a single person or organization. The argument is absolutist and anti-constitutional; Hobbes, and others, drew exactly those conclusions from it—a mixed sovereign, or a number of separate individuals and organizations possessing sovereign power jointly, or a rule-governed procedure or set of procedures being sovereign, is an impossibility.

The argument is persuasive, but fallacious. If it were correct, then constitutions which divide, separate or distribute the powers of sovereignty would not merely be tricky to operate, requiring adherence to constitutional rules and acceptance of the separate jurisdictions of the

officers empowered by the constitution in various spheres, they would
be impossible. The fallacy is contained in holding that the logically necessary characteristics of an independent system of authority must be
possessed by some identifiable part of the system. It is as simple an
error as holding that because clocks tell time, the power of telling the
time must be a characteristic possessed by some identifiable part of a
clock. For a system to be an independent and absolute one, it is only
necessary that there should be no appeal outside it—that it should not
be (normatively) dependent, derivative or subordinate. In other words,
to be an independent, closed, complete and conclusive system merely
requires that there should be a final decider (set by the rules of the
system—its constitution) in any sphere, for any issue or controversy
that may arise; what Hobbes asserts is that there must be the same
final decider for everything. This latter assertion goes beyond what is
logically necessary. The necessity of there being the same final authority in every matter is "necessary" only in the sense that it eliminates
the possibility that there may be conflicting decisions on the same matter by different authorities within the system. Such conflicts might arise
if the constitution provided for jurisdictions which were not mutually
exclusive or if, as is also likely, issues could be interpreted as falling
within the jurisdiction of several authorities. Note that it is a logical
possibility that those with overlapping jurisdictions should disagree; it
is not a logical necessity that they will. But Hobbes held that whenever
such a disagreement was possible, the state of war of all against all was
endemic and so a commonwealth not established. Sovereignty meant
that sovereign powers were indivisible and had to be held by a single
person—a man or institution—who was the Sovereign Representative
of the commonwealth.

According to Hobbes the attempt to establish separate civil and ecclesiastical jurisdictions was to establish two states rather than one:

> Now seeing it is manifest, that the Civill Power, and the Power of the
> Common-wealth is the same thing; and that Supremacy [ecclesiastical
> power], and the Power of making Canons, and granting Faculties, imply-
> eth a Common-wealth: it followeth, that where one is Soveraign, another
> Supreme; where one can make Lawes, and another make Canons; there
> must needs be two Common-wealths, of one & the same Subjects; which
> is a Kingdome divided in it selfe, and cannot stand.

Earlier in the same chapter Hobbes had asserted that dividing sovereign power was "against the essence of a Common-wealth." "For what

is it to divide the Power of a Common-wealth, but to Dissolve it; for Powers divided mutually destroy each other." The idea that there can be mixed constitutions is also scathingly denounced. It is the same false doctrine about the civil power as the one above about dividing ecclesiastical from civil power. Put the power of levying money in a general assembly, the power of command in one man and the power of making laws in those two along with a third, the result is not one state. "For although few perceive, that such government, is not government, but division of the Common-wealth into three Factions, and call it mixt Monarchy; yet the truth is, that it is not one independent Common-wealth, but three independent Factions; nor one Representative Person, but three." Such an arrangement may be possible for God but not for man. "And therefore if the King bear the person of the People, and the generall Assembly bear also the person of the People, and another Assembly bear the person of a Part of the People, they are not one Person, nor one Soveraign, but three Persons, and three Soveraigns."[34]

Thus Hobbes contended that the powers of sovereignty were indivisible; they could not be distributed among a plurality of authorities; they could not be exercised jointly by a number of individuals or organizations in a procedure defined by constitutional rules. Sovereignty had to be possessed by a single identifiable human being or an assembly of human beings. Having such a sovereign defines the existence of a commonwealth. Not having such a sovereign, whether by having an authority more limited than such a sovereign or by having a number of authorities purporting to share sovereignty, is not really having a state at all—it is remaining in the situation of the war of all against all.

Hobbes thought that he was doing something more than issuing admonitions about the practical inadvisability of dividing sovereignty. He tried to show that each of the powers of sovereignty implied the other powers. Since adjudication could produce decisions which varied from the legislative enactments, the legislator must possess the judicial power. Similarly without power to enforce his commands, the sovereign's laws would be ineffective and without the power to tax he would have no money to arm or pay enforcers or to pay those forces he employs to defend the society against foreign enemies; so he must have those powers too. Hobbes was not trying to show that it was practically better not to divide sovereignty. When he uses that type of empirical argument he signals it. For example, when he discusses the question of which type of government is better, monarchy, aristocracy or democracy, he discusses the advantages and disadvantages of these forms, appealing to experience. All three forms of government must have undivided sovereign power; which of them exercises it best may be decided by comparing their advantages and disadvantages.[35] Hobbes's argument for the indivisibility of sovereign powers is couched in no such empirical terms. The rights of sovereignty are "incommunicable and inseparable"; "And because they are essentiall and inseparable Rights, it follows necessarily, that in whatsoever words any of them seem to be granted away, yet if the Soveraigne Power it selfe be not in direct termes renounced . . . the Grant is voyd."[36] Thus the concept of sovereignty is used in an all or nothing way: either there is a sovereign possessing all these powers or there is none; if there is no sovereign then we are not in a civil state, but in the state of nature. Moreover all Hobbes's arguments against mixed government rely on the doctrine that sovereignty is indivisible. As we have seen, Hobbes asserted that a mixed government either contained a number of sovereigns or none. But this does not prove that such governments are impossible, it merely asserts the fallacy that the state must have a sovereign and not just sovereignty in a different way. Mixed government is said to be impossible because there would be more than one sovereign; but there cannot be more than one sovereign because a state must have one and only one sovereign. Instead of proving his case, Hobbes merely repeats his view.

But while Hobbes may have thought that the indivisibility of sovereignty was not merely practically desirable but "necessary," in what sense was it necessary? Often the necessity seems to be logical necessity. But Hobbes may have believed that indivisibility was scientifically demonstrable. Here we must remember that Hobbes's conception of science allowed him to regard scientific proof as establishing something more than merely empirical connections. He may have believed that his arguments showing that one of the powers of sovereignty was necessary to the exercise of another power established a kind of scientific or causal necessity. But, to take one example, is the militia a necessary or a sufficient condition for the existence of the legislative power, or is it a causal factor affecting the degree to which laws are obeyed? The argument that the laws will be better obeyed if these powers are in the same hands is merely an empirical one. Moreover, far from establishing the impossibility of dividing sovereignty, it assumes that sovereignty can be divided. So Hobbes needs to prove that the division of sovereign powers always leads to disagreement among those who hold them and that disagreement cannot be resolved peacefully—it must always lead to contention. All that Hobbes actually shows is that not dividing sovereign power cannot lead to disagreement (and contention) among the holders of power while division may lead to contention.[37]

Once the doctrine that sovereignty is indivisible has been established, the argument for absolutism is completed by showing that the mere normative validity of the sovereign's position will be insufficient to exclude "the private sword" (as Hobbes quaintly calls the situation in which anyone may use force as he pleases in *The Elements of Law*) or the state of nature, which is implicitly if not explicitly the war of all against all.

But if an absolute sovereign is the only logical alternative to the war of all against all (mixed and limited constitutions being excluded), and readers can be persuaded that they do not want a war of all against all, it should not be difficult to persuade them to endow the sovereign with sufficient power (here meaning actual ability, force) to be able to exercise his rights.

The argument for an absolute sovereign (and not just for the sovereignty of the state) was monarchist in its intentions and its implications. To make it explicitly Royalist little was needed—merely to point out that the sovereign in England was the king, as Hobbes casually remarked in *Leviathan,* for example, when arguing that the sovereign is the representative of the people in a state, not some subordinate assembly: "And I know not how this so manifest a truth should of late be so little observed; that in a Monarchy, he that had the Soveraignty from a descent of 600 years, was alone called Soveraign, had the title of Majesty from every one of his Subjects, and was unquestionably taken by them for their King; was notwithstanding never considered as their Representative."[38]

The sovereignty argument, including its fallacy, was by no means exclusive to Hobbes. It was widely used by Royalists in the 1640s. In its simplest form it was assumed, almost without discussion, that sovereign meant king and that an hierarchy of authority existed. According to Henry Peacham, God, the supreme sovereign, had communicated to earthly sovereigns his own attributes, subjects were accordingly bound to obey.[39] Such Royalists as Sir Robert Filmer, however, were far more sophisticated. Filmer's *Patriarcha,* written as Peter Laslett has shown before the beginning of civil war in 1642, asserted the central points of the king's sovereignty: that the king was above the law; the

supreme legislator; supreme judge and interpreter of the law.[40] The
same points are made in *The Freeholders Grand Inquest Touching Our
Soveraigne Lord the King and his Parliament* (1648):

> every supreme court [loosely parliament but more precisely the king sit-
> ting in the house of peers in person, and not the Lords without him] must
> have the supreme power, and the supreme power is always arbitrary; for
> that is arbitrary which hath no superior on earth to control it. The last
> appeal in all government, must still be to an arbitrary power, or else ap-
> peals will be in infinitum, never at an end. The legislative power is an
> arbitrary power, for they are *termini convertibiles.*
>
> The main question in these our days, is, where this power legislative
> remains? . . . we shall find the power of making laws rests solely in the
> King.[41]

Thus Filmer employed both of the notions inherent in sovereignty: that
there was an hierarchical chain of authority and that the chain had to
be closed by a supreme power having no superior on earth. . . .

Hobbes, among the Royalists who turned out to be *plus royaliste
que le roi,* took a more extreme position. He allowed that "in the ad-
ministration" of a state "all those sorts of government may have place
subordinate," but always insisted that sovereign power was indivisible.
On occasion, he wavered to the extent of admitting that men might be
sufficiently tempted by the prospect of a crown to accept it on illogical
and foolish conditions which seem to involve conditional or limited or
divided sovereignty.[42] But such misbegotten states were not really
states at all; only by creating and authorizing a sovereign representative
could men succeed in escaping the state of nature.

As we have seen, Hobbes was by no means peculiar in regarding
sovereignty as a logically necessary characteristic of a state, an independent, non-subordinate political system. Like most other seventeenth-
century Englishmen who used the concept of sovereignty, he followed
Bodin to a great extent in identifying its essential elements. Moreover,
like such Royalists as Spelman, Filmer and Digges he also held the (fallacious) view that sovereign power had to be held by an identifiable
individual or organization. For Royalists, this doctrine, which excluded
what Hobbes called "mixarchy," performed the desirable ideological
function of upholding the King's position and denying the Parliament's
and the subjects' right to resist. It was an especially effective argument,
since as we have seen, many Parliamentary publicists held a similar

conception of sovereignty, but were reluctant to assert the sovereignty of either or both of the houses of parliament. Asserting that parliament without the king, or that the people, was sovereign was a difficult and radical step to take; the argument was difficult to sustain, because however much constitutional and legal evidence one might cite to establish the rights and privileges of Parliament or of Englishmen, no one believed that England was not some sort of monarchy. (Of course the Levellers did take the logical step and assert the sovereignty of the people and of the Commons as the people's representative.)

Hobbes eschewed the extensive compiling of historical evidence indulged in by Prynne, Lilburne, Filmer and Spelman and assumed that once the necessity of an absolute sovereign had been established, there could be little doubt about who that sovereign was—at least in 1640, 1642, or 1647. Of course in 1651 the situation was different; then the rigour of Hobbes's argument and its abstraction from any casuistic discussion about who the sovereign was made it into a case for obedience to whoever held power. Hobbes recognized this point, specifically pointing out in *Leviathan*'s "Review and Conclusion" just when a subject has liberty to submit to a conqueror ("when the means of his life is within the Guards and Garrisons of the Enemy"), emphasizing that it was an error for sovereigns, who must possess "an Absolute and Arbitrary Legislative Power," to "justifie the War, by which their Power was first gotten, and whereon (as they think) their Right dependeth, and not on the Possession" and finally asserting that his only "designe" was "to set before mens eyes the mutuall Relation between Protection and Obedience." Defenders of the Commonwealth of England—as it is now established, without a king or house of lords—appreciated the appropriateness of Hobbes's views.[43]

Hobbes was distinct from others who used the concept of sovereignty then in a number of ways. He was more abstract, less obviously casuistical; if not more logical, he was at least less compromising. Others said the sovereign had to be absolute, then allowed that absolutism to be exercised only through existing legal and constitutional processes; Hobbes's "absolutism" was more absolute.[44] Moreover, Hobbes had built the necessity of a single representative person into his system at a very early stage by making the designation of a sovereign the cause of there being a civil society rather than a state of nature as well as by insisting that the defining characteristic of the state was the existence of such a sovereign. Although there is some development in his account of the generation of a state, he always held that its defining characteristic was the existence of a single representative person or organization which "included" the wills of all the subjects. Without such a sovereign, Hobbes's "mortall God," there could be no state.

Notes

Earlier versions of this article were presented at the Hobbes Tercentenary Congress organized by the Society for Study of the History of Philosophy, the 1979 Annual Meeting of the American Political Science Association and the 1979 meeting of the Political Studies Association of the United Kingdom. I am grateful to the participants at these meetings for their comments and to these organizations and my undergraduate Hobbes seminar at the University of Exeter (1978–79) for reawakening my interest in Hobbes.

1. *Leviathan,* chap. 17, ed. C.B. Macpherson (Harmondsworth, 1968), p. 227. (All citations of *Leviathan* will indicate chapter number followed by the page number in this edition.)

2. *De Cive,* chap. v, sections 7, 9. *De Cive* will be cited by chapter and section number; I shall use the title indiscriminately for the Latin original and for the seventeenth century English translation entitled *Philosophical Rudiments Concerning Government and Society* usually but mistakenly attributed to Hobbes himself. For discussions of this translation see Howard Warrender's forthcoming edition and Tito Magri's translation into Italian of *De Cive* (Rome, 1979), pp. 50–59. Cf. *Elements of Law,* Part I, chap. xix, sections 6, 8 (19, 6, 8), ed. F. Tönnies (London, 1889; reprinted 1969), pp. 103, 104. (The figures in parentheses follow Warrender's numbering system.)

3. *Leviathan* 18, pp. 229–30; *De Cive* vi, 20.

4. *Leviathan* 18, pp. 230–1; cf. *De Cive* vi, 14; *Elements of Law* II, ii, 2 (21, 2), p. 119.

5. *Leviathan* 18, p. 232. These last two points are merely the correlatives of what has been said above. According to *Leviathan* 15, p. 202, injury is the breach of covenant; if the sovereign is not covenanted to the subjects, no breach can occur. Punishment, *Leviathan* 28, pp. 353–56, is evil inflicted for violation of a precedent law by public authority: "Hurt inflicted on the Representative of the Common-wealth, is not Punishment, but an act of Hostility: Because it is of the nature of Punishment, to be inflicted by publique Authority, which is the Authority only of the Representative it self" *ibid.,* p. 356. Thus no one else could punish the sovereign and the sovereign, Hobbes assumes, does not punish itself. Cf. *De Cive* vi, 12; *Elements of Law* II, i, 12; II, ii, 3 (20, 12; 21, 3), pp. 113, 119-20.

6. *Leviathan* 18, p. 232.

7. *Ibid.,* p. 233; *De Cive* vi, 11; opinions are discussed in a different context in *Elements of Law* II, vi, 11–13; ix, 8 (25, 11–13; 28, 8), pp. 157–8, 183–4.

8. *Leviathan* 18, p. 234; *De Cive* vi, 9; *Elements of Law* II, i, 10 (20, 10), p. 112.

9. *Leviathan* 18, p. 234; *De Cive* vi, 8; *Elements of Law* II, i, 9 (20, 9), p. 112.

10. *Leviathan* 18, pp. 234–5; *De Cive*, vi, 7; *Elements of Law* II, i, 8 (20, 8), pp. 111–2.

11. *Leviathan* 18, p. 235; *De Cive*, vi, 10; *Elements of Law* II, i, 11 (20, 11), p. 112.

12. *Leviathan* 18, p. 235.

13. *Ibid.*, pp. 235–6.

14. *Ibid.*, p. 236.

15. *Ibid.* 21, p. 272; 30, pp. 376–7.

16. *Ibid.* 18, p. 236; "if he grant away the Power of raising Mony; the *Militia* is in vain."

17. Sir Robert Filmer, *Patriarcha and Other Political Works*, ed. Peter Laslett (Oxford, 1949), p. 239.

18. See his "Observations upon Grotius," *ibid.*, pp. 261–74.

19. *Ibid.*, p. 240. One of Filmer's pamphlets, *The Necessity of the Absolute Power of all Kings: and in particular of the King of England by John Bodin, A Protestant according to the Church of Geneva,* is extracted from Richard Knolles' translation of Bodin. See *ibid.*, pp. 315–26.

20. Bodin's name occurs frequently in J.H.M. Salmon's study, *The French Religious Wars in English Political Thought* (Oxford, 1959); among those who knew Bodin's work he includes Sir Robert Filmer, Henry Parker, Samuel Rutherford, William Prynne, Dudley Digges, Sir John Spelman, Peter Heylyn and Thomas Hobbes.

21. Jean Bodin, *The Six Bookes of a Commonweale*, trans. R. Knolles (1606), ed. K.D. McRae (Cambridge, Mass., 1962), Book I, chap. 8, p. 84. (Hereafter cited as Bodin, *République* with book and chapter and page numbers from McRae.).

22. *Ibid.*, pp. 85, 88–9. For the development and implications of Bodin's views see J.H. Franklin, *Jean Bodin and the Rise of Absolutist Theory* (Cambridge, 1973); among he useful discussions in *Jean Bodin,* ed. Horst Denzer (München, 1973), see Ralph Giesey, "Medieval Jurisprudence in Bodin's Concept of Sovereignty" for a close examination of *République* I, 8 which shows that the apparent confusions of Bodin's absolute and unlimited sovereign being bound by natural and divine law, his own contracts, fundamental constitutional laws, etc. stem from Bodin's incorporation of previous jurisprudence into his discussion.

23. Bodin, *République* I, 10, pp. 159–82; I, 8, p. 98.

24. *Ibid.*, I, 8, p. 97 and in the French but not the Latin versions III, 7, p. 384 and McRae's note, p. A 129.

25. *Ibid.*, IV, 7, pp. 535–44.

26. For a useful brief sketch of the logic of sovereignty, see Ivor Wilks, "A Note on Sovereignty" in W.J. Stankiewicz (ed.), *In Defense of Sovereignty* (New York, 1969), pp. 197–205. For H.L.A. Hart, see *The Concept of Law* (Oxford, 1961) pp. 97–107; for Hans Kelsen, see *The General Theory of Law and State,* trans. Anders Wedberg (Cambridge, Mass., 1945; rep. New York, 1961), pp. 110–6.

27. Bodin, *République* I, 10, p. 155. See Preston King, *The Ideology of Order: A Comparative Analysis of Jean Bodin and Thomas Hobbes* (London, 1974), pp. 126–57, for a discussion of Bodin's concept of sovereignty.

28. *Leviathan* 22, p. 274; 20, p. 260.

29. *De Cive*, vi, 13, 18.

30. *Leviathan* 29, p. 367.

31. Sovereignty excludes appeals outside the system, requiring that all questions be (legally) finally decidable within the system (that is, by its agencies or agencies designated by it). Thus a state with a constitution that provided for an ultimately authoritative procedure (such as enactment by the crown in parliament or by a legislature followed by approval by some proportion of the electorate in a referendum or by some other process) would still possess sovereignty. So too would a state which restricted final decisions to the "concurrent" agreement to two distinct authorities (e.g., enactment by both federal and regional authorities); so too would a state which distributed final decisions on different subjects to different authorities as the British North America Act gave the Canadian federal government power over criminal justice but reserved commerce to the provinces. Of course such systems may not always exclude the possibility that the empowered authorities will disagree and they may or may not attempt to provide a procedure for reconciling or resolving such disagreements.

32. *Elements of Law* II, viii, 7 (28, 7), pp. 172–3; the last clause closely follows Knolles's translation of Bodin at p. 194.

33. *Leviathan* 19, p. 239; cf. *République* II, 1, pp. 183–97. Some aspects of Hobbes's concept of sovereignty are discussed by F.S. McNeilly, *The anatomy of Leviathan* (London, 1968), pp. 231–40.

34. *Leviathan* 29, pp. 370, 368, 372; cf. *De Cive*, vii, 4, xii, 5; *Elements of Law* II, i, 13–9 (20, 13–9), pp. 113–8.

35. *Leviathan* 19, pp. 241–51; *De Cive* x, 3–19; *Elements of Law* II, v, 3–8 (24, 3–8), pp. 140–43.

36. *Leviathan* 18, p. 237.

37. The possibility that Hobbes held that the division of sovereign power was merely practically undesirable was suggested first to me by Professor David Raphael and subsequently by other scholars. I think that Hobbes saw indivisibility as something more than desirable. Part of the problem results from Hobbes's view of science which blurs the distinction between empirical and logical truth. Perhaps it is worth noting that at one point Hobbes actually uses the fallacious argument in relation to sovereign power that what is true of the state is also true of its ruling part; see *De Cive* xii, 4.

38. *Leviathan* 19, pp. 240–1.

39. Henry Peacham, *The Duty of All True Subjects* (London, 1639), esp. pp. 1–7. The Bodinian notion of sovereignty was obviously used by lawyers earlier in the century, e.g. in the arguments on ship money; see M.A. Judson, *The Crisis of the Constitution* (New York, 1971), pp. 130–31, 138-41.

40. Filmer, *Patriarcha*, pp. 105–13, 119-20; see Laslett's introduction, p. 3.

41. *Ibid.*, p. 157.

42. *Elements of Law* II, viii, 7 (27, 7), pp. 172–3; *Leviathan* 29, pp. 364–5.

43. *Leviathan* Review and Conclusion, pp. 719, 721–22, 728. Quentin Skinner has told the story, "Conquest and Consent: Thomas Hobbes and the Engagement Controversy" in G.E. Aylmer (ed.), *The Interregnum* (London, 1972).

44. See James Daly, "The Idea of Absolute Monarchy in Seventeenth-Century England," *Historical Journal* 21 (1978), 227–50.

3

The Failure of Hobbes's Social Contract Argument

Jean Hampton

> Whilst Mr. Hobbes with one hand speciously offers up to kings and monarchs royal gifts and privileges, he with the other, treacherously plunges a dagger into their very hearts.
>
> Richard Cumberland, *De Legibus Naturae*

A good sign that Hobbes's justification of sovereignty fails is that it is rare to see someone walk away from a reading of *Leviathan* a convinced absolutist. Ever since they were first published, Hobbes's political writings, though often evoking admiration (Skinner 1972), have generally aroused intense opposition from conservative and liberal thinkers alike. As one scholar of the seventeenth century notes, Hobbes was regarded as the "Monster of Malmesbury," the "bug-bear of the nation" (Mintz 1969, vii), and another scholar of the period relates that when Clarendon decided to spend his time during his banishment in France refuting *Leviathan*, he was embarking upon a "reputable and well-thought-of task" (Bowle 1951, 33). Twentieth-century readers, although intrigued by the power of Hobbes's argument, are even more opposed to instituting any of Hobbes's ideas than his contemporaries. What these attitudes indicate is that Hobbes's argument, compelling and sophisticated though it is, fails to justify its conclusion, and in this chapter we will explore exactly where and how it fails.

The argument I will be discussing does not attack the truth of the premises of Hobbes's argument; that is, it does not challenge the argument's soundness, only its validity. Clearly, arguments against Hobbes's psychology, or his shortsightedness account of conflict, or his regress

41

argument, could be launched by disgruntled opponents that, if successful, would call into question the truth of Hobbes's conclusion. I want
to explore what Hobbes would regard as a more serious issue, namely,
whether or not his argument for absolute sovereignty is valid, given the
truth of his psychology, the shortsightedness account, and the regress
argument. If the argument is not valid, then *Leviathan* fails on its own
terms; that is, it does not present a valid geometric deduction of
Hobbes's political conclusions. In fact, we will see that it does so fail.

I will be discussing [an] invalidity argument . . . making use of the
interesting objections and criticisms of the little-known clerics and poli-
ticians who wrote in opposition to Hobbes's theory during the seventeenth century. None of these thinkers was philosophically adept
enough to be able to launch a full-scale counterargument to Hobbes's
theory in the way Locke eventually did, perhaps because they were
accustomed to simple scriptural or theological justifications of political
power, and hence unused to dealing with rational arguments designed
to explain and legitimate a particular conception of the state. Most of
them made their arguments against Hobbes by painstakingly going
through the text of *Leviathan* and attempting to refute his ideas, one
by one, as they came upon them. Their philosophical ineptness caused
Hobbes to refer to them as "beasts" and "flies" in the epistle dedica-
tory to *De Homine*. But he was wrong to be so scornful of them. Because they were sincerely disturbed by the political situation in England, and fervent opponents of the solution Hobbes proposed, they
put a tremendous amount of work into reading and criticizing
Hobbes's writings, work that often paid off in excellent insights into
where and why Hobbes's argument fails. . . .

7.2 Leviathan **Shown to be a "Rebel's Catechism"**

I want to discuss a problem with Hobbes's argument that has been
little recognized in recent years by Hobbes scholars but that was appreciated by a number of Hobbes's important contemporary critics,
including Clarendon, Bramhall, and Filmer. This problem is so serious
that it renders the entire Hobbesian justification for absolute sovereignty invalid. Although, as we saw in the last section, Hobbes's argument does not fail because he cannot establish the rationality of creating an absolute sovereign, nonetheless it fails because he cannot
establish, given his psychology, that men and women are *able* to do

what is required to create a ruler satisfying his definition of an absolute sovereign. That is, if we assume Hobbes's shortsightedness account of conflict, his regress argument, and especially his psychological theories of human nature, we will see that the result of the only kind of "authorization" action they are able to perform will not be the institution of an absolute sovereign. Indeed, whenever Hobbes argues that people can create an absolute sovereign and that it is rational for them to do so, he has subtly but importantly changed his conception of what an absolute sovereign is and what submission to such a ruler entails. It is extremely important to appreciate that Hobbes equivocates at this crucial point in his argument in order to avoid being straightforwardly inconsistent. The purpose of this section is to expose that equivocation so as to reveal this inconsistency.

In chapter 4 of *Hobbes and the Social Contract Tradition*[1] we presented Hobbes's regress argument and the conception of absolute sovereignty that his argument supports. To review: The regress argument holds that in a civil society there must be some decision and enforcement entity that limits other such entities in society but that itself has no limits, and because this entity cannot be a law or set of laws, it must be a person. (Recall also that we argued against Hobbes's claim that this entity could be a set of persons.) Hence, the result of this argument is that civil society must have a person with *unlimited* decision and enforcement powers at its helm: That person is called the sovereign, and he has the power to decide *all* questions in the commonwealth, holding power permanently insofar as he has the power to decide the most important question in the commonwealth, that is, whether or not he should remain in power.

However, can such a sovereign really be created by Hobbesian people? In chapter 5 of *Hobbes and the Social Contract Tradition* we explored Hobbes's contention that a sovereign is created when a person is "authorized" by his subjects, where this means that they "surrender their right to all things" to him. And in chapter 6 we attempted to cash out this metaphorical language consistent with Hobbesian psychology; in particular, we argued that one authorizes a sovereign when one obeys his commands to punish others and, in general, when one does nothing to frustrate his enforcement powers. We found, however, that there had to be one big exception to any person's willingness to support the sovereign's punishment efforts in the commonwealth: One could never willingly obey the sovereign's command to punish oneself, insofar as doing so would endanger one's self-preservation, Hobbes must grant that each human being will "surrender" her punishment powers to the sovereign only insofar as doing so will not endanger her life. Thus, according to Hobbes, each human being carries with her into the commonwealth a "self-defense" right. But if she does, is the resulting ruler a genuine sovereign? Does he still have the power to decide all questions in the commonwealth? Does he still reign permanently? In order to answer these questions, we need to know precisely what this self-defense right is and how extensive it is. It clearly precludes obeying a sovereign's commands to punish oneself, but what else does it preclude?

Hobbes does not clearly define this self-defense right. Indeed, its name suggests that it is only a negative description of the fundamental right of self-preservation. However, Hobbes has to take the position that the self-defense right is only a small part of the larger self-preservation right, distinguishable from the "right to all things" that is surrendered to the ruler so that he is made sovereign. If Hobbes does not, then obviously nothing is surrendered to the sovereign. So let us begin by defining the right very narrowly as the privilege or liberty to defend one's body if it is attacked, or to do what is necessary to procure the means (e.g., food and shelter) to assure bodily survival. On our supposition, Hobbes must expect a subject to disobey *any* command by the sovereign when obedience likely would threaten that subject's bodily survival more than would disobedience.

But if we accept this very natural interpretation of the self-defense right, then isn't this granting the subjects the right of private judgment concerning whether or not their lives have been endangered? Why doesn't it make their obedience to him conditional on his commands not threatening their lives, where *they* are the judges of this question? And because empowerment comes about only from obedience, why doesn't this make the sovereign's empowerment conditional on people's determination that such obedience is rational? Yet, insofar as it does, they do not really empower a truly absolute sovereign at all, because there is no single permanent power to decide all questions and hence ensure peace among men. Conservative readers to *Leviathan* in the seventeenth century were quick to notice these subversive implications of the self-defense right. Filmer correctly perceived that by granting that the subjects had a right to defend themselves, even when the right is very limited in scope, Hobbes makes the subjects the judges of whether or not the sovereign has endangered their survival, and hence allows the subjects to decide whether or not they will disobey certain of the sovereign's commands (1652, 4). This means that the sovereign is not the only authority in a commonwealth and that he will have to reckon with disobedience or rebellion on the part of some or all of his subjects if they decide that his laws or actions jeopardize their lives.

In fact, one of the consequences of allowing the subjects this self-defense right was Hobbes's very peculiar position on the legitimacy of rebellion in a commonwealth, a position that made all royalists who had lived through the events of the 1640s furious. Hobbes says that one is never justified in initiating a rebellion, because no man will be better off if the sovereign is deposed and the state of nature returns. However,

> in case a great many men together, have already resisted the Soveraign Power unjustly, or committed some Capitall crime, for which every one of them expecteth death, whether have they not the Liberty then to joyn together, and assist, and defend one another? Certainly they have: For they but defend their lives, which the Guilty man may as well do, as the Innocent. There was indeed injustice in the first breach of their duty; Their bearing of Arms subsequent to it, though it be to maintain what they have done, is no new unjust act. And if it be onely to defend their persons, it is not unjust at all. (*Lev,* 21, 17, 112–13)

After quoting this passage, Bishop Bramhall asks: "Why should we not change the Name of *Leviathan* into *Rebells catechism?*" (1658, 515).[2] What is upsetting Bramhall and others[3] is that in this passage Hobbes is partially condoning as right certain rebel activity in a commonwealth. He even uses the phrase "not unjust" to describe rebellion if it is done to preserve the rebels' lives, and this usage is quite shocking, because he has defined injustice simply as disobedience to the sovereign's laws, which the rebellious subject is surely committing. But probably Hobbes simply misspoke here, and really meant by "not unjust" the concept "is a prudent course of action." Indeed, it seems plausible that in this passage Hobbes is contending that although people who start a rebellion are not behaving prudently, nevertheless if they know that they will be killed by the sovereign's forces on their surrender, then their continuation of the attack and the bearing of arms becomes prudent. And clearly Hobbes makes this point, because he maintains that the rebels retain a self-defense right and hence cannot refuse to defend their lives when they are under attack. But by taking this position, Hobbes is committed to advocating the continuation of rebel activity in a commonwealth once it has begun, and hence sanctioning the internal warfare and civil strife that the creation of an absolute sovereign was supposed to end. In defense, Hobbes would, of course, stress that he argues against the legitimacy of initiating a rebellion, but his conservative critics angrily appreciate that he also condones (and must condone) as rational the continuation of rebellious activity once it has begun.[4] And not only did these critics find this condoning of rebellious activity offensive; more important, they found it inconsistent with the idea that when one subjugates oneself to a sovereign, one makes him the judge of all questions in the commonwealth and the master of every area of one's life.

However, what upset the conservatives even more was that Hobbes did not limit the scope of the self-defense right to mere bodily survival. In Chapter 21, on the liberties of the subjects, Hobbes uses a very broad notion of this right, that is, that one can rightfully resist or defend oneself against anything that *might lead* not only to death but also to mere injury of one's body, as a foundation for a number of subject liberties that would seriously undermine the supposedly limitless and absolute power of the sovereign. For example, he says that "If a man be interrogated by the Soveraign, or his Authority, concerning a crime done by himselfe, he is not bound (without assurance of Pardon) to confesse it; because no man (as I have shewn . . .) can be obliged by Covenant to accuse himselfe". (*Lev,* 21, 13, 112). Given that such interrogation is not a direct attack on the subject's bodily survival, and given that the subject is supposed to have made the sovereign his master and hence obliged himself to obey the commands of the sovereign, how can he refuse to disobey the sovereign's orders here? Is this "owning all the Actions (without exception) of the Man, or Assembly we make our Soveraign?" (*Lev,* 21, 10, 111). And what about the passage in which Hobbes says

> No man is bound . . . either to kill himselfe, or any other man; and consequently . . . the Obligation a man may sometimes have, upon the Command of the Soveraign to execute any *dangerous,* or *dishonourable* Office, dependeth not on the Words of our Submission; but on the Intention; which is to be understood by the End thereof. (*Lev.* 21, 15, 112; emphasis added)

What? Is Hobbes saying that people have a right to *lie* to their sovereign, that they can refuse not only to kill other men but also to commit those actions that are dangerous or *dishonorable?* Clarendon was shocked that Hobbes would suggest that the right to defend oneself could include defending not only one's body but also one's reputation (1676, 135). In addition, Hobbes says in this paragraph that men have a right to choose not to obey a sovereign's command to kill another. But if all or many of the sovereign's subjects choose to exercise this "right" (believing their disobedience to be prudent), what coercive power does the sovereign have left? How can he amass an army to quell internal rebellion? How can he even create a police force that will pursue criminals, or carry out executions? The self-defense right has now been interpreted so broadly that it is essentially equivalent to the *entire* right to preserve oneself.

However, there is an important reason why Hobbes *must* broaden the self-defense right in this way. Remember that Hobbes's entire justification of the state, as we saw in chapter 6, rests on its being conducive to a person's self-preservation. But according to Hobbesian psychology, the pursuit of this goal is central to a person's life not only outside but also inside a commonwealth. Hobbesian people do not simply forget their ultimate desire to preserve themselves when they enter the commonwealth; it remains their premier goal. But insofar as it does, each of them will determine the rationality of performing any action in the commonwealth by determining to what extent it will further this goal. So Hobbes's psychological views force him to admit that the goal of self-preservation (not merely some limited concern for "self-defense") provides the criterion for determining whether or not to obey *any* of the laws of the commonwealth. And this means that such people are incapable of letting the sovereign determining their every action; their psychology is such that they will obey a sovereign command only when, in their eyes, it will further their lives to do so.

Perhaps even more remarkably, there are two passages in *Leviathan* in which Hobbes actually admits this is so. One of them occurs in Chapter 21 in the midst of Hobbes's attempt to define the self-defense right:

> When . . . our refusall to obey, frustrates the End for which the Soveraignty was ordained; then there is no Liberty to refuse: otherwise there is. (*Lev.* 21, 15, 112)

It appears from this passage that the subjects are supposed to perform some kind of expected-utility calculation about the relative benefits of obeying or disobeying the sovereign's commands, taking into consideration not only the dangers of disobedience but also the effect the action of disobedience will have on the stability and final purposes of government. But if these calculations dictate disobedience, the subject is "right" (i.e., rational) to disobey. So, by taking this position, Hobbes essentially is admitting that the self-defense right retained by each subject in the commonwealth is equivalent to the *entire* right of self-preservation and hence makes the subjects the judges of whether or not they will obey *any* of the sovereign's laws.

The second passage in *Leviathan* in which Hobbes admits that the subjects must be the ones who finally decide whether or not to obey the ruler occurs later in Chapter 21. In this passage, Hobbes contends that the ability of the sovereign to protect his subjects and make their lives secure defines the extent and limits of the subjects' rightful obedience to the sovereign:

> The Obligation of Subjects to the Soveraign, is understood to last as long, and no longer, than [sic] the power lasteth, by which he is able to protect them. . . . The end of Obedience is Protection. [*Lev*, 21, 21, 114; see also DC, *EW* ii, 6, 74–5]

The interesting question one is left with on reading this passage is, *Who decides* whether or not the sovereign is adequately protecting his subjects? If a ruler is absolute sovereign, then he should have final say over what his subjects should and should not do, and hence he should be the judge of whether or not they should continue to obey his laws; but because it follows (as Filmer recognized[5]) from Hobbes's psychology that human beings will always judge any course of action on the basis of how well it furthers their self-preservation, he is committed to saying that the subjects will decide whether or not submission to the sovereign is furthering their lives. Indeed, given that psychology, we can expect them to do nothing else—whether the sovereign likes it or not. But this means Hobbes is forced to say that *an "absolute sovereign" reigns at his subjects' pleasure,* for it is they who decide whether or not obedience will secure them protection! When commenting on this passage, Bishop Bramhall appreciates not only how difficult it is for Hobbes to say anything else but also how disastrous this position is for Hobbes's political argument:

> Either it must be left to the soveraign determination, whether the subjects security be sufficiently provided for, And then in vain is any mans sen-

tence expected against himself, or to the discretion of the subject, (as the words themselves do seem to import,) and then there need no other bellowes to kindle the fire of a civill war, and put a whole commonwealth into a combustion, but this seditious Article. (1658, 513)

Bramhall's point is that insofar as Hobbes is forced to admit that the subjects decide whether or not to continue their obedience to the sovereign, the commonwealth will inevitably degenerate into chaos and civil war.

But is Bramhall right to say this? Insofar as the self-defense right retained by the subject must be understood by Hobbes, given his psychology, as the entire right to preserve oneself, exactly why does this spell disaster for his political argument? That is, why does it mean that Hobbes's argument for absolute sovereignty is *invalid?*

Consider that an absolute sovereign is defined by Hobbes to be someone who is the *final decider* of *all* questions in a commonwealth, and whose subjects are literally enslaved to him. But if the subjects retain a right to determine whether or not to obey the sovereign's laws, then the sovereign not only fails to be the ultimate decider of every issue but also is not the decider of the most important question in the commonwealth: whether or not he will continue to receive power from his subjects. As we saw in chapter 6, the sovereign's empowerment comes about only when the subjects obey his punishment commands. But now we see that *they decide* whether or not it is advantageous for them to obey these commands on the basis of whether or not doing so will further their self-preservation. So these "slaves" are continually deciding whether or not to let their master have the whip! Clearly this is not genuine enslavement at all, and the ruler with the whip is not someone who has absolute power to do what he wishes, but only the power to do what his subjects will *let* him do.

Indeed, as long as the subjects retain the right to preserve themselves in a commonwealth, they cannot be said to have surrendered *anything* to the sovereign. Whatever power he has been granted by the subjects for the purpose of furthering their self-preservation can and will be taken back by the subjects when they determine that doing so will further their self-preservation. And insofar as any sovereign will lose his punishment power if his subjects decide it is no longer advantageous for them to obey his punishment commands, the sovereign's power *must* be understood to be a "loan" from the people, not a permanent grant. The power he wields not only comes from them but also

returns to them if *they* decide his use of it will do more to hurt them
than to help them, and this is exactly the relationship that prevails between any principal and his agent. In fact, the same process of making
agreements in order to institute the sovereign that we explored at
length in chapter 6 can also be used by the subjects to take back the
power they lent to him, and used instead to reach agreement on lend-
ing that power to a different ruler who these subjects believe will be
better able to further their self-preservation. To use Nozickean terminology: If the "protection agency" hired by the people is perceived by
them to be doing a poor job of furthering their self-preservation, they
may find it in their best interest to "fire" that agency and "hire" another. But this means that as long as people retain the right to preserve
themselves in the commonwealth, Hobbes is also forced to admit that
there is really an *agency relationship* between people and ruler, and
this is exactly what he did *not* want to conclude in *Leviathan.*

But readers might question the idea that this conclusion is a disastrous one for Hobbes. Couldn't he contend that the less-than-absolute
ruler-agent that Hobbesian people can create is still powerful enough
to achieve peace among them? Perhaps he can—we shall explore this
possibility in the next chapter—but the fact remains that in *Leviathan*
he explicitly contends in his regress argument that nothing less than a
ruler who reigns permanently and has the power to decide all questions in the commonwealth can end the warfare among human beings.
Thus, if we accept the truth of the regress argument, we are forced to
accept the kind of ruler Hobbesian people are able to create is not
good enough to secure peace. Indeed, it is useful to review compo-
nents of Hobbes's regress argument that we presented earlier in chapter 4 in order to see exactly how, given this argument, the "agency
commonwealth" forced on Hobbes by his psychological views is
doomed to fail. Or, to put it more crudely, it is useful to see the way in
which Hobbes is skewered with his own sword.

Consider that as long as subjects retain the right to preserve themselves, and hence the right to decide whether or not to obey any of
their ruler's commands, *private judgment* has not been destroyed in
the commonwealth, and Hobbes himself contends, using his ethical
and psychological views, that any commonwealth in which private judgment exists will be destroyed from within:

> I observe the *Diseases* of a Common-wealth, that proceed from the poy-
> son of seditious doctrines; whereof one is, *That every private man is*

Judge of Good and Evill actions. . . . From this false doctrine, men are disposed to debate with themselves, and dispute the commands of the Common-wealth; and afterwards to obey, or disobey them, as in their private judgements they shall think fit. Whereby the Common-wealth is distracted and *Weakened.* (*Lev,* 29, 6, 168)

What we have discovered is that Hobbesian people are incapable of giving up their power of private judgment in a commonwealth because they will always retain the ability in a commonwealth to determine whether any action—including the action of obeying the sovereign's commands—is more conducive to their self-preservation than any available alternative. And given what Hobbes says in the foregoing passage, he would believe that the results of each subject retaining this right will be, first, debates whether or not to obey the ruler's commands that cannot be resolved in any way except by violence, followed by seditious actions by dissatisfied subjects fanning this violence, leading eventually to full-scale war. And as we see from their remarks cited earlier, Hobbes's contemporary critics, including Cumberland, Filmer, and Bramhall, agree with this general point. So Hobbes's regress argument in *Leviathan* (based on his psychology) against any political union in which subjects retain the right to make private judgments (and so the right to judge their ruler's performance) is also an argument against the political union Hobbes himself is forced to espouse given that same psychology.

Consider another aspect of the regress argument against agency commonwealths made in Chapter 18 of *Leviathan* involving the existence of a contract between ruler and people in these regimes. Hobbes insists (*Lev,* 18, 4, 89) that any contract-created commonwealth is doomed to fail. Because there can be no legal judge to decide any controversy about how well the ruler is living up to the agency contract, each subject will judge this question on the basis of how well the ruler is advancing her self-preservation. But such individual assessments are bound to conflict, and Hobbes believes that it will be only a short period of time before this sort of contract-created commonwealth will degenerate into a state of war as the subjects turn to violence (just as they did in England during the 1640s) to resolve their disagreements over how well the ruler is performing. But, as we have seen, in a Hobbesian commonwealth the subjects retain, by virtue of their psychological makeup, the right to decide whether or not to obey the sovereign's commands. This means that the sovereign is essentially

empowered by them for as long as they believe that following his commands will be conducive to their interests, so that there is, at the very
least, an *implicit agreement* between him and the subjects specifying
what he must do to retain the power given to him by the subject's
obedience. It follows that this "implicit agency-contract" commonwealth is doomed to fail.

The third and perhaps most significant problem introduced into
Hobbes's commonwealth by the subjects' retention of the right to preserve themselves is the loss of the permanence and continuity of sovereign rule. Recall our discussion in chapter 5 of Hobbes's official explanation of this permanence and continuity: Because the subjects
"surrender their right to all things" to the sovereign, they give him a
property right in them, so that if they try to take back the right they
previously surrendered from either him or his successor (who has been
willed that property right), "they take from him that which is his own,
and so again it is injustice" (*Lev.* 18, 3, 89). There is a peculiar and
intriguing moral tone to this passage that, given Hobbes's subjectivist
ethical position, ought not to be there. We tried to "explain away" this
moral tone in chapter 5 by interpreting the wrongfulness of rebellion
prudentially: Deposing the sovereign or refusing to obey his hand-
picked successor is wrong, not because it violates some deontologically
valid moral law but because it will precipitate violence and civil strife,
endangering not only the lives of other members of the commonwealth but also one's own life.

But note what this prudential explanation of the wrongfulness of
rebellion takes for granted! It assumes that *the subjects* can and will
judge whether it is prudent for them to remain in the commonwealth
or work to depose it. And we can expect that they will (rationally)
choose not to obey these commands whenever doing so will threaten
their self-preservation. This means that a sovereign holds power because most or all of his subjects have chosen to obey him—that is, have
chosen to let him have power, which means that, in the end, he rules
because *they let him rule.* But a sovereign cannot be permanently authorized when the subjects are not only able but also "prudentially
obliged" to secede from his rule when their lives are, in *their* eyes,
endangered. Such a ruler holds power conditionally, not permanently.
And no successor of a sovereign can be assured of his property right
over the subjects if these subjects are not only able but also "prudentially obliged" to rethink the advisability of their allegiance after the
reins of power have been passed on. In the end, this successor receives

power not when the previous sovereign bequeaths it to him, but only when the subjects decide to let him have it by obeying his punishment commands. And that decision might go against him, destroying the continuity of rule in this political society.

I believe that it is because Hobbes *cannot* permanently and absolutely bind people, as he has described them, to any ruler or ruler-successor by arguing for the prudence of their allegiance to that ruler that Hobbes's remarks on a subject's obligation to the ruler continually have a moral tone. Because his argument is critically weak at this point, he "cheats," either consciously or unconsciously, by invoking moral ideas that not only have no place in his argument but also have already been rejected in the course of making that argument. Consider his remarks in Chapter 18 on why "The subjects cannot change the forme of government." He starts out by saying that

> they that have already Instituted a Commonwealth, being thereby bound by Covenant, to own the Actions, and Judgements of one, cannot lawfully make a new Covenant, amongst themselves, to be obedient to any other, in any thing whatsoever, without his permission. (*Lev.* 18, 3, 88)

Why do they need his permission? Perhaps because it is prudent for them to ask for it? But if they think another individual would make a better sovereign because he would further their preservation more effectively than the original sovereign, why doesn't prudence dictate *not* asking the original sovereign's permission and simply making the switch? But, Hobbes might contend, switching sovereigns likely will bring forth a time of bloodshed and chaos, so that it is not in one's best interest to try it. However, what if the subjects believe that the switch can be made with little loss of life, or believe that the switch is so desirable that an expected-utility calculation tells them it is worth the risk of bloodshed? Hobbes cannot rule out the possibility that situations like this could exist. And it is probably because he cannot preserve permanence of rule by appealing to prudence to block rebellion on all occasions that he suggest that the action is wrong in some objectively moral sense.

That moral tone surfaces a few sentences later when he says, as we noted earlier, that deposing the sovereign is taking from him "that which is his own," an act that is "injustice." In chapter 5 we gave a prudential interpretation of this passage, but perhaps the more natural interpretation is a moral one, that is, that it is morally wrong to take the sovereign's power from him because that would be stealing. But where do these scruples against stealing come from? From the laws of nature, whose dictates are not even supposed to be followed if doing so will endanger one's preservation? No, these laws contain nothing that would rule out theft in *all* circumstances. Indeed, stealing (i.e., seizing an object that another has claimed) would seem to be (prudentially) right and rational if the object is necessary for one's preservation and if taking it does not endanger one's life. Hence, far from laying a moral foundation for the *complete* condemnation of stealing, Hobbes's law of nature and his psychology lay the groundwork for explaining when it is rational and (prudentially) correct to be a thief—even a "rebellious" thief of the sovereign's power.

So the moral tone in these passages seems to be Hobbes's attempt to circumvent deep trouble in his argument—a way to try to make the sovereign's rule permanent and his successor's rule secure, when no such permanence or continuity of rule follows from his argument. Critics such as Warrender have been rightfully sensitive to the moral tone of Hobbes's discussion of a subject's obligation to her sovereign, although missing the way in which, given Hobbes's subjectivist meta-ethics and his analysis of the validity of the laws of nature, that moral tone is completely out of place in his argument, and actually signals that argument's failure.

So, we now see that Hobbes's social contract argument is invalid: That argument cannot show that people, as he has described them, can institute what Hobbes defines as an absolute sovereign. Indeed, let us spell out this invalidity precisely:

1. In order for peace to be secured, an absolute sovereign must be created, and an absolute sovereign is defined as one who is master of all his subject-slaves; this absolute sovereign is the final decider of all questions in the commonwealth, including the question whether or not he will continue to hold power, and in virtue of deciding this last question, he holds power permanently.

2. Hobbesian people empower a ruler by obeying his punishment commands, and they do so whenever *they decide* such obedience is conducive to their best interests.

3. But from (2), it follows that the ruler created by Hobbesian people does not decide *all* questions; in particular, he does not decide for his subjects the question whether or not they will obey his commands—including his punishment commands.

4. It follows from (3) that insofar as a ruler holds power only as long as his subjects obey his punishment commands, the subjects determine (by their decision whether or not to obey these commands) whether or not he will continue to hold power.

5. Hence, from (3) and (4), Hobbesian people cannot create a ruler who meets the definition of a sovereign in (1) (i.e., a ruler who decides all questions in the commonwealth and whose reign is permanent), which, from (1), means that they cannot secure peace.

So there is no successful geometric deduction of absolute sovereignty in *Leviathan,* although Hobbes certainly tried mightily to construct one. Although most twentieth-century critics have commonly assumed that Hobbes's political conclusions can be dismissed because they rest on false premises, they have not appreciated the more important fact that the conclusions themselves do not follow from those premises. Indeed, we see that Hobbes's dilemma in *Leviathan* is identical with that of Philip Hunton. Recall the discussion in chapter 4 of Hunton's difficulty in explaining how people who "elected" their sovereign in an original contract were not superior to their ruler even though they were his creators. Hunton ends up maintaining that the subjects *surrender* some or all of their rights to their ruler, thereby enslaving themselves to him, but Hunton also insists that they retain a "moral" power to evaluate his conduct. In the end, it turns out that Hobbes tries to hold a similar sort of contradictory position.

But we really should have appreciated that Hobbes's argument was in trouble by the end of chapter 6. In that chapter we relied on Hobbes's psychology to specify precisely the concrete actions that Hobbesian people would take to institute a ruler. And the actions we specified *presupposed* that people always retained the right to determine if the performance of any of those actions was in their interest. Indeed, this right was at the heart of my attempt to explain how Hobbesian people could create a commonwealth, because at every state of the creation process I was concerned to show that these people would (or could) find the actions required at that stage advantageous to them. So, in setting out to define 'authorization' consistent with Hobbesian psychology, I ended up by cashing out the metaphor not of "surrendering power" but of "loaning power" to the ruler.

Indeed, the fact that I so naturally cashed out the notion of authorization consistent with Hobbes's psychology but inconsistent with his definition of absolute sovereignty suggests why so many critics have not realized that his political argument in *Leviathan* is invalid. Hobbes equivocates: He gives only a metaphoric definition of the notion of authorization, characterizing it as a surrender, such that it appears consistent with his official definition of absolute sovereignty; but when he actually uses the notion of authorization in his argument, he implicitly uses it in the way I defined in chapter 6—assuming that it involves obedience to the ruler *for self-interested reasons*—and linking it with a self-defense right. The fact that this use does *not* cash out the surrender metaphor and is actually inconsistent with the official definition of absolute sovereignty is therefore very difficult to see. . . .

Notes

1. Jean Hampton, *Hobbes and the Social Contract Tradition* (Cambridge: Cambridge University Press, 1986).

2. And see Edward Clarendon, *A Brief View and Survey of the Dangerous and Pernicious Errors to Church and State in Mr. Hobbes's Book, Entitled Leviathan* (1676), 87: "[Hobbes] devest[s] his Subjects of all that liberty, which the best and most peaceable men desire to possess, yet he literally and bountifully confers upon them such a liberty as no honest man can pretend to, and which is utterly inconsistent with the security of Prince and People."

3. See also Robert Filmer, *Observations Concerning the Originall of Government, Upon Mr. Hobs Leviathan.* In *Patriarcha and Other Political Works of Sir Robert Filmer,* ed. Peter Laslett (Oxford: Basil Blackwell, 1949), 8–9.

4. It was because of passages like this that Clarendon thought Hobbes was offering in *Leviathan* a justification of de facto power in general, and Cromwell's rule in particular.

5. See Filmer (1642, 8): "[Hobbes] resolves refusal to obey, may depend upon the judging of what frustrates the end of Soveraignty and what not, of which he cannot meane any other Judge but the people."

References

Bowle, John. *Hobbes and His Critics* (London: J. Cape, 1951).

Bramhall, John. *The Catching of Leviathan or the Great Whale, appendix to Castigations of Mr. Hobbes . . . Concerning Liberty and Universal Necessity* (1658).

Hobbes, Thomas. *Leviathan.* Ed. C. B. Macpherson (Harmondsworth: Penguin, 1968).

Mintz, S. I. *The Hunting of Leviathan* (Cambridge: Cambridge University Press, 1969).

Molesworth, W., ed. *The English Works of Thomas Hobbes* (London: John Bohn, 1840).

Skinner, Quentin. "The Context of Hobbes's Theory of Political Obligation." In *Hobbes and Rousseau: A Collection of Critical Essays.* Ed. M. Cranston and R. Peters (New York: Anchor-Doubleday, 1972), 109–42.

4

Hobbes's Social Contract

David Gauthier

1.

In justifying the sovereign, does Hobbes appeal to a social contract? In her new and important book, *Hobbes and the Social Contract Tradition*,[1] Jean Hampton says "No" (pp. 4, 186–8, 279). Hobbes's "social contract" argument is unfortunately, although no doubt irretrievably, mislabelled. He appeals, not to a contract, but to a self-interested agreement or convention. And this appeal is typical of contractarian strategy; "*there is no literal contract* in any successful social contract theory" (p. 4).

And in authorizing the sovereign, do the subjects alienate their rights to him? Hobbes claims that they do. But Hampton maintains that his claim is unsuccessful, and that *any* alienation theory must be unsuccessful (pp. 256–66). However, beneath the surface, another, successful account of authorization may be found, according to which the subjects appoint an agent to act on their behalf. But this agent lacks many of the characteristics of the Hobbesian sovereign; he is neither absolute nor permanent. According to Hampton, the sovereign whom Hobbesian men can authorize is not Leviathan.

My concern is with the structure of Hobbes's social contract argument. Hampton's revisionist interpretation turns on two contrasts, opposing self-interest agreement to contract, and agency to alienation. Against the claim that the "social contract" is a self-interested agreement with which the subjects appoint an agent, I shall defend the traditional account of a true contract in which the subjects alienate their rights to a ruler. This provides the best reading of Hobbes's argument, and the only one compatible with his political absolutism. But it offers more. For an alienation social contract theory need not be wedded to this implausible and unattractive absolutism, and Hobbes's achievement in being the first systematically to construct such a theory makes him the true parent of rational morality and politics. However, I shall not pursue this larger theme here, confining myself to analyzing, not celebrating, Hobbes's argument.

2.

Hobbes characterizes the natural condition of humankind as a mutually unprofitable state of war of every person against every other person. Since Hobbesian persons value self-preservation above all else, and since universal war affords each person the prospect of a life that is nasty, brutish and short, ending in violent death, some explanation of the natural emergence of such a war is evidently needed. I shall put this question aside here.[2] It will suffice to interpret Hobbes as holding that if fully rational persons were in, *and could not exit from,* a state of nature, then they could not effectively agree on peace, and universal conflict would emerge. But of course Hobbes supposes that persons can exit from the state of nature, and his account of conflict is intended to establish, not that rational persons would face universal war, but that they would accept an institutional structure that provides the coercive force needed to motivate compliance with the laws of nature, which Hobbes describes as "convenient Articles of Peace, upon which men may be drawn to agreement"[3] (p. 63), and so to establish and maintain peaceable cooperation.

How do persons exit from the state of nature, converting it into society? What is needed "to make their Agreement constant and lasting . . . is a Common Power, to keep them in awe, and to direct their actions to the Common Benefit" (p. 87). The second task—the direction of actions to the common benefit—is one of coordination. But to ensure that persons follow the directions given, "to secure them in such sort, as that by their own industrie, and by the fruites of the Earth, they may nourish themselves and live contentedly," the first task—to keep them in awe—is necessary. And this requires a sovereign—someone who rules.

Hobbes's procedure for instituting a sovereign has two parts. The first is a covenant of every person with every other person. The second is the authorization, by every person, of some one person (or group). The authorization provides the content of the covenant; each person covenants, with every other person, to authorize some one person or group, which is to say, to treat the acts of that person or group as her own.

For Hobbes a covenant is a type of contract. And so the institution of a sovereign is effected by a social contract. But Hampton finds this terminology misleading. She claims that the institution of the sovereign requires only a self-interested agreement. What is the point here at issue? And is Hampton correct? She claims that "SI [self-interested] agreements differ from contracts in being coordinations of intentions to act that are kept by both parties *solely for self-interested reasons,* whereas contracts are trades of *promises* that introduce moral incentives that either *supplement or replace* each party's self-interested motivations" (pp. 145, 147). A social contract provides a moral basis for sovereignty; a self-interested agreement provides a purely prudential basis.

But Hampton's distinction needs modification. Consider an agreement made within a framework providing for legal enforcement. And suppose that without the prospect of such enforcement, compliance with the agreement would not be adequately motivated. This is surely a paradigmatic contract. But the incentive provided by legal enforceability need not be thought of as moral. Rather, the agreement simply calls into play a supplementary but necessary incentive, and in so doing reveals its contractual character.

I propose to distinguish contracts from other agreements by characterizing the former as exchanges of intentions to act that introduce incentives, whether internal or external, moral or other, to supplement or replace each party's motivation to attain the true objective of the agreement. In particular, I distinguish contracts from purely coordinative agreements. Both require that each person prefers the outcome of agreement to that of no agreement. In purely coordinative agreements, each also prefers compliance with the agreement to noncompliance, given compliance by her fellows, and this preference for compliance is not induced by sanctions, external or internal. Furthermore, each expects the others to comply, and intends to comply herself. No part of the agreement exists solely to ensure compliance with the remainder, so that, leaving compliance aside, omitting any of the terms of the agreement would be regarded as undesirable by at least one of the parties.

A contract is only partially coordinative. Again, each prefers the outcome of agreement to that of no agreement. But either someone does not expect compliance by the other or others, or would be unwilling to comply herself, in the absence of sanctions or terms introduced solely for the purpose of ensuring compliance with the remainder. Rather, someone expects compliance by the other or others, or intends to comply herself, only because of the additional incentives that the agreement calls into play.

Note that in so characterizing contract I say nothing about a preference for noncompliance over compliance, given that others comply. If each person chooses on the basis of her preferences, and if no problem is created by decision-making or communication costs, then a contract is required only in those cases in which some would prefer noncompliance, given compliance by the others, in the absence of sanctions or specially created incentives. But my characterization of contract allows for cases in which, even if each person would prefer, in some not strictly behavioural sense, to comply given compliance by the others, yet sufficient compliance would nevertheless not be expected in the absence of additional terms or incentives, whether because of the costs of making a purely coordinative agreement, or because of the irrational refusal of some to comply with such an agreement. For in these cases coordination must be induced by supplementary incentives, and this is what distinguishes contract.

Given Hobbes's insistence that agreement alone does not suffice to achieve peace in the absence of a common power, we should interpret the covenant of every person with every other person as a contract, and not as a purely coordinative agreement. For even if we suppose that everyone keeps this covenant for purely self-interested reasons, yet these reasons stem, not simply from the concern to achieve the primary objective of agreement, peace and security, but rather from the power of the sovereign, a supplementary incentive called into play, and indeed created, by the agreement itself. The institution of a sovereign is not the primary objective of agreement, or part of this objective. Were mere agreement on conditions of peace sufficient—were the covenant a purely coordinative agreement—then a sovereign enforcer would be not merely unnecessary, but positively undesirable.

Hampton claims that the agreement to institute a sovereign, considered in itself, is kept for purely self-interested reasons. If she is right, then the institution of a sovereign, *as such,* is purely coordinative and fits her model of self-interested agreement. But to suppose that

Hobbes does not appeal to a social contract is to overlook the context of the institution of the sovereign, and to fail to recognize that it is part of a larger agreement, whose primary objective is peace and security, and that in relation to this larger agreement, it is accepted, despite its cost, to ensure compliance. This overall agreement is the social contract.

3.

Is sovereignty successful? Will each person be sufficiently motivated by considerations of her own interest to obey the sovereign's directives and adhere to the laws of nature? If this is what is required for success, then sovereignty fails. The sovereign's attempt to make his subjects secure gives rise to a free-rider problem which cannot be solved by a direct appeal to self-interest.

If the sovereign is to provide security, what must his subjects do? Hampton argues, plausibly, that a subject must (i) "not interfere with the sovereign's punishment of anyone other than himself," (ii) "actively assist the sovereign when ordered to do so in punishment and enforcement activities involving others," and (iii) "be disposed to obey the punishment orders of only the sovereign" (pp. 174–5). We may agree with her that the first and third of these raise no problems in plausible circumstances; no one would have an interest in opposing an effective sovereign or in supporting a rival. But to give the sovereign active assistance is to risk one's safety and security. Will not each subject prefer to free-ride, letting others (should they so choose) actively assist the sovereign? Will not each subject reason that the incremental effect of adding her assistance in support of the sovereign would yield her so little expected benefit, in comparison with the expected cost to herself of providing the assistance, that it is not in her interest, and so not rational, to assist?

In attempting to obtain the active assistance of his subjects, the sovereign seems to face the usual problem involved in supplying an incremental public good—a good that is non-excludable, so that if it is supplied to one person, it is supplied to all. But Hampton denies that the sovereign need face this problem, because security is not an incremental good, but a step good. The security level is not increased incrementally by each individual act of assistance to the sovereign, but in discrete steps each of which requires the acts of several individuals. And the sovereign can exploit the step character of security to arrange it so that each subject will find it rational to obey his orders, and provide the active assistance he needs.

Consider her example (pp. 176ff.). The sovereign wants a lawbreaker apprehended, and selects a group of persons to carry out the task. If the group is too small it will fail, and no increase in security will result. If the group is too large, no greater increase in security will result than if it were just large enough to carry out the apprehension successfully. Hence if the sovereign commands a minimally sufficient number of persons to constitute the apprehending group, each person selected will reason as follows: "It is very likely that the others selected, and no one else, will participate in trying to apprehend the lawbreaker. If I participate, very likely the group will succeed and security will increase. If I do not participate, very likely the group will fail and security will not increase. So the expected value, to me, of my participation is almost equal to my expected gain in security from apprehending the lawbreaker, and this exceeds my cost of participation. Therefore it is rational for me, because in my interest, to obey the sovereign's command and give him my active assistance."

Hampton agrees that each person will see his contribution as decisive, and so equate the expected value of assisting the sovereign with the expected value to himself of the good achieved by the entire group. But if this moves each member of the group to participate, then the benefit to each from the apprehension of the lawbreaker must exceed his cost in participating. And since the members of the group bear the entire cost of apprehending the lawbreaker, then the total social cost must be less than the benefits to the members of the apprehending group alone. If each person in the society may expect roughly the same gain in security as her fellows from the apprehension of the lawbreaker, then if the sovereign appoints as many as one person out of every hundred members of society to the apprehending group, the total social benefit from apprehending the lawbreaker must be at least one hundred times the cost.

Can the sovereign provide his subjects with peace and security, if he may expect their active assistance only when the good to be provided is so much greater than the cost of providing? Surely not. The sovereign can not motivate the members of a small group voluntarily to provide a non-excludable public good, albeit a step good, unless it offers a net benefit to the small group alone. And such goods will not suffice for peace and security. Hobbes has no general solution to the free-rider problem that confronts a sovereign in need of the active assistance of his subjects, if we assume, as Hampton does and as we have done implicitly in our discussion, that each subject will decide whether to assist the sovereign by a direct appeal to her overall self-interest.

4.

Our discussion of the failure of sovereignty would not surprise Hobbes, who might agree that he has no solution to the free-rider problem as we have posed it. For he never claims that the sovereign must gain the assistance of each subject by making a direct appeal to his self-interest. Such an appeal treats each individual's "private Appetite" as "the measure of Good," and Hobbes insists that so long as this is done "a man is in the condition of mere Nature" (p. 80).

Authorizing the sovereign commits the subject to more than self-interestedly assisting him in his punishment and enforcement activities. It commits the subject to accept the sovereign's *judgment* in place of his own, so that when the sovereign requires his active assistance, he obeys directly and not only if a self-interested calculation shows obedience to be advantageous. Although Hobbes insists that "all men equally, are by Nature Free," yet he treats authorization as limiting that freedom (p. 111). He distinguishes two ways in which such a limitation might arise, either "from the expresse words, *I Authorise all his Actions*" by which the subject places himself under the sovereign, or "from the Intention of him [the subject] that submitteth himself to his [the sovereign's] Power, (which Intention is to be understood by the End for which he so submitteth . . .)" (Ibid.). And this end, Hobbes goes on to say, is "the Peace of the Subjects within themselves, and their Defence against a common Enemy." But the first way, the words themselves, do not limit freedom, or put the subject under any obligation, for in them "there is no restriction at all, of his own former naturall Liberty" (p. 112). And so Hobbes concludes "that the Obligation a man may sometimes have, upon the Command of the Soveraign to execute any dangerous, or dishonourable Office, dependeth not on the Words of our Submission; but on the Intention; which is to be understood by the End thereof. When therefore our refusall to obey, frustrates the End for which the Soveraignty was ordained; then there is no Liberty to refuse: otherwise there is" (Ibid.).

In deciding whether actively to assist the sovereign, the subject is to consider whether refusal to assist frustrates the end that sovereignty exists to realize. How are we to interpret Hobbes's position here? There are at least three possibilities. If, first, we focus on Hobbes's previous statement of the end, then we might read the last sentence quoted as saying: "When an individual's refusal to obey frustrates the maintenance of peace among the subjects, and their defence against an enemy, then the individual must obey (i.e. has an obligation to obey, or has no liberty not to obey); otherwise he may refuse." This treats the end as collective. And it would, seemingly, require an individual to sacrifice himself for that end, if we suppose, as surely we must, that peace and defence may require some persons to perform dangerous and even fatal tasks.

But second, we may recall that Hobbes maintains that each individual is concerned to preserve himself, and has no natural care for the preservation of well-being of his fellows. And so we may suppose that the end is to be understood not collectively but individually; each seeks to be maintained in peace among the other subjects, and to be defended against their common enemy. We might then read the sentence as saying: "When an individual's refusal to obey frustrates his prospect of living in peace among his fellow subjects, or being defended against their common enemy, then he must obey; otherwise he may refuse." On this reading no individual would be obliged to sacrifice himself, since even if his sacrifice would help to preserve the general peace, it would frustrate his own prospect of living in peace.

There is a third interpretation, which may be motivated by reflecting on the significance of commitment in maintaining peace and security. Suppose I am a potential lawbreaker, who prefers lawbreaking with impunity to lawabiding, but lawabiding to lawbreaking and being caught. You prefer that I be lawabiding, but if I break the law, you then prefer that I do so with impunity, to spare you the danger in having to apprehend me. You prefer not to be part of the group the sovereign selects to assist him in maintaining law and order. If I expect you to react to my lawbreaking in accordance with your preferences, I shall blithely go ahead. This is disadvantageous for you. But if you are *committed* to joining the group to apprehend me, then I shall remain lawabiding. Your commitment to act against your preferences yields your best prospect.

More generally, to maximize his expectation of living in peace among his fellows, and being defended against their common enemy, a subject may do best to commit himself to perform certain actions in conditions in which, should he actually then perform them, would not best ensure his living in peace and security. The best deterrent, against the potential hostility both of one's fellows and of external enemies, may be a readiness to retaliate which in itself would be disadvantageous. This suggests that we read Hobbes's sentence as saying: "When an individual's refusal to obey would violate the commitments that maximize his prospect of living in peace among his fellow subjects, or being defended against their common enemy, then he must obey; otherwise he may refuse." This requires each subject to run real risks, but only those to which he would rationally have committed himself as maximizing his expectation of peace and security. It does not require anyone to sacrifice himself for the general peace and security of his fellows. But it does afford the sovereign the assistance that he needs, to punish offenders and maintain peace and security for his subjects.

This third interpretation enables us to make best sense of Hobbes's argument, although he does not introduce the vocabulary of commitment needed to formulate it. His account of individual motivation is directly incompatible with the collective concern necessary to the first interpretation. And the second interpretation leaves the obligation to obey the sovereign too weak, in making it depend directly on one's present interest. If each subject decides whether or not to obey by considering whether to not, in each particular situation, obedience is to his own interest or advantage, then private appetite remains the measure of good and evil, and the sovereign will be unable to elicit the degree of obedience requisite for him to bring about and maintain peace. Each subject must realize that his prospect of living securely and at peace with his fellows is maximized if he is committed to offering active support to the sovereign, even when giving that support is not itself maximally conducive to his peace and security.

Against this interpretation of Hobbes's account of authorization it may be objected that a Hobbesian person is psychologically incapable of committing himself, even in his own interest, to perform actions that would not be in his interest at the time of performance. Although Hobbes does not discuss this matter explicitly, he does insist that "of the voluntary acts of every man, the object is some *Good to himselfe*" (p. 66). However, we may suppose that the problem of commitment was not fully clear to Hobbes. In *The Logic of Leviathan*[4] I endorsed the view that Hobbesian individuals would be psychologically incapable of a commitment to actions not in their interest at the time of performance (pp. 93–9). But I now believe that the Hobbesian text gives no real guidance on this matter. A person's interest must enter at some point into an explanation of each of his voluntary actions: a commitment against interest, to perform an action against interest, would be incompatible with Hobbes's psychology. But this leaves room for a commitment based on interest. Whether Hobbes would have accepted it we can not say, but it opens the door to a much more interesting and defensible interpretation of a large part of his moral and political theory.

In section 2 I argued that the covenant should be considered a contract rather than a purely coordinative agreement because the primary aim of the parties can not be realized without providing for enforcement. I have now argued that the authorization of the enforcer, to be effective, requires a commitment to obedience that overrides self-interest. But such a commitment can not be a part of a purely coordinative agreement. Thus both parts of the procedure for instituting a sovereign fit the model of a social contract rather than that of a mere convention, adhered to because each party considers it in her interest given her expectation of adherence by her fellows.

5.

I turn to the contrast between an alienation social contract theory and an agency theory. The distinction, as formulated by Hampton, is between "the position that the ruler is instituted when the people surrender their power to him" and "the position that the ruler's power is only loaned to him" (p. 3). To authorize someone to act in one's name is to appoint her as one's agent. The subjects authorize the sovereign to act in their name. But this does not suffice to make Hobbes's account an agency theory. The issue is not whether the sovereign is the agent of his subjects, but whether he is *only* their agent. But surely there is no doubt about this; he is more than his subjects' agent and they do surrender their power to him. Hobbes formulates the covenant by which the sovereign is instituted in these words: "*I Authorise and give up my Right of Governing my selfe, to this Man, or to this Assembly of men, on this condition, that thou give up thy Right to him, and Authorise all his Actions in like manner*" (p. 87). To authorize the sovereign is to give up one's right to him, and this is surrender, not loan.

Hampton does not deny that Hobbes formally espouses an alienation contract, but she denies that he needs it, since she supposes that the sovereign can gain the support he needs by a direct appeal to the self-interest of his subjects, and she denies that an alienation contract is possible, because "the cost [of alienation] would always be greater than the increment of benefit attained" (p. 257). We have seen in the preceding sections that she is mistaken on both counts. The sovereign would be ineffective, were the subjects not to commit themselves to an obligation, overriding considerations of self-interest, to obey him, and the prospective subjects may expect to benefit by making such a commitment. And if the subjects commit themselves to an overriding obligation to obey the sovereign, then they give up to him some portion of their right to govern themselves, and accept his judgment as determining good and evil.

However, although Hobbes uses the *words* of alienation in his account of the authorization of the sovereign, yet it may be objected that authorization can not be correctly understood as the giving up or surrendering of right. To authorize someone is to appoint her as one's agent, but this is only to loan her one's right. As Hobbes says, an act *"done by Authority"* is "done by Commission, or Licence from him whose right it is" (p. 81). There is no suggestion or implication that the person "whose right it is" have given *up* that right to the agent. If I authorize you to act on my behalf, then I must acknowledge, or as Hobbes would say, own what you do, as my action. But this does not preclude me from acting on my own behalf, unless I have specifically committed myself, by covenant, not so to act, or from withdrawing my authorization, and subsequently acting on my own behalf, although I may not retroactively *disown* your action if performed with my authorization, any more than I may disown my own action. As Hobbes insists, from the words of an act of authorization "there is no restriction at all, of his own former naturall Liberty," and so no giving up of right (p. 112).

But an act of authorization may involve the giving up of right.[5] If the end for which I authorize someone to act on my behalf requires me not to withdraw my authorization or to act on my own behalf, then I do indeed give up the right so to act. The subject authorizes all of the sovereign's actions. Since her peace and security require that she commit herself to assist the sovereign in his efforts to maintain internal order and defend the society against external enemies, in authorizing the sovereign she does give up some portion of her natural liberty, or her right to do whatever seems best to her for her own preservation and well-being.[6]

Hobbes must espouse an alienation social contract theory in order to defend absolute, permanent sovereignty. If the subjects merely loan their rights to the sovereign, then he is assured neither absolute nor permanent power. But an alienation social contract theory is not therefore incompatible with limited sovereignty. Indeed, if persons have the capacity to alienate certain of their rights in order better to further their interests by undertaking overriding commitments, then internal, moral constraints, holding them to their commitments, will do much of the work that Hobbes assigns to external, political constraints, and, as we should intuitively suppose, *only* limited sovereignty is defensible. An absolute sovereign is neither needed nor wanted among persons who have some capacity to commit themselves to what their peace and security demand.

Hobbes represents himself as timorous, the twin of fear. He is frightened by the potentially destructive effects on peace and order of the individualism which he saw unleashed in his time. He recognizes that each person has reason, based in her own interest, to acknowledge constraints on the pursuit of that interest. He underestimates (or denies) the potential efficaciousness of internal or moral constraints, and so overstates the necessary extent of external or political constraints. Thus he is led to create Leviathan. But he asks the right questions, and begins to understand the form that the answers must take. The idea of an alienation contract—a device by which persons mutually agree to give up certain of their natural liberties, and in particular their self-oriented judgment of good and evil as their sole guide to action—is his enduring contribution to our thought. No secular and rational morality and politics can be built without it.

Notes

A longer version of this paper appears in *Perspectives on Thomas Hobbes*, the proceedings of the Hobbes Fourth Centenary Conference, edited by G.A.J. Rogers and Alan Ryan (Oxford University Press, 1991) with whose permission this version appears. I am grateful to Daniel Farrell for comments when an earlier draft of that version was read at the University of Michigan.

1. Jean Hampton, *Hobbes and the Social Contract Tradition* (Cambridge: Cambridge University Press, 1986).

2. I discuss the question in the longer version of this paper.

3. All page references are to the 1651 (London) edition of *Leviathan*.

4. David Gauthier, *The Logic of Leviathan* (Oxford: Clarendon Press, 1969).

5. The following argument was suggested by a seminar presentation on the relationship of sovereign and subject by Terry Moore.

6. In so interpreting Hobbes, I am departing from my position in *The Logic of Leviathan.*

5

Why Ought One Obey God?
Reflections on Hobbes and Locke

David Gauthier

I

> Lastly, those are not at all to be tolerated who deny the being of a God.
> Promises, covenants, and oaths, which are the bonds of human society,
> can have no hold upon an atheist. The taking away of God, though but
> even in thought, dissolves all.

These words, from Locke's *Letter Concerning Toleration,* ring unconvincingly in our ears. They affirm that the bonds of human society
hold only those who believe in God. This affirmation breaks into two
propositions:

1. the bonds of human society are promises, covenants, and oaths;
2. promises, covenants, and oaths hold only those who believe in
   God.

Much might be said about the first proposition, but not here.[1] Whether
it rings unconvincingly in our ears, surely the second does, and it is
this which I shall address. The supposition that moral conventions depend on religious belief has become alien to our way of thinking. Modern moral philosophers do not meet it with vigorous denials or refutations; usually they ignore it.[2] If the dependence of moral conventions
on religious belief was necessary for Locke, it is almost inconceivable
for us.

"The taking away of God, *though but even in thought, . . .*" It is with thought that we are concerned, with man's conceptions, and most especially his moral conceptions. What lies beyond thought may be relevant to the validation of these conceptions, but validation falls outside my enquiry. Whether there is a God does not affect the argument of this paper, although it may affect the consequences to be drawn from this argument. Here we are concerned with the conception of God, and the role which this conception plays in moral thought. And Locke insists that this role is central.

"The taking away of God . . . *dissolves all.*" These are measured words, which convey Locke's exact intent. They express the core of his moral and political thought. Much of the time they are not in the forefront of that thought, for Locke largely addresses those who share his conviction. But some of the time they come to the fore, since Locke was aware, uncomfortably, of those who did not share that conviction. In particular, Locke was aware of Hobbes.

Locke can be read, and often is read, from our presumptively superior vantage point. We know where his argument leads, and thus can discern its true significance. Hence we suppose that Locke was not really trying to justify individualistic contractarianism by tying it to the natural law of God, but rather that he was defending capitalistic appropriation.[3] Having ourselves abandoned God for Mammon, we read that abandonment back into Locke, and then find, not only that he is the grandfather of the ideology of capitalism, but also that he is the wolf, Hobbes, in sheep's clothing.[4]

Locke would have been unsurprised. Having taken away God, we have dissolved all—all of what Locke understood as morality. And the result is precisely Hobbism. Locke shares his individualism, his emphasis on self-preservation, his subjectivist, hedonic value theory, with his predecessor. And if these are all, then morality fails: "an Hobbist with his principle of self-preservation whereof himself is to be judge, will not easily admit a great many plain duties of morality."[5]

If Locke minus God equals Hobbes, then Hobbes plus God equals Locke. And if among our modern commentators are some who read God out of Locke, there are also some who read God into Hobbes. Hobbes tells us that "the true Doctrine of the Lawes of Nature, is the true Morall Philosophie" (L. 15).[6] Howard Warrender then says:

> If it is denied that God plays an essential role in Hobbes' doctrines, the laws of nature in the State of Nature cannot be taken to be more than prudential maxims for those who desire their own preservation.[7]

Again, the taking away of God dissolves all morality.

Warrender's comment, directed to Hobbes, has for us a further significance. We are concerned with the alleged dependence of moral conventions on religious belief. If we accept Warrender's argument, then it would seem that this dependence is required, at least for that framework of thought, shared by Hobbes and Locke, within which the science of the laws of nature is identified with moral philosophy. If we find it difficult even to understand Locke's insistence that the taking away of God dissolves all, then surely we must find it difficult to understand this framework. And yet, modern moral and political philosophers still appeal to Hobbes and Locke. Kurt Baier compares his conception of morality with that of Hobbes.[8] Robert Nozick revives the doctrine of natural law in a form which he traces to Locke.[9] Baier, of course, does not interpret Hobbes in the theistic manner of Warrender, and Nozick deliberately avoids querying the underpinning of the Lockean system. But perhaps God is lurking there, unwanted and even unconceived, yet not unneeded.

My first concern in this paper is to place the role of God in the thought of Hobbes and Locke. I shall argue that they differ in a manner which I consider characteristic of the difference between secular and religious outlooks. My next concern is to explore the implications of this difference for our understanding of morality. I shall agree with Locke that moral convention depends on religious belief, given his conceptual framework. But I shall argue that Hobbes, within his different framework, is quite able to construct a purely secular morality.

This is not all. If it were, then we might dismiss Locke as holding an outworn theism, and embrace Hobbes's secularism. But I want at least to suggest that Locke is correct about two further matters. First, he is right to insist that "a great many plain duties" cannot be accommodated within the secular morality available to Hobbes and those who share Hobbes's outlook. Second, Locke is right to insist that the taking away of God does indeed dissolve those duties. The morality available to Locke is thus not only conceptually different, but also materially different, from that of a Hobbist.

All this is important if we are to understand more recent moral thought. There is a Hobbist, secular morality, and there is a Lockean, religious morality. But what modern moral philosophers have wanted is a Lockean, secular morality, beginning with the individualism which Hobbes and Locke share with us, and leading, without introducing

God, to the "many plain duties" which Locke affirms.[10] If my suggestions are correct, such a morality is not to be found.

II

Locke's thought contains a set of tight conceptual connections among morality, law, God, nature, and reason.

1. *Morality and law*: A "moral relation" is defined as "the conformity or disagreement men's voluntary actions have to a rule to which they are referred, and by which they are judged of." "*Morally good and evil,* then, is only the conformity or disagreement of our voluntary actions to some law, whereby good or evil is drawn on us from the will and power of the law-maker." (E.II.28.4).[11]
2. *Morality, law and God*: Of three kinds of law distinguished by Locke, "The *divine law* . . . is the only true touchstone of moral rectitude" (E.II.28.8).
3. *Law, God and nature*: The divine law is "promulgated to them [men] by the light of nature, or the voice of revelation" (*Ibid.*). So promulgated, the divine law is the law of nature. "The *Rules* that they [men] make for other Mens Actions, must, as well as their own and other Mens Actions, be conformable to the Law of Nature, *i.e.* to the Will of God, of which that is a Declaration" (2T. 135).[12]
4. *Law, nature and reason*: The law of nature is identified with the law of reason (1T. 101, 2T. 96) and with Reason itself: "The *State of Nature* has a Law of Nature to govern it, which obliges every one: And Reason, which is that Law" (2T. 6).
5. *Reason and God*: Reason is "*the Voice of God in him* [man]" (1T. 86), "the common Rule and Measure, God hath given to Mankind" (2T. 11), that "which God hath given to be the Rule betwixt Man and Man, and the common bond whereby humane kind is united into one fellowship and societie" (2T. 172).

From these interconnected conceptions we may move in two directions: to the content of the law of nature, and to its binding force. I shall make brief reference to the first presently. Since the law of nature

is the expression of the will of God, the second concern directly raises
the question which serves us for a title: why ought one obey God?

Locke answers this question, which must be crucial given the structure of his moral and political thought, very briefly. His answer is formulated first in the sixth of the *Essays on the Law of Nature*,[13] but we
may focus on his later and essentially similar formulations in the *Essay
concerning Human Understanding* and the second *Treatise on Government*:

> That God has given a rule whereby men should govern themselves, I
> think there is nobody so brutish as to deny. He has a right to do it; we
> are his creatures. He has goodness and wisdom to direct our actions to
> that which is best; and he has power to enforce it by rewards and punish-
> ments, of infinite weight and duration, in another life: for nobody can
> take us out of his hands. (E.II.28.8)
>
> The *State of Nature* has a Law of Nature to govern it, which obliges
> every one: And Reason, which is that Law, teaches all Mankind, who will
> but consult it, that being all equal and independent, no one ought to
> harm another in his Life, Health, Liberty, or Possessions. For Men being
> all the Workmanship of one Omnipotent, and infinitely wise Maker; All
> the Servants of one Sovereign Master, sent into the World by his order
> and about his business, they are his Property, whose Workmanship they
> are, made to last during his, not one anothers Pleasure. (2T. 6)

Locke distinguishes three aspects of the obligation to obey God in
these passages. First, he refers to God's power, indeed to his omnipo-
tence, as the basis for the enforcement of the law of nature. Locke
insists that sanctions are necessary if law is to be binding (E.II.28.6),
but he does not argue that sanctions alone create obligation; power,
without right, may compel, but does not obligate.

Second, Locke refers to God's wisdom, and indeed to his omni-
science, in directing our actions to what is best. What is best would
seem to be determined by the interests, the pleasures and pains, of
mankind. Law, Locke says, is *"the direction of a free and intelligent
Agent* to his proper Interest, and prescribes no farther than is for the
general Good of those under that Law" (2T. 57). "Good and evil . . .
are nothing but pleasure or pain, or that which occasions or procures
pleasure or pain to us." (E.II.28.4) But Locke does not suggest that
God's wisdom and goodness, in directing our actions to what is best,
provide the basis of our obligation to obey the law of nature. He admits
that "Could they [men] be happier without it, the *Law,* as an useless

thing would of it self vanish" (2T. 57), yet it is not the usefulness of the law which makes it binding.

Rather, third, the obligation to obey God, and so the law of nature, Locke clearly derives from the rights of God, the Creator, over his creation. We are obliged to obey him because we are all his creatures, his workmanship, his property.

It is as creator that God provides law for all his creation. In the first of the *Essays on the Law of Nature* Locke says:

> The third argument [which proves the existence of a law of nature] is derived from the very constitution of this world, wherein all things observe a fixed law of their operations and a manner of existence appropriate to their nature. For that which prescribes to every thing the form and manner and measure of working, is just what law is. . . . This being so, it does not seem that man alone is independent of laws while everything else is bound. On the contrary, a manner of acting is prescribed to him that is suitable to his nature; for it does not seem to fit in with the wisdom of the Creator to form an animal that is most perfect and ever active, and to endow it abundantly above all others with mind, intellect, reason, and all the requisites for working, and yet not assign to it any work, or again to make man alone susceptible of law precisely in order that he may submit to none.

All creation is subject to law, each creature in that manner appropriate to its nature. We find an equivocation in the application of the concept of law both to descriptions of the workings of things and to prescriptions for the workings of men; Locke finds no equivocation. Man being rational, his law is the command of reason, so that man is given law in a prescriptive manner, but the law he is given, like the law given all other things, is the directive appropriate to his created nature.

From our standpoint the derivation of man's obligation to obey God from God's creation of man requires argument. Creation and obligation are not intrinsically or necessarily connected. But this is the fundamental measure of the difference between Locke's conceptual framework and our own. His framework is theocentric; everything depends on God, for its being, for its nature, and so for its rule. And each thing depends on God in the manner appropriate to its nature, so that man, as rational, depends rationally on God. Reason is God's voice in man, the rule God has given to mankind. No argument from creation to obligation is needed from Locke's perspective. Creation establishes man's dependence on God, and so his dependence on God's rule;

man's created nature establishes the mode of this dependence. Rationality establishes rational dependence, which is obligation to prescriptive law.

The binding force of the law of nature is thus found in man's relation to God, as creature to creator. The fundamental content of this law is preservation. Locke insists that "the *fundamental Law of Nature* being *the preservation of Mankind,* no Humane Sanction can be good, or valid against it" (2T. 135). Preservation of the individual is subordinated to preservation of the species; "the *first and fundamental natural Law,* . . . is the *preservation of the Society,* and (as far as will consist with the publick good) of every person in it" (2T. 134).

Each individual's primary concern is to preserve himself. The positive obligation that each has to do "as much as he can, *to preserve the rest of Mankind,*" depends on the condition that "his own Preservation comes not in competition" (2T. 6). But concern with one's own preservation is not a licence to destroy others; Locke never suggests, as does Hobbes, that "every man has a Right to every thing; even to one anothers body" (L. 14). Indeed, self-preservation is fundamentally not a right but a duty. "Every one . . . is *bound to preserve himself*"; Man "has not Liberty to destroy himself" (2T. 6). When Locke speaks of my "Right to destroy that which threatens me with Destruction," he derives this right from "*the Fundamental Law of Nature, Man being to be preserved*" (2T. 16). Law and duty, not right, is the foundation of Locke's ethics.

III

Turning from Locke to Hobbes, we must consider how far Hobbes's thought exhibits a parallel set of conceptual connections among morality, law, God, nature, and reason.

1. *Morality, law and nature:* "The Science of them [the laws of nature], is the true and onely Moral Philosophy" (L. 15).
2. *Law, nature and reason:* "A LAW OF NATURE . . . is a Precept, or generall Rule, found out by Reason" (L. 14). "The laws mentioned in the former chapters, as they are called the laws of nature, for that they are the dictates of natural reason."[14]
3. *Reason and God:* "God Almighty hath given reason to a man to be a light unto him."[15]

4. *Law, nature and God:* "There may be attributed to God, a two-fold Kingdome, *Naturall,* and *Prophetique*: Naturall, wherein he governeth as many of Mankind as acknowledge his Providence, by the naturall Dictates of Right Reason" (L. 31).

These passages may suggest a framework of thought very similar to that of Locke. But they do not adequately represent Hobbes's position. We need also to consider these further excerpts:

5. *Reason:* "REASON . . . is nothing but *Reckoning* . . . of the Consequences of generall names agreed upon, for the *marking and signifying* of our thoughts" (L. 5); "All the voluntary actions of men tend to the benefit of themselves; and those actions are most Reasonable, that conduce most to their ends" (L. 15).
6. *Reason, law and God*: "These dictates of Reason, men use to call by the name of Lawes; but improperly: for they are but Conclusions, or Theoremes concerning what conduceth to the conservation and defence of themselves; whereas Law, properly is the word of him, that by right hath command over others. But yet if we consider the same Theoremes, as delivered in the word of God, that by right commandeth all things; then are they properly called Lawes" (*Ibid.*).
7. *Law, God and nature*: "There being no Court of Natural Justice, but in the Conscience onely; where not Man, but God raigneth; whose Lawes . . . in respect of God, as he is the Author of Nature, are *Naturall*; and in respect of the same God, as he is King of Kings, are *Lawes*" (L. 30).

Taking all of these passages together, we may suppose that two, quite different positions are present in Hobbes's thought. On the one hand, moral philosophy is the science of rational precepts concerning preservation or conservation, within a natural order created but not otherwise affected by God. On the other hand, moral philosophy is the science of those precepts commanded by God as King of Kings. Does Hobbes hold both, or indeed either, of these views?

To answer this, let us return to our initial question: why ought one obey God? This question is never raised in *Leviathan,* where Hobbes considers only God's right to rule:

The Right of Nature, whereby God reigneth over men, and punisheth those that break his Lawes, is to be derived, not from his Creating them, as if he required obedience, as of Gratitude for his benefits: but from his *Irresistible Power.* I have formerly shewn, how the Soveraign Right ariseth from Pact: To shew how the same Right may arise from Nature, requires no more, but to shew in what case it is never taken away. Seeing all men by Nature had Right to All things, they had Right every one to reigne over all the rest. But because this Right could not be obtained by force, it concerned the safety of every one, laying by that Right, to set upon men . . . by common consent, to rule and defend them: whereas if there had been any man of Power Irresistible; there had been no reason, why he should not by that Power have ruled, and defended both himselfe, and them, according to his own discretion. To those therefore whose Power is irresistible, the dominion of all men adhaereth naturally by their excellence of Power. (L. 31)

But this argument is insufficient for Hobbes's purposes. The right of nature, as he defines it, is merely permissive, a liberty, determining what one may do, but implying no obligation or duty on others. But God's right to rule must surely be a claim right, with a consequent obligation on the part of men to obey.

In *De Cive* Hobbes proceeds to establish an obligation, to obey the holder of the natural right to rule. I have argued elsewhere that Hobbes deliberately omitted this account of man's obligation to obey God from *Leviathan,*[16] but since no alternative account is open to him, we may consider the argument of *De Cive* here:

> Now if God have the right of sovereignty from his power, it is manifest that the *obligation* of yielding him obedience lies on men by reason of their weakness. . . . There are two species of *natural obligation.* . . . [The first is irrelevant.] The other, when it [liberty to resist] is taken away by hope or fear, according to which the weaker, despairing of his own power to resist, cannot but yield to the stronger. From this last kind of obligation, that is to say, from fear or conscience of our weakness in respect of the divine power, it comes to pass that we are obliged to obey God in his natural kingdom; reason dictating to all, acknowledging the divine power and providence, *that there is no kicking against the pricks.*[17]

Although no covenant is introduced, Hobbes's account of our obligation to obey God parallels his introduction of the covenanted obligation to obey a conqueror. In both cases we yield from weakness, rationally accepting an obligation of obedience in the interest of our preservation.

The laws of nature are *laws* insofar as God is King of Kings, that is, insofar as he is omnipotent. They are laws because they are his commands, and we, insofar as we are rational, cannot but yield obedience to them. But none of this matters to the structure of Hobbes's moral and political theory.

Hobbes is no atheist. He accepts the existence of God as a fact. But what is the practical or moral relevance of this fact? God is omnipotent, and so threatens our existence. We must, to maintain ourselves as best we can, accept his rule and oblige ourselves to obey him. This is to act in accordance with the second law of nature, insofar as it enjoins a man "*as farre-forth, as for Peace, and defence of himselfe he shall think it necessary, to lay down* . . . [his] *right to all things*" (L. 14), to lay down, that is, some portion of his initially unlimited permissive right of nature. Thus the second law of nature, as the command of God, obliges us only because the same second law, as a dictate of reason, requires us to oblige ourselves to obey God. The ultimate validity of the second law therefore turns on its status as a rational precept, not on its status as a divine command.

Moral obligation does not depend on God. It arises whenever, in accordance with the rational requirements of the laws of nature, we grant away some portion of our initially unlimited right. We do this in our relationship with God, but we do it also in our relationships with our human fellows, to secure ourselves against their power.

Hobbes's presentation of his argument parallels its logical structure. The laws of nature are introduced as theorems of reason, and only afterwards as commands of God. The obligation to obey the temporal sovereign is established in terms of these theorems of reason, and only at the conclusion of Hobbes's political argument is man's relationship with the spiritual sovereign introduced. Although Hobbes is no atheist, he is what we may call a practical atheist—as indeed we, his successors, all are. God makes no difference to the structure of Hobbes's moral and political system, and indeed, since God in his commands simply reinforces the laws of nature, God makes no difference even to the content of Hobbes's system.

But, we may ask, does Hobbes even present a moral system? If the laws of nature are but rational requirements for preservation, then is not Warrender right to insist that they are mere maxims of prudence? If they are not truly laws, then as Locke says, "Man would not be able to act wrongfully, since there was no law issuing commands or prohibitions, and he would be the completely free and sovereign arbiter of his actions."[18] Locke insists that the binding force of the laws of nature cannot be explained if every man's own interest is taken to be their basis.[19]

Hobbes's laws of nature are more than principles which prescribe the necessary means to self-preservation. They are precepts which each man is rationally required to follow, provided every other man does so. And this double generality—that the laws apply to every man but to each only insofar as they apply to every other man—distinguishes the laws of nature from mere principles of prudence, and establishes their moral significance. In a crucial passage Hobbes explains:

> The Lawes of Nature oblige *in foro interno*; that is to say, they bind to a desire they should take place [which we may gloss as a desire they be accepted by all]: but *in foro externo*; that is, to the putting them in act, not alwayes. For he that should be modest, and tractable, and performe all he promises, in such time, and place, where no man els should do so, should but make himselfe a prey to others, and procure his own certain ruine, contrary to the ground of all Lawes of Nature, which tend to Natures preservation. And again, he that having sufficient Security, that others shall observe the same Lawes towards him, observes them not himselfe, seeketh not Peace, but War; & consequently the destruction of his Nature by Violence. (L. 15)

To follow the laws of nature is not to act directly in accord with immediate interest. Mutual adherence to the laws is the "cooperative" outcome of a multilateral Prisoner's Dilemma, optimal, better for each than mutual violation, which is the "competitive," directly self-interested outcome.[20] I have argued elsewhere that what distinguishes this type of morality is that each person benefits more from the cooperative behaviour of others than he loses by refraining from competitive behaviour.[21] Hobbist moral principles are thus those maxims which it is in the interest of each to adopt, as overriding the direct pursuit of the objects of his own appetites, provided his adoption is both the necessary and the sufficient condition of their adoption by others.

Hobbist morality is entirely conventional, and strictly instrumental in relation to each individual's ends. Hobbes and Locke agree that men exist within the order of nature, but for Locke, although not for Hobbes, the order of nature is a moral order. For Hobbes, men must create a moral order, because without it they are unable to achieve security. Morality is then neither an expression of man's nature, nor an expression of the natural order within which he finds himself, but rather the product of his rational capacity to impose costs on himself, for the sake of greater benefits. And these benefits relate only to individual conservation and delectation; they do not, and cannot, themselves possess any moral significance. For Locke, morality confers value on man's non-moral ends; preservation is a duty. For Hobbes, morality takes its entire value from these non-moral ends, having no value of its own to confer upon them.

Locke, like many more recent thinkers, never grasps the real nature of Hobbism. For him, the only possibilities are recognition of the laws of nature as divine commands, or pursuit of immediate advantage. Hobbes does not adequately clarify his "middle way," partly because his defective psychology forces him to the implausible claim that morality is directly, rather than indirectly, advantageous to each individual.[22] But the real structure of his argument reveals a conception of morality which addresses the condition of the self-interested, secular individual who faces the conflicts of naked egoism.

IV

To confirm the differences between Locke's theocentrism and Hobbes's anthropocentrism, I propose now to ask them another question: what considerations provide reasons for acting? The conception of a reason for acting is, of course, not to be found in their writings, but we may nonetheless consider how each would understand it, consistently with what is found in those writings.

By a reason for acting, I denote a consideration with practical force which directly affects the rationality of action. To speak of practical force is to insist that the consideration must be capable of playing an explanatory role; reasons for acting must be capable of being reasons why one acts. The reverse does not hold; explanatory reasons may be irrelevant to, or may even detract from, the rationality of action. Reasons for acting are thus a proper subset of reasons why one acts.

If a consideration is capable of being an explanatory *reason*, then it must be possible to act on it intentionally. Otherwise it would not belong to that subset of causes which are also reasons. One may say that what one does intentionally, one wants to do; hence to act on a reason is to want so to act. One may then be tempted to suppose that one can have a reason to do only what one wants, or in other words, that reasons why one acts, and so reasons for acting, must be or be derived from the wants and desires of the agent.

But this is not so. One need not have a reason to do anything one wants to do, except that in treating a consideration as a reason for acting, one *thereby* wants to act on it. We must sharply distinguish the view that we have certain wants, which thereby become or may become our reasons for acting, from the quite different view that we find certain considerations to be reasons for acting, which thereby become, or may become, what we want.

I shall say that a reason for acting is *internal* to an agent, insofar as its status as a reason depends on its prior connection with that agent. And I shall say that a reason for acting is *external* to an agent, insofar as its status as a reason is independent of, or prior to, its connection with that agent. If a person's own wants and desires provide him directly with reasons for acting, then such reasons are internal. If, on the other hand, the wants and aims of other persons provide him directly with reasons for acting, then such reasons are external. Let me state, quite dogmatically, a fundamental theorem of practical rationality: internal reasons for acting do not entail external reasons, or vice versa. I shall not attempt here to defend the view that internal reasons are perfectly acceptable.[23]

One might suppose that the distinction between internal and external reasons corresponds necessarily to the distinction between the wants of the agent and all other factors, considered as reasons for acting. But this supposition rests on a particular conception of human nature. If one were to hold, with Aristotle, that man by nature has an *ergon,* a function or role,[24] then one would suppose that this *ergon* as part of each person's nature, provides him with reasons for acting, whether or not his actual wants accord with it. And if one were also to hold, with Plato, that desire is an inferior part of human nature, which should be mastered by the rational individual,[25] then one would suppose that desires provide reasons for acting, not directly in virtue of being part of human nature, but only insofar as they receive the endorsation of man's superior faculties. It may be foolishness to us to suppose that wants provide only external reasons for acting, and that other factors can and must provide internal reasons, but it was not foolishness to the Greeks.

Within the tradition of possessive or appropriative individualism, internal reasons for acting must be, or must be derived from, the wants of the agent. The plausibility of the more extreme but mistaken claim that all reasons for acting must, as a matter of logical or conceptual necessity, rest on wants, arises from taking for granted this conception of man. If each man is an independent appropriator, then natural human activity must be a function of appropriative desires, themselves perhaps founded on more basic desires for preservation. Reason plays an instrumental role on this conception of man, so that appropriative desire is the natural and final ground of all rational action. If, as is commonly done, we identify Locke with this individualistic tradition, then we shall have to conclude that in his account reasons for acting, or at least internal reasons for acting, must be derived from and only from the agent's wants and desires.

We may draw this conclusion, but we must draw it carefully, without oversimplifying the complexities which Locke's theocentrism introduces into his account. Although he says that "If it be . . . asked, what it is moves desire, I answer, Happiness, and that alone" (E.II.21.41), and he continues, "What has an aptness to produce pleasure in us is that we call good, and what is apt to produce pain in us we call evil; for no other reason but for its aptness to produce pleasure and pain in us, wherein consists our happiness and misery" (E.II.21.42), yet we may not straight-forwardly conclude that since "all good be the proper object of desire" (E.II.21.43), therefore desire gives rise to our reasons for acting.

For Locke, the function of reason is to acquaint us with God's law, so he must relate our desires to the divine will, as the ultimate basis of all reasons for acting. Thus he argues:

> For the desire, strong desire of Preserving his Life and Being having been Planted in him, as a Principle of Action by God himself, Reason, *which was the Voice of God in him,* could not but teach him and assure him, that pursuing that natural Inclination he had to preserve his Being, he followed the Will of his Maker, and therefore had a right to make use of those Creatures, which by his Reason or Senses he could discover would be serviceable thereunto. (1T. 86)

God, as author of our being, has planted our reason, our desires, and our sensations in us. Reason, together with our sensations, makes us aware of God, and of our dependence on him; Locke establishes this in the *Essays on the Law of Nature.* This dependence has its practical consequences; only in relating a ground of action to God does reason approve it. Hence when reason considers our desires—those factors which naturally and directly motivate us—it regards them as providing reasons for acting, not in themselves, but in virtue of their divine origin.

It is because God has planted a desire in me, as part of my nature, that it comes to be my reason for acting. Desires give rise to reasons for acting, not in themselves but nevertheless because of their prior connection with the agent, and so, in terms of our distinction, provide internal reasons for acting.

But if reason validates our desires by relating them to their divine origin, it also, together with our sensations, makes us aware of God's will, and of his law for mankind. This law is the "Rule betwixt Man and Man" (2T. 172), making each person "know how far he is left to the freedom of his own will" (2T. 63). Hence the law of nature imposes a constraint on each individual's pursuit of happiness, a constraint derived from God's concern with the preservation of all mankind, which the law commands.

When Locke states that we are "sent into the World . . . about his [God's] business," so that each of us is bound "not to quit his Station wilfully" (2T. 6), one might suppose that Locke is ascribing a role to man, independent of his wants, which gives rise to further internal reasons for acting. But this would be a misinterpretation; our awareness of God's business, and of our station, is not an awareness of our own nature, but of God's edicts. We apprehend God's business as affording us reasons for acting, because we apprehend it as part of his will for us, contained in his law. Although Locke agrees with Aristotle that the universal order includes a role for man, he treats this role as related externally to the individual, constraining his pleasure-based will, and so as providing external reasons for acting.

Hobbes presents a simpler account, for he unequivocally embraces the position that all reasons for acting are internal, resting on the agent's wants, and that no reference to God, or to any other being, is required to establish these wants as reasons. Hobbes begins with an account of human motivation, and his subsequent treatment of rationality is strictly derivative from it. To show some consideration to be a reason for acting is to relate it, directly or indirectly, to man's basic motivations. Thus the first step in Hobbes's discussion of those considerations which determine what we ought to do, the introduction of the unlimited, permissive right of nature, is established by relating this right to each man's concern for his own preservation, and for the means required best to assure it. The unlimited right of nature is simply the reformulation, in the language of reason, of Hobbes's claim that "in the first place, I put for a generall inclination of all mankind, a perpetuall and restlesse desire of Power after power, that ceaseth onely

in Death" (L. 11). The two subsequent steps in the argument, the limitation of the right of nature, or assumption of obligation, in accordance
with the prescriptions of the laws of nature, and the authorization of
the sovereign to enforce the laws of nature and the obligations assumed under them, are both established by demonstrating the insuffi-
ciency of the preceding step, and the consequent necessity of the new
step, given only each individual's concern with his own end, "which is
principally their owne conservation, and sometimes their delectation
only" (L. 13).

V

I shall turn now to some of the fundamental consequences for moral
theory which are entailed by the contrasting standpoints of Locke and
Hobbes. In particular, I shall focus on the autonomy of the moral agent,
and on the overriding character of moral requirements.

A person is autonomous, a law unto himself, if and only if reasons
for acting require the endorsation of his will. A person is morally autonomous if and only if he is morally bound by and only by his own will.
Since Locke supposes that the law of nature provides what I have
termed external reasons for acting, it may seem evident that his system
provides no place for moral autonomy. External reasons for acting
oblige independently of any connection with the will, and so cannot
require its endorsation.

But this argument needs more careful elaboration. To talk of the will
is of course to invite difficulties, for the concept is notoriously obscure,
but we may at least distinguish Hobbes's conception, in which the will
is *"the last Appetite in Deliberating"* (L. 6) from Kant's, in which "the
will is nothing but practical reason."[26] If we accept Kant's view, then the
rational apprehension of certain considerations as reasons for acting is
the rational willing of those considerations. And so autonomy is not
violated by the existence of external reasons so apprehended. External
reasons have no prior connection with the agent, but, in a Kantian
framework, they oblige only as apprehended and willed by the agent.

Locke's conception of the will is, of course, closer to that of Hobbes
than to that of Kant. He does not reduce the will to an appetite, but he
supposes that the will is determined, not by reason, but by uneasiness,
a form of desire. (E.II.21.31) The apprehension of the law of nature as

the rational ground of human action is therefore not equivalent to the willing of that law.

As we noted in considering Locke's view of reasons for acting, he insists that the law of nature limits man's will. Locke returns several times to this point.

> For God having given Man an Understanding to direct his actions, has allowed him a freedom of Will, and liberty of Acting, as properly belonging thereunto, within the bounds of that Law he is under. (2T. 58)

And in speaking of the right every man has to enforce the law of nature in the state of nature, Locke contrasts will and reason:

> And thus in the State of Nature, *one Man comes by a Power over another*; but yet no Absolute or Arbitrary Power, to use a Criminal when he has got him in his hands, according to the passionate heats, or boundless extravagancy of his own Will, but only to retribute to him, so far as calm reason and conscience dictates, what is proportionate to his Transgression. (2T. 8)

Man is not a law unto himself, but a subject of God's law. God's law is apprehended by man's reason, and is promulgated in the interest of mankind, but it is not expressive of man's own will, or based on his individual interest. Thus our initial conclusion is correct; Locke rejects moral autonomy.

Hobbes, on the other hand, uncompromisingly affirms the autonomy of the individual. A man is morally bound only by his own will. Obligations are self-imposed, "there being no Obligation on any man, which ariseth not from some Act of his own; for all men equally, are by Nature Free" (L. 21). Each man places himself under obligation only by his own acts of covenant, acts whereby he denies himself some portion of his initially unlimited right of nature, in return for similar denial by those with whom he covenants. If men in Hobbist society are bound inescapably to the sovereign, and to the sovereign of sovereigns, God, yet they are bound entirely by chains of their own making, expressive of their own will, and based on their own individual interest.

Hobbes is able to affirm autonomy, however, only by supposing that morality overrides individual interests in the minimum possible way. A man's direct and immediate pursuit of his own conservation and delectation is overridden by the laws of nature only insofar as it is in his interest that everyone's similar pursuit of conservation and delectation be so overridden. The only checks which anyone accepts rationally on the exercise of self-interest are those which, imposed on everyone, enable him better to attain his principal ends.

No man can oblige himself not to resist when his survival is directly threatened:

> For . . . no man can transferre, or lay down his Right to save himself from Death, Wounds, and Imprisonment, (the avoyding whereof is the onely End of laying down any Right,) and therefore the promise of not resisting force, in no Covenant transferreth any right; nor is obliging. (L. 14)

Checks on the exercise or self-interest which do not better enable a man to secure his conversation could only be curbs on, and not expressions of, his individual will.

Locke, it will be remembered, accuses the Hobbist of not admitting "a great many plain duties of morality." We have established the basis of this accusation, in showing that Hobbist morality can override interest only to secure greater mutual advantage. No man can be expected to sacrifice more, by his moral actions, than he can expect to benefit, from the moral actions of others. For Locke, and for most of us, this is not enough.

Moral autonomy and the overriding character of moral requirements are not reconciled satisfactorily either by Hobbes or by Locke. Given the individualistic conception of man, in which human nature is characterized by desire, for appropriation, and ultimately for self-preservation, the will must be determined by appetite. Man can then be autonomous only insofar as appetite is accepted as his proper basis, and his only ultimate proper basis, for action. A morality based on appetite can be only a morality of the Hobbist type—a morality the laws of which curb the pursuit of advantage only better to secure advantage. A stronger morality, of the Lockean variety, requires a basis in some power outside of and superior to man, and thereby cancels human autonomy in overriding man's appetite-based will.

VI

Our argument has been concerned with differences between Hobbes and Locke at the level of moral theory; before concluding, we should draw at least one implication at the level of moral practice. I have endorsed Locke's insistence that Hobbes's doctrine will not admit many plain duties; let us, then, consider a fairly plain duty. Let us consider the morality of refraining from pre-emptive war.

Hobbes and Locke agree that war is the great evil in human affairs. For Hobbes, it is that "Warre, where every man is Enemy to every man," which makes

> the life of man, solitary, poore, nasty, brutish, and short. . . . And Reason suggesteth convenient Articles of Peace, . . . which otherwise are called the Lawes of Nature. (L. 13)

For Locke:

> To avoid this State of War (wherein there is no appeal but to Heaven, and wherein every the least difference is apt to end, where there is no Authority to decide between the Contenders) is one great *reason of Mens putting themselves into Society.* (2T. 21)

Nevertheless, war stands on a very different footing in their accounts.[27] Hobbes insists that in the state of nature it is rational to resort to pre-emptive violence:

> And from this diffidence of one another [endemic to the state of nature], there is no way for any man to secure himself, so reasonable, as Anticipation; that is, by force or wiles, to master the persons of all men he can, so long, till he see no other power great enough to endanger him: And this is no more than his own conservation requireth, and is generally allowed. (L. 13)

It is rational to seek peace, but where agreement on peace is not to be found, it is rational to engage in unlimited war:

> It is a precept, or generall rule of Reason, *That every man, ought to endeavour Peace, as farre as he has hope of obtaining it; and when he cannot obtain it, that he may seek, and use, all helps, and advantages of Warre.* (L. 14)

For Locke, only defensive war can be rational. He argues:

> And one may destroy a Man who makes War upon him, or has discovered an Enmity to his being, for the same Reason, that he may kill a *Wolf* or a

Lyon; because such Men are not under the ties of the Common Law of Reason, have no other Rule, but that of Force and Violence, and so may be treated as Beasts of Prey. (2T. 16)

In other words, those who initiate war have abandoned the rule of reason for that of unjust force; only as a response to such a rejection of reason is force just and rational.

If morality is an agreed rule for mutual preservation, then where there is no agreement on preservation, there is no morality. In the state of nature there is no such agreement; hence Hobbes concludes logically that "where there is no Common-wealth, there nothing is Un-just" (L. 15). Pre-emptive war falls outside the framework of morality; we may condemn it from the vantage point of those who have agreed to peace, but we may not condemn those who lack such agreement if they engage in it.

If, on the other hand, morality is an imposed rule for common pres-ervation, then morality binds in the state of nature as in society. Locke correctly insists that "Trust and keeping of Faith belongs to Men, as Men, and not as Members of Society" (2T. 14). War, as inimical to com-mon preservation, is irrational and immoral from every standpoint, and pre-emptive war may be condemned, not only from the vantage point of those who have agreed to peace, but also for those who, lacking such agreement, must be prepared to defend themselves, but may not otherwise "take away, or impair the life, or what tends to the Preserva-tion of the Life, Liberty, Health, Limb or Goods of another" (2T. 6).

Although it is easy to find instances of pre-emptive war throughout human history, only in the nuclear age has it been openly advocated as a justifiable practice. We may find in this one piece of evidence for a shift, in our society, from Lockean to Hobbist rationalizations. If we have lost the conceptual basis of Locke's thought, while embracing Hobbes's secular individualism, this shift should not surprise us. I can-not consider here whether it is, indeed, pervasive.

VII

Why ought one obey God? We are unwilling to be his creatures; indeed, we are unable to be his creatures because we have forgotten the mean-ing of the status of creaturehood. Locke's theocentrism is an answer we no longer understand, but insofar as it is an answer to the question of the foundations of morality, our failure to understand does not remove the problem.

That there is no kicking against the pricks is an answer we can understand, but of course Hobbes's truer answer to why one ought to obey God is that obedience to God is no more than adherence to those rational precepts which he calls the laws of nature. And that answer to the question of the foundations of morality we can also understand; morality is founded in advantage.

But it was not the foundations of this morality—the morality of advantage—that we were seeking. As I have suggested, modern moral philosophers want to begin with the conception of man as an individual appropriator, and derive a Lockean, strongly overriding morality within the framework of Hobbist secularism and autonomy.

Locke's affirmation of God will not satisfy us. But we must realize that if, and since, it does not satisfy us, in embracing Hobbes's practical atheism we cannot deny its consequences for morality. Perhaps this should be our conclusion. But if, in turn, Hobbist morality does not satisfy us, then we must realize that we have no adequate conceptual foundations for the conventions of morality, or for the bonds of human society which these conventions maintain. "The taking away of God . . . dissolves all."

Notes

An earlier draft of this paper was read to the Canadian Philosophical Association. I am grateful for comments received on that occasion.

1. The first proposition suggests a rather literal version of social contractarianism. Substituting hypothetical contractarianism, as defended by John Rawls, or as dissected in several of my recent papers, would not affect Locke's affirmation.

2. The phrase "modern moral philosophers" is intended to evoke G.E.M. Anscombe's paper, "Modern Moral Philosophy," *Philosophy* 33 (1958), pp. 1–19. Anscombe's discussion of the "*law* conception of ethics" and her suggestion that the status of the notion of "obligation" in recent moral thought is "the interesting one of the survival of a concept outside the framework of thought that made it a really intelligible one" are directly relevant to the underlying argument of the present enquiry.

3. C. B. Macpherson, *The Political Theory of Possessive Individualism: Hobbes to Locke,* Oxford, 1967, is of course the classic statement of this view of Locke. According to Macpherson, Locke's achievement is that "he provides a positive moral basis for capitalist society" (p. 221). It is interesting to find that Macpherson is alive to complaints about ahistorical interpretations of Locke; he

objects on this ground to those who read "modern liberal-democratic beliefs" back into Locke.

4. Richard H. Cox, *Locke on War and Peace,* Oxford, 1960, offers the most extended statement of this view; see especially pp. 18–28, 136–147. He is following in the footsteps of Leo Strauss. See *Natural Right and History,* Chicago, 1953; a typical statement is: "It is on the basis of Hobbes's view of the law of nature that Locke opposes Hobbes's conclusions" (p. 231).

5. Locke MS., quoted by John Dunn, *The Political Thought of John Locke,* Cambridge, 1969, pp. 218–219.

6. Quotations from Hobbes's *Leviathan* are indicated by "L," followed by the chapter number.

7. Howard Warrender, *The Political Philosophy of Hobbes: His Theory of Obligation,* Oxford, 1957, p. 99.

8. Kurt Baier, *The Moral Point of View: A Rational Basis of Ethics,* Ithaca, 1958, pp. 308–315.

9. Robert Nozick, *Anarchy, State, and Utopia,* New York, 1974, p. 9.

10. Modern moral philosophers do not actually say that this is what they want. But I believe that it is illuminating to read them from this assumption. John Rawls erects the most impressive edifice.

11. Quotations from Locke's *Essay Concerning Human Understanding* are indicated by "E," followed by the book, chapter, and paragraph numbers.

12. Quotations from Locke's *Two Treatises of Government* are indicated by "1T" or "2T," followed by the section number.

13. *Essays on the Law of Nature* VI: "Are men bound by the law of nature? Yes." The crux of Locke's argument is in this passage:

. . . we say that the law of nature is binding on all men primarily and of itself and by its intrinsic force, and we shall endeavour to prove this by the following arguments:

(1) Because this law contains all that is necessary to make a law binding. For God, the author of this law, has willed it to be the rule of our moral life, and He has made it sufficiently known, so that anyone can understand it who is willing to apply diligent study and to direct his mind to the knowledge of it. The result is that, since nothing else is required to impose an obligation but the authority and rightful power of the one who commands and the disclosure of his will, no one can doubt that the law of nature is binding on men.

For, in the first place, since God is supreme over everything and has such authority and power over us as we cannot exercise over ourselves, and since we owe our body, soul, and life—whatever we are, whatever we have, and even whatever we can be—to Him and to Him alone, it is proper that we should live according to the precept of His will. God has created us out of nothing and, if He pleases, will reduce us again to nothing: we are, therefore, subject to Him in perfect justice and by utmost necessity.

In the second place, this law is the will of this omnipotent lawmaker, known to us by the light and principles of nature; the knowledge of it can be concealed from no one unless he loves blindness and darkness and casts off nature in order that he may avoid his duty.

(Translated from the Latin by Wolfgang von Leyden, *John Locke: Essays on the Law of Nature,* Oxford, 1954, pp. 187, 189.)

14. Hobbes, *De Corpore Politico,* I.5.1.

15. *Ibid.,* 1.5.12.

16. *The Logic of Leviathan,* Oxford, 1969, pp. 188–199.

17. Hobbes, *De Cive,* XV.7.

18. *Essays on the Law of Nature* I. Von Leyden, *op. cit.,* p. 121.

19. *Essays on the Law of Nature* VIII: "Is every man's own interest the basis of the law of nature? No."

20. The Prisoner's Dilemma is by now well established in philosophical literature. For a very brief account, see my paper "Reason and Maximization," this *Journal* 4 (1975), p. 422.

21. "Morality and Advantage," *Philosophical Review* 76 (1967), pp. 461–464, 468–470.

22. Hobbes is thus led to his discussion of "the Foole" (L. 15). See my account in *The Logic of Leviathan,* pp. 61–62, 76–98.

23. The most developed attack on the acceptability of internal reasons is offered by Thomas Nagel, *The Possibility of Altruism,* Oxford, 1970. My terminology differs from Nagel's, but I think that my internal reasons are a subset of the reasons he classifies as subjective. Opposed to subjective reasons are objective ones, which, he concludes after an intricate argument, are "the only acceptable reasons" (p. 96).

24. Aristotle, *Nicomachean Ethics,* 1097b25ff.

25. Cf. Plato, *Republic,* 441e–442b.

26. Kant, *Groundwork of the Metaphysic of Morals,* translated H. J. Paton, *The Moral Law,* London, 1948, p. 80.

27. See Cox, *Locke on War and Peace,* pp. 164–171, 184–189, for an opposed interpretation of Locke, which would make pre-emptive violence justifiable for him as for Hobbes.

6

Locke's State of Nature

A. John Simmons

The state of nature is in many ways the central concept at work in Locke's *Two Treatises of Government*. It is the concept with which Locke chooses to introduce the *Second Treatise.*[1] And it is only against and by means of the state of nature that Locke offers us accounts of political obligation and authority, the limits on political power, and the occasions for justified resistance. But the state of nature is probably also, as John Dunn has observed,[2] the most misunderstood idea in Locke's political philosophy. Progress has been made, of course, largely because of Dunn's own work[3] and an influential paper by Richard Ashcraft.[4] It is, as a result, no longer fashionable to simply dismiss Locke's claims about the state of nature as bad history or bad psychology.[5] Nor is it as easy as it once was to accuse Locke of blatant inconsistency or deceptiveness in his descriptions of the social conditions men would endure in the state of nature.[6]

In spite of this progress, however, widespread obscurities and errors persist in discussions of Locke's state of nature, mistakes that often conceal the nature and virtues of the concept with which Locke chose to work. Most of these mistakes, I will suggest, stem from two sources: running together (in various ways) Lockean and Hobbesian conceptions of the state of nature and taking as *definitions* of the state of nature in Locke, his statements of mere *conditions* (necessary or sufficient) for men's being in the state of nature. I will try in this article to remedy those mistakes, but I have three more general aims. First, I want to (finally) present a clear account of and definition of Locke's state of nature. With this definition in hand, many of the familiar worries about Locke's account are much easier to unravel. Second, I will point to what I believe are Locke's true confusions about the state of nature, which lie in rather different areas than is generally supposed. Third, I hope to cast some light on the point and the virtues of the particular concept of the state of nature we find Locke employing in the *Two Treatises*.

I.

Locke begins Chapter II of the *Second Treatise* by asking us to "consider what state all men are naturally in," the state of nature. If we come to Locke fresh from a reading of Hobbes (as students often do), it is perhaps natural to suppose that Locke means by the state of nature roughly what Hobbes meant. For Hobbes (to simplify a bit), the state of nature can be defined as the state men are (or would be) in living together without effective government over them. "Effective government" here means something like "government able to provide its citizens with adequate security against domestic and foreign assaults on their persons or property." To be sure, Hobbes fills out his picture of life in the state of nature in a way no one would confuse with Locke's picture.[7] But it is easy enough to believe that in their *definitions* of the state of nature, Hobbes and Locke simply agree.

Let me be more precise. We can distinguish in Hobbes the *definition* of the state of nature (as life without effective government) from the *social* and *moral* characterizations of that state and from claims about that state's *historical* instantiations. The social characterization of the state of nature in Hobbes is familiar (and quite different from what we find in Locke). Life in the state of nature is "solitary, poor, nasty, brutish, and short," a condition of war "of every man against every man," a war in which there is no industry, no culture, and no real society.[8] The moral condition of persons in the state of nature for Hobbes is less clear, though it seems fair to say that they have no moral rights or obligations at all in the ordinary sense—"the notions of right and wrong, justice and injustice, have there no place."[9] As for historical instantiations of the state of nature (that is, actual occasions where men lived together without effective government), Hobbes mentions savages in America, "civilized" men during a civil war, and (at the international level) independent sovereigns.[10] Now Locke, of course, would accept little of this. His social characterization of the state of nature seems considerably less bleak than Hobbes's; his moral characterization includes individuals with full-blown moral rights and obligations; and in Hobbes's list of historical instantiations of the state of nature, Locke would certainly make changes. But for all of these disagreements, it is not difficult to suppose that Hobbes's and Locke's *definitions* of the state of nature are roughly the same.

This supposition is a common one among Locke scholars, who frequently claim that for Locke the state of nature is the condition of men without (effective) government.[11] That view is, however, mistaken in both obvious and more subtle fashions. In the most obvious case, men can for Locke be living under effective, highly organized governments and still be in the state of nature—provided only that those governments are illegitimate with respect to them. Prominent instances mentioned by Locke are men living under arbitrary, tyrannical governments (§§ 17–20) and under foreign powers which have dissolved their society by conquest (§ 211). In both cases effective government and the state of nature are consistent. At the very least, one wants to build into a definition of the state of nature that it is the condition of men living together without *legitimate* government. Even this addition, however, will not suffice, for Locke mentions several classes of persons who can live under legitimate governments while remaining in the state of nature—visiting aliens (§ 9), minors under the age of consent (§§ 15, 118), and those of defective reason (§ 60). What is clearly needed in any adequate definition of Locke's state of nature is some element that captures the distinctive moral component of that state. I will suggest such a definition momentarily.

But there is a second set of problems confronted in approaching the Lockean state of nature from a Hobbesian direction. For Hobbes, the state of nature is a condition men are either in or out of (*simpliciter*).[12] He virtually always writes of it as a condition that only *groups* of persons can be in or out of. Neither of these points squares well with Locke's concept of the state of nature (though Locke's own language is sometimes misleading). In the first place, Locke often writes of people being in the state of nature with respect to certain people and out of it with respect to others (at the same time). Thus, the princes of (legitimate *or* illegitimate) independent governments are in the state of nature with respect to each other (§ 14), though legitimate princes are (at the same time) out of that state with respect to fellow citizens of their commonwealths. A visiting citizen of an alien legitimate state is the state of nature with respect to the state he visits (§ 9), but out of that state with respect to citizens of his own state. This suggests that the state of nature must for Locke be a *relational* concept, something not at all obviously true of Hobbes's parallel notion.[13] Second, where Hobbes virtually never writes of individuals being in the state of nature while those around them are not[14] (making his state of nature essentially a property of groups of persons), Locke's individuals are frequently in that position. Visiting aliens are, of course, in that position, and since every person for Locke is born into the state of nature (§ 15), it is impossible to imagine a realistic society (no matter how legitimate) within which there are not *many* persons in that position.[15] Locke's state of nature is, then, both a more individualistic and a more relational concept than that of Hobbes. The more closely we pattern our analysis of Locke's state of nature on Hobbesian notions, the more completely we will miss these essential features.

Now it may seem that in concentrating on the Hobbesian leanings of some scholars' accounts of Locke's state of nature, I have thus far managed to ignore Locke's most important claims about that state. Indeed, many take Locke to have given us a clear *definition* of the state of nature. "Want of a common judge with authority, puts all men in the state of nature" (§ 19). "Men living together according to reason, without a common superior on earth, with authority to judge between them, is properly the state of nature" (§ 19).[16] Here (and elsewhere) Locke claims that wherever no one is entitled to settle controversies between two persons, wherever there is no authorized umpire to judge between them, those persons are in the state of nature. This appears to be believed by most of the scholars who are not influenced by Hobbesian notions to be (at least the essence of) Locke's definition of the state of nature.[17]

It is worth noting, first, that Locke's claims about the "common judge with authority" do not have the *form* of a definition; they have, rather, the form of a statement of a *sufficient condition* for being in the state of nature. Locke never, for instance, claims that it is *only* when there is no common judge that men are in the state of nature (he never, that is, claims that this condition is a *necessary* one). For all we know (on the strength of these passages alone) there may be many quite different conditions also sufficient to put men in the state of nature. A statement of a sufficient condition need not even approach a definition.

But lest this seem an idle, academic point, of no relevance to intelligent interpretation of Locke's text, I believe there is good reason not to *want* Locke to be offering his claims about the common judge as a definition of the state of nature. This is most easily seen if we remember Locke's claims about private contracts in the state of nature:

> For 'tis not every compact that puts an end to the state of nature between men, but only this one of agreeing together mutually to enter into one community, and make one body politic: other promises and compacts, men may make one with another, and yet still be in the state of nature. . . . For truth and keeping of faith belongs to men as men, and not as members of society. (§ 14)

In other words, people may make promises and contracts with one another, transfer rights and undertake obligations, without leaving the state of nature. Only one particular and very special agreement takes men out of the state of nature. Is that "special agreement" simply any agreement to set up a judge between persons? Is it simply any instance of one person transferring to another his natural right to judge for himself and punish violaters of the law of nature (what Locke calls the "executive power of the law of nature")? It is hard to see how either of these claims could be plausibly maintained. If it is possible for a large group of persons to surrender (in creating a commonwealth) the rights necessary to make a "common judge with authority," surely it is possible for a small number of people, *without* creating a commonwealth, to erect a common judge with equally legitimate authority. Why may not two persons in the state of nature authorize a third to settle conflicts between them (that is, both surrender to the third their rights to judge for themselves)? I can see nothing in the nature of the rights or the transaction that would preclude this for Locke. Yet if two persons thus agreed to set up a common judge, surely this would be a purely *private* contract, after which they would still be in the state of nature. Simply erecting an authorized umpire would not be sufficient to constitute creation of a commonwealth or civil society. Among other things, this "common judge" would lack the right to make law for those he judges between (a right governments receive in Locke as a result of transfers in trust of other rights that citizens relinquish, *in addition to* the executive right [§§ 128–130]). Nor would there be a sufficient number of people involved in the agreement to create a functioning commonwealth.[18] The one very special agreement that creates a commonwealth is considerably more complex, and involves the surrendering by citizens of far more rights, than an agreement to set up a common judge with authority. Thus, while the absence of a common judge between persons is clearly a sufficient condition for those persons being in the state of nature, it does not appear to be a necessary condition. Common judges with authority may be present even in the state of nature (a fact presupposed in Robert Nozick's well-known discussion of these issues).[19] Nothing Locke says conflicts with this possibility, nor is there any compelling reason to suppose that he would want to outlaw private contracts to create common judges.

Exactly when an agreement is an agreement that creates a commonwealth, and when sufficiently many people are involved to create one, are questions to which Locke provides only the frameworks for answers. He rightly concentrates his attention on one particular aspect of the agreement (the creation of an authorized judge) in his discussion of the state of nature, for it is this aspect of the agreement that solves the fundamental problems of life in the state of nature. It is, however, still only one aspect of the special agreement that creates a civil society. Without the rest of the agreement, men remain in the state of nature. Thus, any acceptable definition of Locke's state of nature must make reference to (or otherwise capture the significance of) the full agreement that alone creates civil society and removes men from their natural condition. Reference only to a part of that agreement, the creation of a common judge with authority, will not suffice.

II.

We might try to give an account of Locke's state of nature that refers to the full agreement as follows:

> A person (A) is in the state of nature if and only if A has not voluntarily agreed to join some legitimate political community.

This definition (in the non-technical sense of "definition"), while exceedingly simple, succeeds where the others we have considered failed in capturing the crucial element distinguishing the civil from the natural state—the voluntary agreement by an individual to perform according to the special terms of the contract that alone creates a commonwealth. This definition leaves open the precise content of the contract necessary to create a civil society (Locke, of course, fills in some of that content for us). It also preserves the individualistic character of Locke's concept, since it allows that a single person may be in the state of nature (in virtue of not having agreed to join) while those around him are out of it.

But this definition is still flawed in two regards. First, it does nothing to capture the relational character of Locke's concept of the state of nature. Second, this definition does not account for the cases of those who are returned to the state of nature from civil society. I propose, then, as an acceptable definition of Locke's state of nature the following:

> A is in the state of nature with respect to B if and only if A has not voluntarily agreed to join (or is no longer a member of) a legitimate political community of which B is a member.

And then as a special case, falling under this account, we can say:

> A is in the state of nature (*simpliciter*) if and only if A has not voluntarily agreed to join (or is no longer a member of) any legitimate political community.

Obviously, my definition has a great deal in common with those we considered earlier and rejected, but it squares with claims made by Locke for which they cannot account. Thus, while on my definition those not living under legitimate governments are, of course, in the state of nature, the definition accounts as well for Locke's claims that aliens, children, and madmen are in the state of nature even within legitimate political communities (their having either not agreed at all or not agreed voluntarily to join).[20] Although those who retain their executive rights and thus erect no judge over them are, of course, on this definition in the state of nature (the transfer of those rights being essential to any agreement to join a political community), the definition allows as well that private transfer of the executive rights leaves one in the state of nature.

The following picture, then, flows from this definition. Each person is born into the state of nature (*simpliciter*), and, barring a universal community of man, each person *stays* in the state of nature with respect to at least some (and possibly all) others. Those incapable of consent (voluntary agreement) and those who choose never to consent remain in the state of nature (*simpliciter*). Those whose communities are dissolved (for example, by foreign conquest) and those who are abused by otherwise legitimate governments are returned to the state of nature (*simpliciter*).[21] Persons who enter civil society (includ-ing princes) leave the state of nature with respect to fellow citizens, but remain in it with respect to all alien nations and with respect to all noncitizens (that is, those still in the state of nature [*simpliciter*]). All of these consequences of the definition I have offered seem to square precisely with Locke's claims about the state of nature.

Perhaps the most important point to note about this definition is its strong *moral* flavor. We have already distinguished between the defi-nition of the state of nature and the social, moral, and historical charac-terizations determined by it. Locke's definition clearly leans toward the moral characterization, making prominent use of distinctively moral notions (like legitimacy and voluntary agreement). No obvious social characterization flows from this definition, the state of nature being consistent for Locke with many different social circumstances. Hobbes's definition of the state of nature, by contrast, clearly leaned toward the social characterization; it was primarily the brute fact of absence of physical security that defined the state of nature for Hobbes, and an obvious social characterization (of life without secur-ity) follows immediately from his definition (given his account of human nature). It might be fair to say that for Hobbes, the moral di-mension of interpersonal life rests on and follows from the social di-mension.[22] The sharp contrast between the social character of Hobbes's account of the state of nature and the moral character of Locke's illuminates, as we shall see, some major controversies in the literature on Locke's state of nature.[23]

III.

Locke's state of nature, then, is a concept with strong moral content. But thus far our account of that content has been purely *negative*—that is, the state of nature is the state a person is in with respect to another when he has *not* consented to join with him (or has subse-quently left) a legitimate commonwealth. Can we not give a full and positive moral characterization of Locke's state of nature? What is the moral condition of a person in the state of nature, and what are his rights and duties? Locke often talks as if the moral condition of men in the state of nature is reasonably simple to summarize: (1) Persons have all (and only) the duties defined by the law of nature, that law being eternal and immutable (for example, § 135) and there being in the state of nature no legitimate commonwealth that could impose on them any other duties. While the "particulars" of the law of nature are not discussed by Locke (§ 12), the general form of the duties it defines are briefly elaborated—duties to preserve oneself and others (by, for instance, not harming others in their lives, liberty, health, limbs, or goods [§ 6]). (2) Persons enjoy in the state of nature their full complement of natural rights (which correlate with the natural duties of others to respect those rights). Each person is "born to" this set of rights and possesses them fully on reaching maturity (§§ 55, 59). A person's natural rights are a "grant or gift from God,"[24] which he possesses intact until (if ever) he consents to enter a legitimate civil society, surrendering some of these rights in the process. While Locke is again sketchy on the particular rights we possess, they include rights to freely pursue harmless activities, to do what is necessary to preserve oneself and others, and to "execute" the law of nature (§§ 4, 129). This is the account of man's moral condition in the state of nature that can be drawn most easily from Locke's texts.

But it simply cannot be the *whole* account, nor do I think Locke intends it to be. This account is perfectly adequate as an account of (what we might call) the "original" state of nature in which a newly mature individual finds himself.[25] But if my claims about Locke's state of nature have thus far been even reasonably accurate, a full moral characterization of the state of nature would seem to be impossible. In the first place, we must specify at least two sorts of moral conditions for persons in the state of nature—the conditions of mature, rational individuals, and the conditions for children and incompetents. Where mature persons in the state of nature may possess the "full complement" of rights and duties, those who are not fully rational (and are thereby also in the state of nature) clearly do not. Because a law only binds those to whom it is promulgated, and because the law of nature is promulgated by reason, those deficient in reason are not properly under the law of nature at all (§§ 57–60). Presumably, this means that children and incompetents lack at least some (and probably all) of the duties and rights defined by the law of nature.[26]

But even leaving aside children and incompetents, it is easy to see that the moral characterization of the state of nature offered above cannot be adequate. We need only remember our earlier observation about private contracts being consistent with Locke's state of nature. Since the point of contracts is precisely to alter the existing structure of rights and duties, mature persons in the state of nature are perfectly capable of changing the rights and duties that were their "original" grant from God. Originally free to pursue any harmless activity, I may by promise or contract transfer a portion of this right to another and undertake a duty to respect that right (as when I promise to help you on Friday, thereby giving you the right I initially possessed to determine how I shall spend Friday). The one to whom I make my promise has greater right and less duty toward me than he had before the promise. My point is not that the law of nature somehow ceases to bind; there is a clear sense in which it is eternal, as Locke claims. The point is rather that the specific rights and duties granted originally to each under natural law may be altered. Consent, as it were, carves the boundaries of natural law. Any rights that can be transferred in the trust that creates civil government can in principle be transferred in private transactions within the state of nature. As we have seen, this includes our natural executive rights. The only rights that could not be transferred would be those which are in principle inalienable (though Locke's position on that subject is far from clear[27]).

If this is correct, there is no specific moral characterization of the state of nature that can be given even for mature adults. No adult in the state of nature will necessarily possess any particular set of rights or duties. Which rights and duties he possesses will follow from his specific moral history (the nature of his promises, contracts, and other morally relevant activities). The best we can do is this: since being in the state of nature consists in not having made (or having been released from) one special sort of transaction (that one which alone creates a legitimate civil society), each person in the state of nature lacks the one distinctive sort of moral obligation that transaction creates— what we normally refer to as "political obligation."[28] All persons in the state of nature, then, have no political obligations. That moral characterization of Locke's state of nature, however thin and negative, is, I think, the best we can offer.

IV.

What, then, of the *social* characterization of Locke's state of nature? By contrast with Hobbes's thoroughly bleak characterization (to which any form of effective government at all would be preferable), the Lockean state of nature receives mixed reviews. It is a state of limited safety and considerable uncertainty, a state of significant but not desperate "inconveniences," a state to which only certain limited forms of political society will be preferable. The state of nature is one of "uncertain peace" in which people are able to follow the law of nature, but do not always do so,[29] a state caused by the "tension between man's natural sociableness and his equally natural desire for personal happiness."[30] Indeed, even if there were not this natural tension in human nature, it would be surprising if Locke's social characterization of the state of nature were not "mixed," for in both *Treatises* there are ample suggestions that the state of nature might take many different forms.[31] At the lower end of the spectrum, the state of nature could be a reasonably primitive state, with no ownership of land and few moveable possessions. For the inconveniences of this state of nature, where there is so little to covet, Locke allows that monarchical government would be appropriate (§ 107). At the upper end of the spectrum, the state of nature could be quite civilized, with property in land, money, commerce, cities, and so on (all things that would be impossible in Hobbes's state of nature and things that, in Locke's view, call for greater safeguards in government than a simple monarchy could supply [§ 111]). It would be surprising if all points on this spectrum involved the same kinds of social problems and benefits, and Locke never suggests that they do. What he does suggest is that the state of nature will always have one specific kind of social problem, and it is on this problem that he concentrates his attention. In every state of nature there will be the problem that men are judges in their own cases. Where there is no common judge with authority, men may be partial or vengeful in exercising their natural executive rights, possibly leading to feuds, conflicts, and war (§ 13). This kind of social problem plagues all forms of the state of nature, and the insecurity it causes is the primary reason for seeking the protection of a (properly limited) civil government (§§ 13, 21).

Just how bad will this problem be? On his answer to that question, of course, Locke has taken something of a beating. He seems to describe the state of nature first as "a state of peace, good will, mutual assistance, and preservation" (§ 19) and then as a state we should be very eager to escape (§ 21). The first description leaves us wondering why a civil society would seem a desirable alternative to the state of nature at all; the second leaves Locke looking like Hobbes after all, and the inconsistency leaves Locke looking confused. The range of explanations for these passages, sympathetic and unsympathetic, is familiar to any student of the literature on Locke's political philosophy: Locke's

real position is like Hobbes's,[32] a position to which he was converted
as he wrote;[33] Locke is deliberately inconsistent in order to conceal
gaps in his argument;[34] he has different views of the state of nature
before and after the invention of money;[35] this last hypothesis is mistaken, and Locke was just inconsistent;[36] Locke is not inconsistent at all
and there is no confusion.[37]

What is puzzling about the various charges of confusion and indeci-
sion is that they charge Locke with a particularly silly and shallow sort
of confusion. This is not a deep, theoretical problem on which even a
very intelligent man might be expected to become muddled. Indeed,
the charges often amount to a claim that Locke was inconsistent or
changed his views over the course of three or four paragraphs of text.
Only the strong antecedent desire to defend a particular interpretation
of the text would make such a reading attractive. In fact, the apparent
inconsistencies are strikingly easy to explain. Locke never really characterized the state of nature as "a state of peace, goodwill, mutual assistance, and preservation" any more than he describes it as a state of
"enmity, malice, violence, and mutual destruction" (§ 19). Both descriptions are of *possible* states of nature, but neither is of *the* state of
nature. The contrasting descriptions in § 19 are quite plainly intended
as descriptions of the best and the worst that the state of nature can
be. Where persons almost always abide by the laws of nature, the state
of nature will be one of peace, goodwill, and the like; where persons
disregard the law, the state of nature will be a state of enmity, malice,
and so on.[38] But since people will almost always behave in a way that
falls between these extremes, the social characterization of the state of
nature that dominates the *Treatises* is also a mixed account of the sort
with which we began. No amount of struggling will make other passages in Locke yield anything but a "mixed" social characterization.[39]

Whatever stand we choose to take on that question, however, it is
worth noticing that *any* social characterization of the state of nature
given by Locke would represent a confusion on his part. The problem
is not that the state of nature might be either very primitive or reasonably civilized and so no one description applies uniformly. As we have
seen, Locke tried to isolate that "inconvenience" that would plague
any state of nature—namely, the want of a common judge with authority. But what Locke seems not to keep carefully in mind in his descriptions is that his state of nature is not just (as Hobbes's was) a state
without government. It is rather a state where one is not a member of
the same legitimate commonwealth as another. It follows from this, of

course, that the want of a common judge characteristic of the state of nature will not create anything like the same problems for various state of nature situations. *Prepolitical* men, of course, and men whose society has collapsed, will suffer the kinds of insecurity and inconvenience Locke describes in the *Second Treatise*. Persons living under a depressive and tyrannical government will face a quite different set of problems. They are equally in the state of nature and equally lack a common judge with authority, but they *do* have a common judge *without* authority. Illegitimate governments may nonetheless be highly structured with complex legal systems. The social problems of life in such a state will be very different from those of that state of nature in which all men are judges in their own case (and in which the outbreak of war between private individuals is the primary worry). Others living in the state of nature (without a common judge with authority) may face no serious problems at all. Children or aliens living in a commonwealth that is legitimate with respect to most of its citizens will presumably be living in a moderate, peaceful society. Although they have no judge over them (with authority to settle disputes between them and citizens of the commonwealth), they will probably be treated well, leading lives burdened with few of the inconveniences Locke describes. Life in *this* state of nature may be quite acceptable. The point here is only that Locke's concept of the state of nature is compatible with an extremely wide range of possible social circumstances.[40]

For Hobbes, the definition of the state of nature was social in character. It was thus compatible with only a very limited range of social characterizations. For Locke, however, the state of nature is a moral condition of man (and a relational one). Locke's concept of the state of nature, unlike Hobbes's, does nothing to limit the possible social descriptions of persons in that condition. When Locke attempts a social characterization of the state of nature in response to the social characterizations offered by others, he succumbs to a confusion, for he is entitled to no particular social characterization. The state of nature is not necessarily characterized by the inconvenience of having no common judge. There is only the inconvenience of having no *legitimate* common judge, which may or may not be a *social* problem (and where it is a social problem, it will not always be of the same sort). The best Locke can do is to describe the social position of persons in one kind of state of nature. We can, I suppose, take Locke to be intending to do just that in the *Second Treatise*. But it surely seems more likely that Locke was simply confused on this point, either by the genetic account he offers of the formation of political society (which concentrated his attention on the social condition of prepolitical and nonpolitical states of nature), or by the fact that earlier theorists who employed a concept of the state of nature had offered social characterizations of it (which they, unlike Locke, were entitled to do).

V.

I turn now to Locke's historical arguments and his claims about historical instantiations of the state of nature. Like Hobbes, Locke offers us observations about times and places when actual groups of persons have been in the state of nature. Unlike Hobbes, however, Locke spends rather a long time with historical claims. His historical worries about the state of nature begin as early as § 14, and a large part of Chapter VIII (especially §§ 100–115) is devoted to them. In light of the moral character of his state of nature, what (if anything) can these arguments be supposed to add to the support of Locke's position? Locke concerns himself with finding historical examples of groups of people in the state of nature who voluntarily band together to form commonwealths. Why does he bother? What does it matter to his project whether or not he can present such examples?[41] Presumably, all he needs to show to support his claims about the state of nature is that everyone (including those persons born in political society) is in the state of nature originally. He need not show that everyone was in that state at some time or that everyone in each community was in that state at the same time, or even that the *origin* of *any* political community was legitimate (i.e., the voluntary consent of all involved). On the face of things, at least, even if Locke were able to show none of these things, his moral concept of the state of nature would in no way be suspect. He notes himself that "at best an argument from what has been, to what should of right be, has no great force" (§ 103), and his most central arguments in these passages (e.g., § 113) are logical, not historical.[42] So what is Locke up to with his historical arguments?[43]

Undoubtedly, one answer is that Locke wishes to meet Filmer (whose arguments are primarily historical) on his own ground. He wants to respond to Filmer's claims that patriarchal monarchy is the natural (and legitimate) form of government, claims to which Locke actually makes several concessions. He tries to show, against Filmer, that it is just as natural to form other kinds of governments (given other kinds of social conditions), that there is historical evidence of men having done just that, and that even the establishment of a monarchy is evidence that individuals were naturally free to establish a government. Now this would all be well and good if Locke were (oddly) presenting his case as a detached criticism of another author whose positions bore no logical relation to his own, but the arguments of Chapter VIII are *not* presented in this way. They are presented as if they lend support to Locke's own position, and, in particular, they are presented as if they are evidence for the conclusion that men are *naturally free* (that is, born into the state of nature with the right to determine the course their political, and nonpolitical, lives will take). Because being "naturally free" for Locke does *not* mean being *physically free* to create, join, or remain outside of a commonwealth, but rather means having the *right* to do so, it is hard to see how historical evidence could in any way bear on his conclusion. Is Locke, then, hopelessly confused in these passages?

The more reasonable answer, I think, is that Locke was both rather unclear in his wording and a bit carried away by his arguments. What I believe Locke is really driving at is that history shows that we all *regard* ourselves as naturally free, act as if we are, and have always done so (this belief, then, is not, for instance, simply a product of recent social conditioning or a particular ideological stance). This is in fact the way he puts some of the conclusions he draws from his historical arguments: "Tis plain mankind never owned nor considered any such natural subjection" (§ 114); there is little room for doubt "what has been the opinion, or practice of mankind, about the first erecting of governments" (§ 104). These are conclusions one could be entitled to reach from historical inquiry.

Now, of course, these conclusions *prove* nothing that is logically related to Locke's main position on the state of nature. Even if everyone did believe himself born free of subjection to any government, a fact Filmer and others (e.g., Hume) have denied, this would in no way prove that we are all naturally free. Locke can, perhaps, be excused for excessive enthusiasm in his conviction that the opinion of mankind through the ages shows us "where the right is" (§ 104). Insofar as we believe men to be on the whole rational beings, it would be surprising if the consensus of men throughout history did not point us in at least the general direction of the truth. This is particularly the case where *moral* truth is concerned and where one believes (as Locke, of course, did) that moral distinctions are perceived by reason with relative ease

(§ 12).[44] So Locke's historical arguments are at least relevant to the support of his position on the state of nature. They help to show "how *probable* it is, that people . . . were naturally free" (§ 112, emphasis mine). This is a respectable, if not decisive, role for history to play in Locke's arguments.

VI.

With this understanding of Locke's definition of the state of nature (and of the force of his various claims about that state), the point of using a concept like the state of nature appears more clearly. Its role in Locke's political philosophy can be seen to share some features of its role in Hobbes, for instance, but to depart from Hobbes in other regards. Both Hobbes and Locke, at the most obvious level, use the idea of the state of nature to offer a vivid portrayal of the stakes in the choice between government and anarchy (in Locke's sense of that word—that is, having "no form of government at all" [§ 198][45]). For Locke, of course, the only intelligible choice is between some limited form of government and anarchy, the absolute government favored by Hobbes appearing to him clearly worse than the worst consequences of anarchy (perhaps a dubious assumption by Locke). In any event, anarchy loses out for both Hobbes and Locke. Both use the idea of the state of nature to formulate general conditions for governmental legitimacy, the rule being (roughly) that a government is legitimate if it fosters conditions preferable to those in the state of nature. For Hobbes, a government has authority and ought to be obeyed if it passes this test;[46] for Locke, a government is *capable* of having authority if it passes (only citizens' consent gives authority, but arbitrary governments that *fail* the test are ones to which binding consent cannot even be given [§ 23]). We can see now, of course, that in none of this can Locke be taken to be comparing limited government with *the* state of nature, since not all instances of the state of nature are anarchical (i.e., one can be under government *and* in the state of nature). The contrast Locke draws bears not so much on the choice each must make between joining an already existing commonwealth or not doing so, but rather on the choice between having governments at all or not having them (and, in this sense, the point is reasonably close to Hobbes).

In other respects, however, the distance between the uses of the state of nature in Hobbes and Locke must be greater. It is often said that the point of Locke's use of the state of nature is to elucidate human nature through his account of how life would be (is) in that state.[47] This is certainly part of Hobbes's aim in utilizing his socially defined state of nature. And while to a certain extent this is clearly true of Locke as well, it cannot (or, at least, should not) be Locke's primary intention. Locke's state of nature, as we have seen, simply has no determinate social characterization. There is no one picture that can be offered of what the state of nature is like and so no simple conclusion that can be drawn from that picture about the character of human nature. A point we can draw from this, and one to which Hobbes would have done well to attend, is that human nature is revealed as much in our responses to social and political settings as it is in our responses to social chaos and insecurity. But in Locke the primary point of the state of nature is not to reveal human nature in any of its particular guises, it is rather to describe a certain *moral* condition of men.[48] It is tempting to say that the moral condition in question is the condition into which God placed man (or the condition into which a mature person rises when he receives his moral birthright) or that the relevant condition is the moral condition of man prior to its modification by his complex social and political interactions. There is no denying that Locke sometimes speaks in these ways, but as we have seen, none of these ideas can be quite right, for Locke's state of nature has no precise moral characterization either. The moral condition the state of nature describes is simply the moral condition of the *noncitizen*—the condition of not being a member (with others) of a legitimate civil society. It is hardly surprising that this should be the point of a central concept in a book whose primary focus is the nature and importance of legitimate government.

A final point about the purpose of Locke's employment of the state of nature device should solidify the desired comparison of Locke and Hobbes on this subject. The idea of the state of nature obviously plays a central role in the voluntarist program in political philosophy. The assertion that each person is born free in the state of nature is one way of asserting that we are not born *into* political communities, however clearly we may be born within their territories. We are not naturally citizens; we must do something to become citizens. The course our lives take should be determined as fully as possible by our own voluntary choices, and birth within the territory of a commonwealth is not the product of any choice we make. This is to stress the *artificiality* of government (however natural it may be for us to create it), and to stress that its moral rights against us (and duties toward us) can only be the sum of what it receives from us in the process that creates it. If we are not naturally citizens, we must be naturally something else, and the state of nature is a way of talking about that "something else," a "something else" we sometimes remain (by disability or by choice) and which we always remain in part.

Both Hobbes and Locke are participants in the voluntarist program in political philosophy and much of the point of "state of nature talk" in both can only be appreciated in light of this fact.[49] But it is worth noticing that the state of nature defined by Locke functions much more naturally within this program than does the parallel notion in Hobbes. This can be seen by attending to their respective moral characterizations of the state of nature. In Locke, persons in the state of nature have full-blown moral rights, rights that correlate with the duties of others to refrain from interfering with their exercise (what, in the by-now-familiar language of Hohfeld, are called "claim rights"). Although only knowing a person's history in Locke's state of nature will tell us *which* rights he has, whatever rights he has will have this character. In Hobbes, by contrast, persons in the state of nature have not full-blown rights, but mere liberties (what Hohfeld calls "liberty rights"). Each person has the "right of nature," which is a "right to everything, even to one another's body."[50] Competitive rights of this sort (where each person has a right to everything) can only be understood as the moral liberty each person has in the absence of obligation (that is, "person A is at liberty to do act X" means only "A has no obligation not to do X"). What these "rights" lack, which leaves them short of "full-blown" rights, is the duty others have to refrain from interfering with the right's exercise.

But the Hobbesian picture of men in the state of nature, armed only with their "rights of nature," severely undercuts the voluntarist conception of *authorizing* a government (or a community) by transfer of right. Our normal idea of authorization is that it is a way of improving the moral position of another, giving him an authority he lacked— when I authorize your actions I make things permissible for you that were previously forbidden. In Hobbes, however, authorization of the sovereign cannot fit this model. The sovereign (as a person or group that also began in the state of nature) *already* had a right to everything. Everything was permissible for him before the "authorization," so there is no way that the contract with his subjects can improve his moral position. There is no sense in which, for instance, if I had not authorized him he could not have legitimately controlled me (if he had the physical power to).[51] Thus, Hobbes can make no real sense of the voluntarist idea of authority or of the view that a government's rights can only be those that its citizens transfer to it.

In this regard, Locke's state of nature fares much better. Because it is populated by persons with full-blown moral rights, Locke's state of nature can fit with the voluntarist conceptions of authorization and transfer of rights to produce a coherent voluntarist account of the nature of the citizen-state relationship. Its role in this account explains much of the point of Locke's concept of the state of nature. Insofar as we find this voluntarist program compelling, we have reason to take seriously Locke's state of nature as a central concept in political philosophy.

Notes

1. John Locke, *Second Treatise of Government,* § 4. Subsequent references to the *Second Treatise* will be by paragraph.

2. John Dunn, *Locke* (Oxford: Oxford University Press, 1984), 46.

3. John Dunn, *The Political Thought of John Locke* (Cambridge: Cambridge University Press, 1969).

4. Richard Ashcraft, "Locke's State of Nature: Historical Fact or Moral Fiction," *American Political Science Review* (September 1968).

5. For criticisms of this sort, see Richard I. Aaron, *John Locke,* 3rd ed. (Oxford: Oxford University Press, 1971), 273; Willmoore Kendall, *John Locke and the Doctrine of Majority-Rule* (Urbana: University of Illinois Press, 1959), 75; J. W. Gough, *John Locke's Political Philosophy* (Oxford: Oxford University Press, 1950), 89.

6. Variants of this attack can be found in C. B. Macpherson, "Introduction" to John Locke, *Second Treatise of Government* (Indianapolis: Hackett, 1980), xiv; Leo Strauss, *Natural Right and History* (Chicago: University of Chicago Press, 1953), 224–226; J. D. Mabbott, *John Locke* (London: MacMillan, 1973), 143–146; Richard Cox, *Locke on War and Peace* (Washington: University Press of America, 1982), 76–80; J. J. Jenkins, "Locke and Natural Rights," *Philosophy* (April 1967), 152–153.

7. Claims to the contrary are surprisingly frequent; however, I argue below against such views. Among those who argue for a "Hobbesian" Locke on this issue are Cox, *Locke on War and Peace,* 79, 104, and Mabbott, *John Locke,* 145–146.

8. Thomas Hobbes, *Leviathan,* ch. 13, §§ 8–9.

9. Hobbes, *Leviathan,* ch. 13, § 13. Natural law binds only "in foro interno" in the state of war (*Leviathan,* ch. 13, § 35); however we understand this claim,

it does not refer to moral bonds of an "ordinary" sort. Similarly, the "rights" held by persons in this state are mere "liberties" (see Section VI). I refrain here from further comment on what I concede are difficult points in Hobbes scholarship.

10. Hobbes, *Leviathan,* ch. 13, §§ 11–12.

11. See John Plamenatz, *Man and Society* (London: Longman's, Green, 1963), vol. 1, 220–221; John Colman, *John Locke's Moral Philosophy* (Edinburgh: Edinburgh University Pres, 1983), 177–178; John W. Yolton, *Locke: An Introduction* (Oxford: Basil Blackwell, 1985), 57; Mabbott, *John Locke,* 142; Richard Cox, "Introduction" to Locke, *Second Treatise of Government* (Arlington Heights, IL: Harlan Davidson, 1982), xxi; Kendall, *John Locke and the Doctrine of Majority-Rule,* 64; W. von Leyden, *Hobbes and Locke* (New York: St. Martin's Press, 1982), 99–100; J.E.J. Altham, "Reflections on the State of Nature," *Rational Action,* ed. by R. Harrison (Cambridge: Cambridge University Press, 1979), 134. To be fair, Colman characterizes the state of nature as the condition of men "living together without *civil* society" (my emphasis), and "civil" conveys for Locke some notion of minimal legitimacy. Yolton may have something similar in mind. I argue below that this addition is inadequate. Part of the requisite contrast between Hobbes and Locke on this point is captured in Dunn, *Locke,* 46–47.

12. It may seem that the sovereign in Hobbes is a counterexample to this claim, since it (or he) appears to be both in the state of nature (with other sovereigns) and out of it (with the citizens of its own commonwealth). This appearance dissolves when we remember that for Hobbes the sovereign *remains* in the state of nature, even with regard to the subjects who are out of it. See *Leviathan,* ch. 28, § 2.

13. Locke's clearest indication of the *relational* character of the state of nature comes in § 145, where he uses the "in reference to" construction prominently. Since writing this essay, I have found that Gregory S. Kavka makes similar claims about the relational aspects of Hobbes's state of nature (*Hobbesian Moral and Political Theory* [Princeton: Princeton University Press, 1986], 88–89). I am not sure that I see the textual warrant for this interpretive claim, though Hobbes certainly could have held such a view without doing violence to his other positions.

14. Even in those cases where the subject may legitimately resist the sovereign, it appears that this fact is no evidence that the subject is returned to the state of nature. See Hobbes, *Leviathan,* ch. 21, §§ 11–21.

15. It appears that *individuals* within otherwise legitimate states may be returned to the state of nature by governmental violations of their rights. Note § 168 ("any single man") and § 208 ("some private men's cases"). This is an additional instance of persons being in the state of nature while those around them are not. Of course, were it not for Locke's odd account of tacit consent being given by mere residence (§ 119), many more people would be in this position (that is, those who resided in but did not consent to membership in a legitimate commonwealth). The individualistic character of Locke's state of nature is stressed, though in rather puzzling ways, in Hans Aarsleff, "The State of Nature and the Nature of Man in Locke," *John Locke: Problems and Perspec-*

tives, ed. by John W. Yolton (Cambridge: Cambridge University Press, 1969), 101, and in Robert A. Goldwin, "Locke's State of Nature in Political Society," *Western Political Quarterly* (March, 1976), 128–134.

16. See the parallel claims in § 91.

17. See, for instance, Peter Laslett, "Introduction" to John Locke, *Two Treatises of Government,* rev. ed. (Cambridge: Cambridge University Press, 1963), 111; Goldwin, "Locke's State of Nature in Political Society," 126–127; Aarsleff, "The State of Nature and the Nature of Man in Locke," 100. Ashcraft comes closer to what I take to be the proper definition in his "legal statement of the state of nature," but still concentrates solely on establishing a judge ("Locke's State of Nature: Historical Fact or Moral Fiction?" 901). Cox (along with others who *are* influenced by Hobbes) also uses this definition (*Locke on War and Peace,* 73).

18. Locke does, of course, say that "any number of men" may create a community or civil society (§ 95). I do not find plausible the conclusion that three persons can make a civil society, but this point is not centrally important to my argument here.

19. Robert Nozick offers interesting observations about the possibility of private contracts to create common judges in the state of nature and about when (and how) private associations become states. Much of this discussion is untainted by his peculiar notion of legitimacy and his unfortunate formulation and manipulation of the "principle of compensation" (whose only apparent justification is its necessity for arriving at the desired conclusion). See *Anarchy, State, and Utopia* (New York: Basic Books, 1974), especially chs. 2–6.

20. It is, of course, an embarrassment for Locke that after saying visiting aliens have not joined the community (§ 9), he goes on to say that they have consented to the laws of their host countries in as full a sense as have most permanent residents (§ 119).

21. Locke is careful to distinguish between dissolution of government and dissolution of society (§ 211). In the latter case, men are returned to the state of nature (§ 211), while in the former it appears that the society regains those rights it entrusted to government, but no *individual* citizen returns to the state of nature (§ 243). This is discussed in Richard Ashcraft, *Revolutionary Politics & Locke's Two Treatises of Government* (Princeton: Princeton University Press, 1986), 575–577. I believe Locke *means* to say here that citizens remain *out* of the state of nature with respect to each other, but enter *into* it with respect to those (governors) who have abused their powers. The difficult case, of course, is that in which the government abuses only particular individuals, remaining legitimate with respect to the majority. As I observed in Note 15, Locke appears to say that these individuals *are* returned to the state of nature (*simpliciter*).

22. I mean this only in the following senses: (1) natural law seems only to bind us to perform ("in foro externo") when physical security (a "social fact") is guaranteed (Hobbes, *Leviathan,* ch. 15, § 35); (2) consent (a moral notion) seems to follow from the mere presence of physical security (Hobbes, *Leviathan,* A Review and Conclusion, § 7) and from the ability of others to take our lives when they please (other "social facts," Hobbes, *Leviathan,* ch. 20, §§ 4–11).

23. I have not yet mentioned the most interesting alternative account of what Locke means by the state of nature—the account offered by Dunn. For him the state of nature is:

> the condition in which God himself places all men in the world, prior to the lives which they live and the societies which are fashioned by the living of those lives. What it is designed to show is not what men are like but rather what rights and duties they have as the creatures of God. (*Locke*, 47, and parallel claims in *Political Thought of John Locke*, 97, 103).

It is hard to argue with claims that capture so much of the true spirit of Locke's account, but Dunn's position seems to me not quite accurate. Men can be in the state of nature long after they have changed the condition God set them in. As I argue below, there is no particular set of rights and duties possessed by all persons in the state of nature. Perhaps we can say that Dunn's claims give a fair characterization of that "original" state of nature to which each person is born, leaving aside later instantiations of that state.

24. This phrase is used by Locke several times in the *First Treatise of Government*, for example, § 116.

25. This, I believe, is what Dunn's analysis adequately captures. See Note 23.

26. This is, I think, a particularly difficult point in interpreting Locke's *Treatises*. Locke talks only occasionally of immature children having rights (e.g., *First Treatise*, §§ 88–90; *Second Treatise*, §§ 78, 183, 190), and even then almost exclusively of rights that they have against their *parents*. He almost never speaks of immature children having duties (again with the exception of duties of obedience to their parents [e.g., *Second Treatise*, § 65]). I confess to puzzlement as to how a child can have natural rights and duties without being under the law of nature, and I suspect that Locke's best position might be to simply deny that young children and incompetents have such rights and duties. To see that this need not be so callous a position as it first seems, see, e.g., H.L.A. Hart, "Are There any Natural Rights?", *The Philosophical Review* 64 (1955), p. 181.

27. See my discussion of this question in "Inalienable Rights and Locke's *Treatises*," *Philosophy & Public Affairs* (Summer 1983).

28. I explain this concept and discuss Locke's theory of political obligation in *Moral Principles and Political Obligations* (Princeton: Princeton University Press, 1979).

29. Ashcraft, "Locke's State of Nature: Historical Fact or Moral Fiction," 902–903.

30. Colman, *John Locke's Moral Philosophy*, 185. A similar version of this tension is described in Geraint Parry, *John Locke* (London: George Allen & Unwin 1978), 61.

31. See the suggestions throughout *Second Treatise*, chs. 5 and 8.

32. Strauss, *Natural Right and History*, 224–232.

33. Cox, *Locke on War and Peace*, 74–79; Mabbott, *John Locke*, 143–146.

34. Jenkins, "Locke and Natural Rights," 152–153.

35. David C. Snyder, "Locke on Natural Law and Property Rights," *Canadian Journal of Philosophy* (December 1986), 745–748.

36. C. B. Macpherson, *The Political Theory of Possessive Individualism* (Oxford: Oxford University Press, 1962), 240–246.

37. Ashcraft, "Locke's State of Nature: Historical Fact or Moral Fiction," 901–907; Colman, *John Locke's Moral Philosophy*, 180–185; Aarsleff, "The State of Nature and the Nature of Man in Locke," 99.

38. The state of war, while not a necessary feature of the state of nature, is consistent with it. See Parry, *John Locke*, 60, and Colman, *John Locke's Moral Philosophy*, 183.

39. Even the "worst" of Locke's other descriptions (e.g., § 123) in no way contradict his claims that the state of nature is preferable to many possible forms of political life (e.g., § 93), and do not even approach the descriptions offered by Hobbes. I take my position in this section to be thus far broadly consistent with those defended by Ashcraft and Colman (who offer further support for the claims I make here).

40. This may be part of what Dunn is driving at when he writes that the state of nature has no "empirical content" (*The Political Thought of John Locke*, 103, 110). See also Ashcraft, *Revolutionary Politics & Locke's Two Treatises of Government*, 581.

41. Worries about this portion of Locke's argument have often led to quick claims of a basic confusion on his part. See, for example, Thomas I. Cook, "Introduction" to Locke, *Two Treatises of Government* (New York: Hafner, 1947), xv–xvi, and Kendall, *John Locke and the Doctrine of Majority-Rule*, 75.

42. Locke seems extremely sensitive to the dubious value of historical argument to his project. Not only does he offer the reminder in the midst of his historical arguments in the *Second Treatise* (§ 103), but the *First Treatise* is full of such warnings (e.g., §§ 58–59, 106). This care makes his use of such arguments even more curious.

43. One response that has been offered is that Locke was not really up to much of anything of importance. See Aarsleff, "The State of Nature and the Nature of Man in Locke," 103.

44. Exactly how easy this perception is, of course, is a point on which Locke was not obviously consistent. Later in the *Second Treatise,* for instance, he says that the state of nature lacks a "known law" that is accepted as the "standard of right and wrong" (§ 124). In other works he emphasizes the "great labor" (*Essays on the Law of Nature*) and "the long and sometimes intricate deductions" (*The Reasonableness of Christianity*) required for knowledge of morality.

45. See Ashcraft's discussion of Locke on "anarchy" in "Locke's State of Nature: Historical Fact or Moral Fiction," 901–902.

46. Hobbes, *Leviathan,* ch. 21, § 21. Consent is also necessary for authority in Hobbes, of course, though it can be acquired simply by sufficient exercises of force. For an argument that Hobbes really relies here on *hypothetical* contractarian ideas, see Kavka, *Hobbesian Moral and Political Theory*, chs. 5 and 10.

47. See, for instance, Cook, "Introduction" to Locke, *Two Treatises of Government,* xv–xvi; Aarsleff, "The State of Nature and the Nature of Man in Locke," 100; M. Seliger, *The Liberal Politics of John Locke* (London: George Allen & Unwin, 1968), 83, 90, 93–94, 99–100.

48. It is on this point that Dunn's account is most helpful, though I go on here to disagree with his claims, in part. See Note 23.

49. The voluntarist character of both of their theories is diminished by certain aspects of their positions—Hobbes's by his belief that coerced consent is binding, Locke's by his view that (tacit) consent can be given passively (by mere residence, for instance). See my discussion of these matters in "Voluntarism and Political Associations," *Virginia Law Review* (February 1981), 19–21.

50. Hobbes, *Leviathan,* ch. 14, §§ 1–5.

51. The only moral effect of authorizing the sovereign in Hobbes is to convert his liberty right to everything into a *protected* liberty right (or *claim* right) to everything; that is, the subjects undertake the obligation to allow the sovereign exercise of his right (*Leviathan,* ch. 28, § 2). Nothing new becomes morally permissible for the sovereign as a result of the contract which gives him his new "authority."

7

Political Consent

A. John Simmons

3.1. The Content of Lockean Consent

Artificial political bodies (civil societies) and governments cannot for Locke (or Lockeans) possess rights naturally; only persons have that capacity. The question then arises: how may political communities and governments obtain rights from (and over) free persons who possess them in their natural condition? Locke's famous answer defines the essence of the political relationship for the voluntarist.[1] It identifies only one possible process by which such political rights ("power") can be secured. Only fully voluntary alienation by the rightholder—consent (contract, trust)—can give another person or body political power over the rightholder:[2] "Men being . . . by nature, all free, equal and independent, no one can be put out of this estate, and subjected to the political power of another, without his own consent" (II, 95). "No government can have a right to obedience from a people who have not freely consented to it" (II, 192).

These claims are intended to mean, I believe, that for Locke only consent can ground a person's political obligations (the logical correlates of political power), and that only consent can remove a person from the state of nature (see II, 15; and 1.2 above). And Locke's wording, here and elsewhere, makes it clear that by "consent" he means the actual, personal consent of each individual (as I argue at length in 7.2). It is consent alone that makes civil society (i.e., legitimate political society), along with the political rights and obligations such a society necessarily involves.

By political power, remember, Locke means the right of making law for the society and of using that society's force to execute the law and protect the society (but all only for that society's own good) (II, 3). This includes the right to have morally acceptable, lawful commands obeyed by the society's members (political power is the right "to command and be obeyed" [I, 120]). The logically correlative obligation of each member of the society, the member's "political obligation," is (a) to obey valid laws (which for Locke means obedience only to those civil laws whose demands do not contradict those of natural law) and (b) to support the society in those other ways necessary to its continued effective (just) functioning (which will typically include paying necessary taxes, contributing one's physical "force" to assist in domestic law enforcement or national defense, etc.).[3]

Consent can take persons out of the state of nature into civil society in one of two ways: they can join together with other persons who are also in the state of nature (simpliciter) to make "one people," a new body politic; or they can "incorporate with any government already made" (II, 89) (i.e., join with others who are still in the state of nature with respect to them, but not with respect to one another). While the process will clearly differ in the two cases, the moral content of the consensual transactions is, Locke claims, largely the same.[4] Whether joining or creating a commonwealth, the same rights are surrendered by the individual to the body (and the same obligations to it are correlatively undertaken). These acts constitute the "one very special agreement" (referred to in 1.1 above) that alone begins the political relationship among persons and creates civil society.

In the most general terms, each person's consent must surrender to political society "all the power necessary to the ends for which they unite into society" (II, 99), that is, "as much of his natural liberty in providing for himself, as the good, prosperity, and safety of the society shall require" (II, 130). Each surrenders these rights and undertakes an obligation to respect the exercise of these rights by their new holders. More specifically, Locke suggests that each person gives up two different kinds of rights on entering civil society. The natural executive right each "wholly gives up" (II, 130),[5] transferring this right to one "common judge" over all the members (who also judges in "federative" matters between members and nonmembers). This right, then, when ultimately exercised by government, becomes its executive and federative powers (II, 144–48)—that is, its right to interpret the law and direct the community's use of force. Second, each relinquishes a portion of the right of self-government—that right made up from the "liberty of innocent delights" and the right "to do whatsoever he thinks fit for the preservation of himself and others within the permission of the law of nature" (II, 128). The right of innocent delights is retained, while the rest is given up only as "far forth as the preservation of himself and the rest of society shall require" (II, 129).[6] This right, in the hands of government, becomes a significant part of its legislative power (II, 143),[7] while the well-known limits on legislative power specified by Locke (in II, 135–42) are determined in part by the natural rights that individuals retain even within civil society.[8]

The simple distinction Locke draws between two kinds of rights that must be surrendered on entrance to civil society is, I think, both extremely important and, quite simply, the correct position to take in a voluntarist account of the political relationship.[9] If the government's right to make and enforce law were only its subjects' natural executive rights (suitably transferred to government), the government could only legitimately make and enforce civil laws whose requirements coincided with those of natural law (as we saw in 2.1). For the natural right to punish, as exercised by independent individuals in the state of nature, is only a right to punish transgressors of *natural* law (II, 7). But while many of the acts a political society will wish to legally proscribe will, of course, also violate natural law (e.g., murder, violence, theft), many others quite clearly will not. Regulatory statutes of all sorts, many tax laws, many "morals" laws, laws designed to control the society's economy, and so on, all prohibit (or require) acts that are not prohibited (or required) by any plausible description of natural law. Governments, then, can only legitimately prohibit activities in such areas if they secure from their subjects additional rights to make laws in areas of morally "indifferent" conduct (those areas where each can in the state of nature do "whatsoever he thinks fit"), conduct *not* specifically required or prohibited by natural law. I take this insight, and the required solution to the problem, to be the point of Locke's arguments in II, 128–30.[10]

Laws concerning "indifferent" conduct must still, of course, be *consistent* with natural law in order to be legitimate: "the rules that they make for other men's actions must . . . be comfortable to the Law of Nature" (II, 135). But the natural executive right possessed outside of civil society does not include the right to make laws for others and punish them for violations where the conduct in question is morally indifferent. I may not, in the state of nature, make it a law that your tribe can only gather acorns east of the river and south of the large rock, and then punish you for violations; for there is no natural law restriction on the area in which your tribe may gather. But a lawful government might be entitled to make such a law, in order, say, to better coordinate gathering activities. It is only by surrendering a portion of the right of self-government that the citizen can legitimate such civil laws, laws that prohibit (or require) actions that are naturally indifferent, thus making it permissible that "the laws of the society in many things confine the liberty he had by the Law of Nature" (II, 129).

The political power of government, then, is the sum of those rights government ultimately receives from all of the individuals who consent to be members of the society it governs.[11] Political power's "domestic" component essentially consists of the rights to make laws limiting members' liberty for the public good and to enforce those laws with punishment.[12] Locke sometimes identifies this power in other terms: the "power of the magistrate" (II, 65), the "authority to command" (I, 81), the "right to obedience" (I, 81; II, 151), and the "power or right of government" (I, 120); and he even occasionally uses the language of "sovereignty" to characterize it.[13] But in whatever terms, political power is simply "that power which every man, having in the state of nature, has given up into the hands of the society, and therein to governours" (II, 171).

The account here offered of the moral content of Lockean political consent is not uncontroversial. Many have argued, for instance, that Locke's citizens must be understood to have surrendered all of their natural rights in creating or joining civil society, retaining none.[14] And while the passages cited above seem reasonably clear in implying the contrary, there is no denying that other passages in the *Second Treatise* could be marshalled to support such a reading—for instance, where Locke writes that "men give up all their natural power to the society which they enter into" (II, 136; see also II, 131). The choice, then, is between a reading of Locke on which individuals retain certain natural rights (i.e., those whose surrender is not needed for peaceful society)—rights held against the community, not just its government—and one on which all rights are given up to the community, to be redistributed to individuals by the community (depending on its needs) in the form of civil or institutional rights (a la Rousseau).[15] On the latter view, only the community (not individual citizens) can have rights against the government, and individual citizens have only those rights the community grants them (i.e., they have no secure, permanent rights even against the community, having surrendered all to the community's judgment).

Locke's *Treatises* are probably as unclear on this crucial point as on any other. Which reading we choose will vitally affect our view of the entire tenor of Locke's project, our view, for instance, of whether we take Locke's methodological individualism to have led him to any serious form of political individualism. Locke's lack of clarity in the *Treatises* is complicated by the fact that his early views of these matters, in the *Two Tracts on Government,* quite clearly *do* favor one reading over the other. They favor the second reading outlined above, the reading of the *Treatises* that I have opposed.[16] In the First Tract, for instance, Locke writes that it is "the unalterable condition of society and government that every particular man must unavoidably part with this right to his [entire] liberty and entrust the magistrate with as full a power over all his actions as he himself hath" (p. 125); and in the Second Tract: "every individual surrenders the whole of this natural liberty of his, however great it may be, to a legislator" (p. 231).

Nonetheless, I will argue for the first reading, on which persons retain a portion of their natural rights (and here, I think, the influence of the Levellers on Whig, and consequently on Locke's, thought is apparent). Locke's views on the political transfer of rights, I will suggest (in chapters 5 and 6), changed with his views on the right to toleration and the right of resistance. We cannot, I think, make sense of his claims in either area in his later works, without embracing the first reading. And it is easy to see how it was Locke's argumentative needs in the *Two Tracts* that there required him to defend the view that individuals must surrender all of their rights (a view he was later to abandon). For Locke there wants both to deny to citizens a right of resistance and to defend the magistrate's right to legislate indifferent religious matters (i.e., matters of worship neither required nor forbidden by God's law). The first ambition is obviously aided by denying any retained liberty to subjects. And the second ambition is advanced by Locke by arguing that a magistrate may lawfully command whatever a subject may rightfully do (First Tract, 125–26; Second Tract, 231), a claim that follows trivially from the position that subjects transfer all of their rights to the magistrate. But once Locke surrenders these ambitions, as he clearly does by the time of the *Two Treatises* and *A Letter Concerning Toleration,* there is no further need for that view of the political transfer of rights. Locke's views changed, both on what rights *must* be transferred to government, and on what rights *can* be transferred.[17] I have argued elsewhere, for instance, that Lockean citizens in civil society must be supposed to retain significant portions of their natural rights in land and all of their rights in other material property.[18] Similarly, the right of innocent delights is clearly excluded by Locke (in II, 128–30) from the consensual transfer that creates political power. (And who, in any event, could imagine Locke denying that a citizen has a clear right to smoke a pipe or whistle a favorite tune?) And the language of II, 129 is obviously intended to convey as well that the rest of our right of self-government (what Locke calls "the first power") is surrendered only in part, to the extent necessary for society's preservation.

This is not, of course, to argue that Locke's (mature) position on the political transfer of rights is without difficulties for him. Locke argues, for instance, that each citizen surrenders (in part) the right "of doing whatsoever he thought fit for the preservation of himself and the rest of mankind" on entrance into civil society. But if the law of nature, which commands the preservation of humankind, is "an eternal rule to all men" (II, 135), then each person always has a duty to preserve self and others, in or out of civil society.[19] And if each has that duty, each also has the right to preserve self and others (i.e., the right to do one's duty). How, then, can Locke claim that even a part of this right has been given up by citizens (a question to which we will return in chapter 5)? One simple answer available to Locke is claiming that the "part" of this right that is surrendered is only the privilege of acting *first* in attempting to preserve self and others. The community obtains from each the right to act first in preserving its citizens and promoting their good (analogous to the "right of first try" that parents possess in rearing their children[20]), by obtaining from each the right to act before that individual. This precludes the anarchic results that might seem to result from citizens following their own judgments while legislators and judges try to follow theirs. Where the community is unable or unwilling to preserve its citizens, however, individuals retain the right (and duty) to "act second" themselves, even to the point of actively resisting a government that fails to observe natural law.[21]

3.2. Consent, Contract, and Trust

With this understanding in hand of the moral content of the transfer of right that creates political society, we can look more closely at the process of transfer (which is more complicated than I have thus far indicated). A complete political society, Locke suggests, is created in two logically separable stages (which may or may not be separated by an interesting temporal gap). The society itself is created by a contract among all those who wish to be part of it. The society's government is formed by society's granting a separate trust, which conveys to government the political power which was previously invested in the society by its members.[22] Political power is given first "into the hands of the society, and therein to the governors whom the society has set over itself, with this express or tacit trust: that it shall be employed for their good and the preservation of their property" ([II, 171]; see also II, 243). While the creation of the "Legislative" (the "soul" of the commonwealth) is "the first and fundamental act of society" (II, 212), the body politic is created "by barely agreeing to unite into one political society" (II, 99).[23] Consent to membership in the body politic must be unanimous ("by the consent of every individual" [II, 96]), for only a person's *own* consent can remove that individual from the state of nature. But this consent *entails,* Locke believes, consent to rule by the majority of the members in all subsequent matters (including, of course, the creation of government) (II, 95–99; I return to this matter in 4.2).

After the first creation of the commonwealth (or after an initially *illegitimate* society has been rendered legitimate), individuals may join it by consenting to those same terms of incorporation to which the original members agreed (II, 89) (or should have agreed), including majority rule and the authority of any legitimate government the previous members may have installed.[24] The new member's rights are simply "added to" the political power of the society (and from there entrusted to government).

All of this is accomplished only by consent. Locke's most famous discussion of consent, of course, concerns the consent given by those who join (or otherwise enjoy the dominions of) already existing commonwealths. But I will take the term "consent" to be for Locke a blanket term covering all instances of deliberate, voluntary alienation of rights (and undertakings of obligation)—including not only what we might narrowly call consenting, but also promising, contracting, entrusting, and so on.[25] This is not just Locke's account of consent, but a quite plausible account in its own right. While we can obviously distinguish in certain ways such acts as consenting, promising, contracting, and entrusting, there is also a perfectly natural sense of "consent" on which promising, contracting, and entrusting are simply *kinds* of consenting.[26] We can describe as acts of consent any acts that deliberately and suitably communicate to others the agent's intention to undertake obligations toward and/or convey rights (or permissions) to those others. One can, on this account, consent insincerely (by deliberately communicating to others an intention one in fact lacks). And acts of consent can, of course, fail to alter the existing distribution of obligations and rights, for consent is not sufficient to ground obligations and convey rights.[27] But consent can be defined in terms of the agent's deliberate and effective communication of an intention to bring about this kind of change.[28]

Regardless of how broadly we understand the term "consent" (or Locke's use of it), however, Locke clearly intends as well to point to (and rely upon) substantive and important differences among the various kinds of voluntary alienations. In particular, the distinction just discussed between the *contract* that creates society and the *trust* that creates its government is meant by Locke to bear considerable weight. It is certainly important to Locke both that invoking the concept of a trust makes this political relationship mirror certain aspects of his view of our relation to God and that doing so constitutes a significant departure from medieval assertions of a contract between people and ruler.[29] Locke's employment of the idea of a trust is especially important in its consequences for his theory of resistance, as one of his clearest discussions of the idea reveals:

> The Legislative being only a fiduciary power to act for certain ends, there remains still in the People a supreme power to remove or alter the Legislative, when they find the Legislative act contrary to the trust reposed in them. For all power given with trust for the attaining an end, being limited by that end, whenever that end is manifestly neglected or opposed, the trust must necessarily be forfeited and the power devolve into the hands of those who gave it. (II, 149)

This passage isolates a number of important features of Locke's understanding of trusts, which make the idea particularly suitable for effectively conveying a particular conception of the moral relation between a people and their government.[30]

(1) Unlike a contract, which binds parties to specific performances, a trust sets an end to be pursued (and grants rights only for the purpose of pursuing that end).

(2) The end establishes a responsibility on the part of the trustee (in this case, "to preserve the members of that society in their lives, liberties, and possessions" [II, 171]). A contractually alienated right, by contrast, typically carries no specific limitations on the new rightholder's use of it.

(3) Pursuit of an end requires discretion (think here of Kant's characterization of imperfect duties). Thus, a trustee must be allowed prerogative in the employment of entrusted rights for pursuing the end (II, 159–68).

(4) Because it is a trust, and not a contract, no consideration need be given for it to bind. The trustee need not personally benefit in order to be bound to pursue the assigned end.[31]

(5) Because a trust conveys more of a privilege than a claim (unlike a contract), and so is only a conditional alienation, the settlor may withdraw the trust without injury to the trustee. Trusts are revokable in a way that executed contracts are not, so that entrusted rights are not irrecoverably lost.[32]

(6) The settlor is the judge of when and whether the trustee has acted contrary to the trust, thus forfeiting the entrusted rights.[33]

Legitimate governments, then, hold their political power only for the purpose of advancing the good of the people who created them (or subsequently consented to their authority), never for advancing their own good. They may act outside of the law (and otherwise use discretion) in order to more effectively serve this purpose. But when the people judge them to have failed in their task, their power is forfeit and resistance to them becomes legitimate. It is this arrangement to which each member of the commonwealth is committed by political consent, and this limit on the power of governors over the governed that consent establishes.

3.3. The Appeal of Consent Theory

Political power, Locke tells us, "has its original *only* from compact and agreement, and the mutual consent of those who make up the community" (II, 171; my emphasis). Let us draw from this claim (and from those examined above) the essential premise of Lockean consent theory: that free consent by citizens is not only (normally) sufficient, but *necessary* for legitimate political authority and political obligation (see

7.1). That this consent theory has great appeal, far beyond the structure of Locke's work or the character of Locke's time, is undeniable. Americans learn at their mothers' knees that governments derive "their just powers from the consent of the governed," and it is a view that is widely (and uncritically) accepted today by most citizens of modern democracies (among others). What accounts for the attractiveness of the doctrine that only consent can make a government legitimate?[34]

Some of what made the doctrine attractive to Locke would undoubtedly not interest us today. But at least a large part of what appealed to Locke about consent theory, I contend, is precisely what continues to appeal to us today. In the first place, for instance, consent (voluntary alienation) is a convincing source of our political ties for both Locke and ourselves, because, more than any other, consent is a clear and uncontroversial ground of special obligation and right-transfer.[35] For Locke, consent (promise, contract) binds even God, its moral force is so clear and indisputable (I, 6; II, 195); indeed, Locke wonders if there can "be anything more ridiculous" than to make a pledge and then break it (II, 194). It is consent that makes society possible on Locke's view.[36] And we share with Locke, I am suggesting, this intuitive conviction: "that men should keep their compacts is certainly a great and undeniable rule in morality" (E, 1.2.5).

Other sources of the appeal of consent theory are also common to Locke and many of us today. For Locke, the emphasis on consent is an emphatic denial of the legitimacy of force and conquest as a source of political authority.[37] Free consent (as the only legitimate source of such authority), of course, is the ground most clearly opposed to force. I assume that on our agreement with Locke in this matter, no argument is necessary. Nor is it necessary to dwell long on our agreement with Locke on the right of a people to resist a government that oppresses them or acts consistently contrary to their expressed aims and commitments. Consent theory is specially connected to this view of the right of resistance.[38] While other theories may also, of course, affirm the right to resist illegitimate government, on other theories a government that acts contrary to its people's will may still have moral standing for unrelated reasons (its institution by God, the historical contract in which it originated, the benefits it still provides, etc.). According to Lockean consent theory, a government that steadily and deliberately fails to act within the terms of its trust has no moral standing at all (as a government), and so may be resisted without fear of moral impropriety.[39]

But all of this still ignores the deepest and most important continuity between Locke's reasons for embracing consent theory and our own. Because many of us agree with Locke about the importance of the individual's right of self-government or autonomy, we are with Locke drawn to the conclusion that consent is the only ground of political obligation and authority that is consistent with the natural moral freedom to which we are committed. The Lockean person's natural condition, remember, is one of perfect freedom (from the political authority of others). Persons are not born subjects, just because they happen to be born within the territories of states (II, 118).[40] It follows from this, of course, that attempts by others to govern us will require some special justification—a justification consistent with and respectful of our natural freedom. But what kind of justification could this be? If another's being wiser or more able were sufficient justification for his governing and controlling us, we would have to concede that we had, after all, no natural claim to choose for ourselves how our lives will go.[41] Only the view that the free choices of those subject to political authority are necessary to legitimate it seems consistent with the natural right of self-government.[42] Consent is an act only a free person can perform; it is a use, not a breach, of one's freedom. Because consent is an *intentional,* deliberate act, which requires knowledge and awareness of circumstances, one's freedom cannot be undermined by allegedly consensual obligations (or alienation of rights) that are accomplished unwittingly or under duress.[43] Indeed, it is virtually analytic for Locke that the political transfer of rights can only be achieved by consent. For a person's rights are personal property (e.g., II, 87), and property cannot be taken without its owner's consent (II, 138).[44]

No government can allow complete liberty (this *is* analytic: E, 4.3.18). But the method of consent comes as close to this ideal as possible. Consent invests governmental acts with the moral significance of the free choices of individuals. It has been argued, by contrast, that Locke was mistaken in thinking that his acceptance of our natural freedom committeed him to consent theory. For once governments are established that protect *others'* freedom, we have a duty to accept the authority of these governments, whether we have agreed to be subject to them or not.[45] This claim, however, betrays a misunderstanding of the substance of Locke's (and the Lockean) doctrine of natural freedom. Others act wrongly if they act in ways that limit our natural freedom to dispose of our rights as God's law and our own wills dictate. Others cannot acquire authority over us by wrongly making it difficult or impossible to reject that authority without disadvantaging them. Indeed, others may only permissibly form a society among themselves (without me) provided that their doing so does not harm me in my freedom: "This [joining to form a commonwealth] any number of men may do, *because it injures not the freedom of the rest*; they are left as they were in the liberty of the state of nature" (II, 95; my emphasis). No one, then, whether born in the territories of an established state or not, is either born obligated to obey any political authority, or born with an obligation to consent to any particular political society's authority.[46] These are fundamental tenets of Lockean consent theory. They are a significant source of its enduring appeal, in my view, largely because they are correct.

However appealing we might find it, though, we should not try to pretend that Lockean consent theory offers the only account of political obligation and authority that has any real potential. Opposing views with many serious and thoughtful adherents are ranged in a wide variety of theoretical distances from Lockean voluntarism. We saw in 1.3, for instance, that Lockean individualism and voluntarism are opposed most dramatically by various naturalist and communitarian theories, according to which the obligation to obey one's political superiors follows simply (or even trivially) from one's identity as a person or as a member of a certain kind of community. Less dramatically, of course, Lockean theory is opposed by more individualistic virtue theories, which maintain that political obedience, allegiance, or civility are important aspects of moral virtue.[47] Less dramatically still, Lockean consent theory can be contrasted with straightforwardly individualistic theories that simply identify different (or additional) grounds of political obligation than consent. Thus, "benefit/reciprocation theories" take political obedience (etc.) to be morally required reciprocation for benefits received or accepted from the workings of one's legal and political institutions. Such theories might appeal either to a principle of gratitude or to one of fairness to justify their claims. "Quality of government theories," while also typically individualistic in character, reject the idea that political obligations must flow from specific transactions between citizens and states, basing those obligations instead on the independent moral importance of supporting just, useful, or worthy (etc.) laws or governments. I class both utilitarian and hypothetical contractarian theories of political obligation as quality-of-government theories.

We will return to some of Lockean consent theory's individualist competitors in 7.2 and 8.4. But the contrast on which I want to concentrate for a moment here is in a way the least dramatic of all, and hence a matter of rather subtler theoretical distinctions. Many (especially recent) political philosophers have, like Locke, employed in their theories of obligation or authority the ideas of consent or contract; but they have at the same time rejected the Lockean consent theory outlined above. Their theories thus constitute the most immediate challenge to Lockean consent theory. For they threaten to capture what is appealing about Lockean theory while dispensing with central aspects of that theory.

All of the theories I have in mind here, while utilizing some notion of consent, reject the central Lockean claim that an actual act of consent is necessary for each person's political obligations or duties. Hypothetical contractarians maintain, for instance, that our political obligations (duties) are to support those institutions that *would be* agreed upon by hypothetical persons of some description (typically, rational, self-interested, and in some ways ignorant) in an original position of equality and nonsubjection.[48] The actual consent of specific persons (or the absence of such consent) is irrelevant (or at least secondary) to a determination of their political duties. Yet, it is claimed, this view captures much of the force and appeal of classical Lockean consent theory:

> No society can, of course, be a scheme of cooperation which men enter voluntarily in a literal sense. . . . Yet a society satisfying [hypothetical contractarian demands] comes as close as a society can to being a voluntary scheme, for it meets the principles that free and equal persons would assent to under circumstances that are fair. In this sense its members are autonomous and the obligations they recognize self-imposed.[49]

Radical participation theorists also reject the idea that specific acts of consent are necessary (or sufficient) for each person's obligations, although they stress as the alternative not some hypothetical version of consent. Rather, their emphasis is placed on "the theory and practice of participatory or self-managing democracy":[50] only serious, ongoing participation in the practices of such a democracy counts as giving true consent (and hence creating and maintaining political obligations). Others agree that political consent is better thought of as "ongoing and diffuse" than as a specific act,[51] and they insist as well on a less individualistic conception of consent than is utilized in classical consent theory. But now we are asked to think of the "consent of the governed" not in terms of acts or ongoing performances by citizens, but instead in terms of the responsiveness of the state to its people (conceived of as a single corporate agent). States that are responsive and unoppressive toward those who reside in their territories are legitimate and are owed obligations of obedience; they enjoy the consent of the governed.[52]

I cannot here respond to these "revisionist consent theories" with the care they clearly merit. But my advocacy of the Lockean perspective requires at least a brief reply, as well as a defense of my view that only the Lockean version of consent theory preserves the intuitive appeal of consent theory summarized above. To radical participation theory the Lockean can respond primarily by insisting on additions. For the Lockean need not insist that only discrete acts (however we might try to explain such a concept) can properly be counted as acts of consent. Ongoing (voluntary, informed, serious) political participation can be counted by the Lockean as giving consent of the appropriate sort, just as Locke himself (although not very convincingly) was willing to count the ongoing process of continued, voluntary residence as giving consent. The Lockean must insist, however, against much participation theory, that discrete acts of consent *can* ground political obligations, provided these acts are genuinely voluntary and adequately informed. And the Lockean will have good reasons for this insistence: for many of the same values (and, from the Lockean point of view, the most important ones) that are promoted by schemes of active, democratic political participation are also promoted by allowing individuals free choice in where their political allegiance will lie, and by permitting persons to commit themselves to their choices by discrete acts of consent. Our practices of promising and contracting have quite apparent justifications. And provided only that the range of possible commitments is appropriately limited (as it will be in any Lockean theory), there is no reason to suppose that political versions of promises and contracts are morally suspect.

As for hypothetical contractarianism and "consent-as-responsiveness theories," the most obvious objection to them (as developments of consent theory) is that both actually constitute clear retreats from genuine consent theory to what I earlier called "quality-of-government theories." Both are only superficially forms of consent theory at all. For both really base our duties or obligations not on anyone's actual choices, but on whether our governments (states, laws) are sufficiently just, good, useful, or responsive to secure the hypothetical support of ideal choosers. And the choices of such ideal parties are, of course, necessarily guided solely by the actual merits of the governments (institutions, schemes) in question; they can only choose that which is in fact best for them. But then it seems only honest to acknowledge that the "contract" in hypothetical contractarianism is simply a device that permits us to analyze in a certain way quality of government, rather than the actual ground of political duty. And once consent is abandoned as the ground, we have also abandoned much of what is most compelling about classical consent theory—namely, the clear, uncontroversial ground of obligation on which it relies, and the high value of self-government with which it remains consistent. Theories that simply base political duties in governmental justice or responsiveness (etc.) plainly lose the latter source of consent theory's appeal (for individual choice or rejection of allegiance becomes unimportant to obligation); and they arguably lose the former as well.[53] It simply will not do to respond that the Lockean consent theorist's demand for actual consent (in the interest of individual autonomy) is silly, given that no actual societies permit (or can permit) their residents full autonomy.[54] For it may well be, as Lockeans insist, that societies that refuse to permit or fail to facilitate free choice of political allegiance are simply illegitimate, however many such societies might actually exist.

Notes

1. This voluntarism, of course, was not much in evidence in Locke's early works (such as the *Two Tracts* and the *Essays on the Law of Nature*), where the lawmaker's rights are, for instance, said to be "borrowed from God" (e.g., ELN, 187) and our obligations to obey are derived simply from God's command that we obey magistrates (e.g., First Tract, 159; Second Tract, 226). Locke's voluntarism apparently emerged only with the maturity of his thought (perhaps as a result of his practical political experience and more active political plans). The claim that Locke's doctrine was essentially the same in his early and later works (as advanced by, e.g., Macpherson in *Possessive Individualism*, 258–61) is mistaken in its identification of both the rights that individuals surrender and how governments obtain them (as I argue below). On the development of Locke's voluntarism, see Riley, *Will and Political Legitimacy*, especially 69–71.

2. Neither forfeiture nor prescription can yield political power. Other kinds of power, such as paternal or despotical power, arise from other sources. Locke occasionally overstates his position by claiming that consent is necessary for subjection "to any earthly power" (e.g., II, 119). But his considered position is clearly only that consent is the sole possible source of *political* power.

3. Each member "engages his natural force . . . to assist the executive

power of the society, as the law thereof shall require" (II, 130), this being taken by Locke to include assistance in federative matters, where "the force of the public" is employed in making war (II, 145–48). Similarly, each must be understood to have agreed to pay "his proportion" of the necessary expenses involved in maintaining a government and extending to all members the protection it provides (II, 140).

4. This claim requires qualification, given Locke's view that the obligations of tacit consenters, while otherwise identical in extent, have a different force or duration than those of express consenters (see 4.1 below). What is certainly true is that the moral content of the consensual transactions is the same for those who either expressly create a society or expressly join an already existing society.

5. Although we should note that Locke appears to claim elsewhere that individuals always *retain* their right to take reparation for damages done them by offenders against the law of nature (II, 11).

6. Among those who argue (correctly, in my view) that some natural rights are retained by individuals after consenting to enter civil society are Plamenatz, *Man and Society*, 1:217; Goldwin, "John Locke," 496; Aaron, *John Locke*, 279; Brandt, *Ethical Theory*, 443; Hacker, *Political Theory*, 226; Barker, "Introduction," xx; DeBeer, "Locke and English Liberalism," 41. It may be worth remembering that the Ninth Amendment to the American Constitution refers explicitly to the rights "retained by the people."

7. Note that legislative power is defined by Locke as "a right to direct how the force of the commonwealth shall be employed for preserving the community and the members of it" (II, 143). This is clearly just the political version of the first power specified in II, 126 (i.e., it is clearly the collection of all the members' "first powers").

8. These limits are that legislative power (a) cannot be arbitrary (II, 135); (b) must operate by means of promulgated laws and known, authorized judges (II, 136–37); (c) cannot be used to take property without the owner's consent (II, 138); and (d) cannot be transferred by government to other hands (II, 141). (Locke's final list of these limits in II, 142 is slightly different from, but consistent with, the limits emphasized in the preceding text, as summarized above.) As we will see in chapter 5, these limits are set in part by the limits of each person's rights over *self* (as specified by the law of nature). But the legislative power must also be limited by the rights that each person retains in society (e.g., retained property rights, which are the justification for limit [c]). Note that Locke says the "bounds" of the legislative power are set both by the law of nature and by the content of the trust (II, 142)—and the content of the trust is itself limited by the rights individuals retain, since all of the rights that they surrender are eventually put in the hands of government.

9. See my more complete defense of these claims in *Lockean Theory of Rights*, section 3.6.

10. Locke's sensitivity to the problem is evident even in his early *Two Tracts*, where he distinguishes between the magistrate's power to require morally obligatory conduct and his power in the area of indifferent conduct. Locke claims there that if the magistrate is not left free to legislate concerning indiffer-

ent conduct, then he could only require again that which is already required by natural law, in which sphere "the power of the magistrate seems to be no greater than that of any private citizen" (Second Tact, 228). Locke solves the problem in the *Second Treatise* by distinguishing two kinds of rights that subjects might transfer to their political superiors.

11. See Pitkin, "Obligation and Consent—I," 994–95.

12. Locke likes to emphasize specifically the right to impose capital punishment in discussing political power, although this is clearly only one kind of punishment that a legitimate government might employ (see, e.g., II, 3, 65). It is tempting to read Locke as trying to identify with this emphasis one particularly central or essential component of political power. But while this may well be Locke's view, it is hard to see why governments that decline to use the death penalty should be taken to be exercising an interestingly impoverished form of political power.

13. As in I, 129–32, where the "marks of sovereignty" he identifies include aspects of political power, as that power is subsequently defined. Locke, however, generally avoids directly utilizing the idea of sovereignty in the central aspects of his positive presentation in the *Treatises*. See Grant, *Liberalism*, 76–79. This essay contains no extended discussion of sovereignty or of how traditional conceptions of sovereignty relate to Locke's position, in part because I can add little to Franklin's careful study of these matters (*John Locke and the Theory of Sovereignty*). In chapter 6, I do comment briefly on the significance of Locke's theory of resistance for classical conceptions of sovereignty.

14. Kendall, *Majority-Rule*, e.g., 62, 103–4, 112–13, and "John Locke Revisited," 221; Strauss, *Natural Right*, 231–32; Cox, *Locke on War and Peace*, 115–23, 148; Macpherson, *Possessive Individualism*, 256–61; Waldron, "Enough and as Good," 327 (although Waldron's position on this point is unclear; see note 21 below). Parry makes the puzzling claim that Locke's contractors "surrendered their right to enforce the law of nature and no other rights" (*John Locke*, 98); his view seems to have been anticipated in Grady, "Obligation, Consent," 282, 284; and followed in Den Hartogh, "Express Consent," 660, 667; and Lessnoff, *Social Contract*, 61–62.

15. There is a third choice, closely related to the first: that the contract amounts to a kind of "limited blank check," an agreement to give up the rights required by society (but *only* those) when they are needed (as opposed to determining in advance which rights are needed). On this reading, like the first, citizens retain those rights that are not needed by society, but, unlike the first, surrender rights in stages as the needs of society become apparent.

16. This, of course, is part of Macpherson's reason for favoring the second reading. See note 1 above.

17. This change was related to Locke's change of view on the best strategy for managing religion in civil society. Whether civil peace and prosperity (the proper ends of civil government) are best served by imposing religion or by tolerating it will partially determine which rights must be transferred from citizens to government. And on this question of strategy, Locke's views clearly changed. See Kraynak, "John Locke," 53–55.

18. What is surrendered is only those rights over property necessary for societal or governmental jurisdiction (II, 120–22); and jurisdiction over property is not identical to community or governmental possession of all rights in the property at issue. See *Lockean Theory of Rights,* sections 4.4 and 6.1; and Waldron, *Private Property,* 137.

19. This claim is independently plausible from an intuitive Lockean perspective. For it seems clear that Locke would want to contend that even citizens in a legitimate commonwealth have duties to refrain from suicide, keep their promises, or save a starving man—whether or not these acts are commanded by the state as legal duties.

20. See *Lockean Theory of Rights,* 178–84.

21. Interestingly, the only place where Locke explicitly approaches this style of reasoning seems to be in connection with the *executive* right, which Locke says is "wholly" given up in civil society. Locke argues that I have a right to preserve myself (by, e.g., killing a thief) even in civil society, if the law "cannot interpose to secure my life from present force" (II, 19).

22. See, e.g., Parry, *John Locke,* 99; Pateman, *Political Obligation,* 69–79; Mabbott, *John Locke,* 151; Pitkin,"Obligation and Consent—I," 994. Sabine claims that Locke did not explicitly employ a "two-stage contract," since he had no real interest in formal clarity (*History of Political Theory,* 532–33). This assertion seems mistaken, at least if one counts the trust as analogous to the second stage in earlier contractarian accounts.

23. Thus, political society logically precedes government for Locke. Grant argues that Locke can be understood to be using two senses of the term "government" in his work. In the technical sense, government is that which is created by the trust from society. But the society itself, at its creation, is also a kind of government: "then the form of government is a perfect [majority rule] democracy" (II, 132). Locke does sometimes use "community" and "government" interchangeably (e.g., II, 95), and the society and the government it entrusts do hold the same political power (although on different terms). So Grant's suggestion seems reasonable. See *Liberalism,* 103–6; and Tarcov, "Best Fence," 205.

24. The differences between express and tacit consent, with regard to membership in the commonwealth, are discussed below in 4.1. On the content of a "joiner's" consent, see Grant, *Liberalism,* 119–21.

25. See Pateman, *Political Obligation,* 71. Note that consent is given in Locke not only to society, but also to government (e.g., II, 121).

26. Raz, *Morality of Freedom,* 82–83; Green, *Authority of the State,* 167. This seems to me more plausible than the view that consent is really a kind of promise, as claimed in Weale, "Consent," 68–69; and Den Hartogh, "Made by Contrivance," 214.

27. We can consent to (virtually) anything; but we can only convey to others rights over a very limited class of acts or objects (Weale, "Consent," 66–67; Raz, *Morality of Freedom,* 84).

28. Raz prefers to analyze consent in terms of the agent's beliefs rather than intentions (*Morality of Freedom,* 81–83). But as Green argues (and as we will see in 8.4), while we might sometimes call an act one of "consent" even where

the intention to bind oneself was lacking, the principle in such cases under which we argue for holding a person liable for that "consent" is very different than that to which we appeal in cases of intentional undertakings of obligation. Where intention is absent, we appeal rather to a principle of "estoppel" (to protect the interests of those who relied on the "consent") (*Authority of the State*, 163–64).

It is important to see that the intention relevant to a proper analysis of consent is the intention to alter the existing distribution of obligations and rights, and not the intention to "induce reliance" in another (as is claimed in Weale, "Consent," 68–69, and rejected in Raz, *Morality of Freedom*, 96). While consenting to something may (or may not) induce others to rely on one, one's obligation to abide by one's consent is not explained by this reliance. Another's reliance is not necessary for me to have a consensual obligation. Nor is even quite deliberate, voluntary creation in another of reasonable expectations sufficient to generate an obligation not to frustrate those expectations (if, for instance, conventional or otherwise appropriate means of creating expectations were not employed; see my "Reasonable Expectations").

29. See *Lockean Theory of Rights*, 53–54, 77–78, 97–99, 260–64. On the history of the use of "trust" in political theory, see Gough, *Political Philosophy*, chapter 7. On Locke's use of the concept in his theory of resistance (noted below), see ibid., 161. Hampton has argued that Locke is not really using the idea of a trust in his theory at all (*Hobbes and the Social Contract Tradition*, 248n). My arguments here and in chapter 6 are, I think, good grounds for believing her claim to be false.

30. Specifically, the people in Locke occupy two of the three standard roles in fiduciary relations—they are both settlor (trustor) and beneficiary, with their government as trustee. See Barker, "Introduction," xxiii–xxiv. Von Leyden's account of Locke on trusts emphasizes (4), (5), and (6) below (*Hobbes and Locke*, 128–32). Dunn's account, by contrast, concentrates on (1), (2), and (3) below (*Political Thought*, 162, and "The Concept of 'Trust,'" 296–97). Both aspects of the fiduciary relationship Locke has in mind need emphasis. Lessnoff argues that trusts should actually be thought of as special kinds of contracts, involving promises by both settlor and trustee, with at least one promise (presumably the settlor's) being conditional on proper performance by the other party (*Social Contract*, 4–6). As the analysis below suggests, this does not capture the full measure of the differences between contracts and trusts (at least as these notions are used by Locke).

31. Gough, *Political Philosophy*, 139.

32. See Cranston, "Government by Consent," 74; Tuck, *Natural Rights Theories*, 146–47; Gough, *Political Philosophy*, 122n; Barker, "Introduction," xxiii–xxiv.

33. "Who shall be the judge whether his trustee or deputy acts well, and according to the trust reposed in him, but he who deputes him, and must, by having deputed him have still a power to discard him when he fails in his trust?" (II, 240). Whether the people wrong their trustee (government) by removing it when they mistakenly judge it to have breached its trust is a question to which I return in 6.4.

Le

34. See my earlier discussion of this question in *Moral Principles and Political Obligations,* chapter 3.

35. Ibid., especially 69–70.

36. See *Lockean Theory of Rights,* 65; Dunn, "Concept of 'Trust,' " 287–88, and *Locke,* 52. The importance of promise-keeping to society's maintenance in Locke can be plainly seen in the limits on toleration that he stresses: papists are not to be tolerated (in part) because the pope can release them from oaths and promises to their rulers (ECT, 188); atheists are not to be tolerated because "promises, covenants, and oaths . . . can have no hold upon" them (L, 156).

37. See 2.3 above. This point is made forcefully in Dunn, *Political Thought,* 144–45, and "Consent," 47.

38. See Shapiro, *Evolution of Rights,* 288.

39. This, it seems to me, is the "logical connection" between Locke's consent theory and his theory of resistance. Plamenatz denies that any such connection exists (*Man and Society,* 1:231–32). We will see in chapter 6, however, that this Lockean position, as I have just expressed it, needs to be in certain ways qualified (e.g., to take account of the necessity of the people's judgment that government is in breach of its trust).

40. See 1.3 above; and Dunn, *Political Thought,* 136–38.

41. See the discussion of these points in Beran, "What Is the Basis of Political Authority?" 490–93, and *Consent Theory,* 34–36.

42. See Pateman, "Women and Consent," 150–51; Richards, *Toleration and the Constitution,* 101; Lemos, *Hobbes and Locke,* 81.

43. *Moral Principles and Political Obligations,* 69–70.

44. This claim requires careful statement. Rights can be forfeited to others without the consent of their original holder, but not "taken from" the rightholder. And only wrongdoing can accomplish a forfeiture (see 2.2).

45. Plamenatz, *Man and Society,* 1:224.

46. See my discussion of this point in *Lockean Theory of Rights,* 66–67; and Lessnoff, *Social Contract,* 62, 98. Even if Locke's view is (as I believe it is not) that each person has an obligation to consent to and enter civil society (a familiar enough Puritan view), this still does not amount to an obligation to enter any particular political society (e.g., the one I happen to have been reared in): each reaches maturity as "a freeman, at liberty what government he will put himself under" (II, 118). This, of course, is the crucial point for the force of consent theory.

47. Hume, *Treatise,* 3.2.7–10; Green, *Authority of the State,* chapter 9.

48. Lessnoff (*Social Contract,* 91) distinguishes hypothetical contract theories (which appeal to what people could or would have chosen) from ideal contract theories (which appeal to what they ought to have chosen). Where the choosers are idealized (as in the theories I am discussing here), however, the distinction tends to dissolve.

49. Rawls, *Theory of Justice,* 13. Indeed, Locke himself has been read as a defender of hypothetical contractarianism, although I postpone until 7.2 my full defense of reading Locke as an actual-consent theorist.

50. Pateman, *Problem of Political Obligation,* 1.

51. Herzog, *Happy Slaves*, 193, 196.

52. Ibid., 202–15.

53. It is not unreasonable (or even unusual) to ask why we should take ourselves to have a duty to support arrangements that merely would be chosen by ideal choosers (Kavka, *Hobbesian Moral and Political Theory*, 399). The counterfactual claim at issue, remember, is not that the choice is one that *I* would have made (as when the doctor tries to justify treating my unconscious body [without my actual consent] by appealing to what I would consent to were I able). It is rather that the choice is one that ideal persons in special circumstances would have made. And if the theory tries to make the choosers *less* ideal (so they are more like me, and their choices more like the ones I would make), the theory loses whatever advantages it gained by associating justification and legitimation with the "best" (soundest, most rational) choices. In any event, however, it is certainly possible for the Lockean consent theorist to argue that one's free *acts* have a very different moral significance than even extremely reliable counterfactual claims that could be made about how one *would* act.

54. Herzog takes the classical consent theorist's demand for individual autonomy to be an impossible demand that each person "have his way" even in society (*Happy Slaves*, 201–2). But this is not, of course, a fair rendering of that demand. The Lockean demand is only a demand either to be left alone (to one's natural freedom) or to be allowed to freely choose the political society within which one will surrender the right to "have his way." And, in any event, the right to "have one's way" is at its fullest (for the Lockean) only a right to act in ways consistent with one's own duties and the rights of others. The Lockean demand for individual autonomy is only a demand for that which is consistent with all others possessing the same.

8

Structure, Choice, and Legitimacy: Locke's Theory of the State

Joshua Cohen

I. Introduction

Locke held that human beings are by nature rational and equally free.[1] On the basis of that rationality and equal freedom he argued against political absolutism and in defense of a constitutional state. Much more than his distinctive *institutional* views about popular sovereignty, legislative supremacy, or the separation of powers, it was these *foundational* beliefs that distinguished Locke from contemporary constitutionalists.[2]

But Locke also believed in the legitimacy of a class state, that is, in a constitutional state subject to the formal authority, and not just the substantive control, of property owners.[3] In this respect Locke was indistinguishable from virtually all his contemporaries. But are these two views really consistent? Is Locke's foundational commitment to equal freedom and rationality consistent with his institutional belief in the legitimacy of a property owner's state? In view of the intimate connection between Locke's conception of equal freedom and his commitment to a contractual theory of political legitimacy (see below, pp. 312–314), this question can be explicated in a way that will make it more susceptible to a precise answer: Could free and equal parties to a social contract rationally consent to a system of political association featuring the formal inequality of political rights that defines a property owner's state?

First, some terminology. By a *constitutional state* I will mean a political order characterized by: (1) the rule of law. That is, effective restriction on the use of state power to the enforcement of general and public rules: "one rule for rich and poor, for the favourite at court, and the country man at plough" (2.142; see also 2.137). Locke's remark about "rich and poor" suggests that he understood the requirement of generality in a way that would rule out legally codified barriers to interclass mobility;[4] (2) separation of legislative and executive powers; (3) legislative control of taxation; and (4) an independent judiciary. By a "property owner's state" I will mean a constitutional state in which the legislative function is formally controlled by a propertied class. That is: (5) the franchise is restricted to those with a specified level of property ownership; and (6) eligibility for elected office is restricted to the same propertied group. While (1)–(4) promise *universal* protections of civil rights and liberties, (5) and (6) accord one class special political standing. Finally, I will use the term "democratic state" to mean a constitutional state with universal political rights, a state without the franchise and office-holding restrictions characteristic of the property owner's state. For other purposes it would be important to provide more detailed conditions and to draw further distinctions. But for present purposes, these brief characterizations suffice, and so we can return to the main question: Could free and equal rational agents consent to a property owner's state?

To clarify the terms of the question and the constraints on an acceptable answer, I want to consider two familiar answers: (1) there could be an "agreement," but only if the agreement involved fraud; and (2) there could be an agreement, but only if the "consent" were forced. What we want to know is not *whether* Locke wanted to rule out forced and fraudulent agreements—of course he did—but how he did it, so that we can eventually see if there is an agreement to a property owner's state that satisfies these and other constraints.

1. A Lockean agreement to a property owner's state would be based on *fraud* if some form of deception of the propertyless were required to secure their agreement to such a state. The propertyless might, for example, be led to believe that their fundamental interests would be best protected under a state controlled by the propertied, when in fact some other arrangement would provide greater protection, and the propertied know this. Locke himself does not address this issue. But there are various ways that such an agreement would not satisfy plausible extensions of Locke's own strictures. Here I will suggest just one, namely, that he would not consider such an agreement *rational.* That is, a rational social contract is not simply a social pact in which the

parties maximize expected benefits *given their current beliefs.* Instead, it must also be the case that no one would choose differently if they knew the beliefs of others. The parties need not have the same beliefs; they might agree to disagree. And their beliefs need not be true. But it cannot be that the outcome would be different if everyone's beliefs were common knowledge.[5]

2. The second alternative is an agreement based on *force.* In this case, those with property parlay their property advantage into control of the means of violence, and use that control to extract consent. But, for Locke, forced consent is no consent at all: "It remains only to be considered, whether promises extorted by force, without right, can be thought consent, and how far they bind. To which I shall say, they bind not at all" (2.186; also 2.1, 2.176). Consent is forced and therefore not binding (or really no consent at all) when it is given as a consequence of a threat—whether direct or indirect—to the preservation of the consenting agent.

Two points about such threats will play a role later on. First, Locke construes indirect threats to preservation very broadly. Any threat either to my liberty or to any of my property counts as a threat to my preservation (2.18). Secondly, Locke will not count the *failure to increase* someone's chances of preservation as a threat to their preservation. This point is suggested by Locke's remark that "The only way whereby any one divests himself of his natural liberty, and puts on the bonds of civil society, is by agreeing with other men. This any number of men may do, because it injures not the freedom of the rest; they are left as they were in the liberty of the state of nature" (2.95).

These points about force and fraud are straightforward enough. The reason for entering them is not to endorse Locke's construal of force and fraud, but rather to indicate some requirements on an answer to our question that respects the main lines of Locke's conception (allowing for the moment that there may be no such solution). Specifically, an agreement to a property owner's state justifies that state only if the agreement is based on common beliefs, and is not dependent upon direct or indirect threats to preservation.

II. Macpherson's Solution

The most systematic answer to the question that I have raised is provided by C. B. Macpherson in his *Political Theory of Possessive Individ-*

ualism.[6] In part because I agree with much that he says, and in part because my own account can be motivated by considering the short-comings of Macpherson's view, I want to review his reconstruction and suggest a few lines of criticism. Before considering the details, however, I will sketch what I take to be the *intuitive* motivations for his account.

Consider again our question: How could a social contract justify a political order with unequal political rights? Why, in particular, would the propertyless rationally consent to their own political subordination? There is a strong temptation to suppose that they would not consent, and to hold, therefore, that a property owner's state could only issue from an (unforced and nonfraudulent) social contract if the propertyless were excluded from that contract. But to justify their exclusion, one would need to argue that they lack rationality and/or freedom, that they lack, that is, the qualifications for giving rational consent. And this is just the view that Macpherson attributes to Locke.

According to Macpherson, Locke: (1) proposes a theory of property which provides nonutilitarian foundations for capitalist property relations, in particular, for the existence of labor markets; (2) construes this defense of capitalist property relations as justifying the claim that there are natural class differentials in *rights* and *rationality;* and (3) concludes that these differences in rights and rationality entail the exclusion of the propertyless from the social contract, and therefore entail that the outcome of that agreement will be a property owner's state, or what Macpherson calls a "joint-stock company whose share-holders [are] the men of property" (Macpherson, p. 195). Some recent scholarship has challenged Macpherson on point (1), defending both the historical thesis that talk about capitalism in seventeenth-century England is anachronistic and the interpretive claim that close attention to Locke's theory of property indicates that he is in fact a critic of wage labor. My main concern here is with points (2) and (3), and so for the purposes of this article I will simply assume what I take to be true, namely, that Macpherson is right about (1).[7]

What of Macpherson's second claim? According to him, Locke holds that there are natural differences between the rights and rationality of propertied and propertyless, *natural* in that they can be accounted for without assuming the existence of a state, and that in justifying political arrangements they provide part of the background of the agreement. Furthermore, he holds that Locke aims to defend this view about natural differences with an argument that takes *equal* rights and rationality as its point of departure.

Here I will consider just the case of differential *rights*.[8] Macpherson argues that Locke begins from a situation in which no one has any *jurisdiction* or authority over anyone else. He then shows how this equality of jurisdiction is transformed into an inequality of jurisdiction between propertied and propertyless prior to the formation of a state. This transformation of equal into unequal natural rights occurs together with the more advanced evolution of property rights. The introduction of money permits what was previously impermissible—that people own more than they themselves can use. But the resulting accumulation of property by some leads finally to circumstances in which one group owns the land and other conditions of production (call them "the propertied"), while the members of another group (call them "the propertyless") own only their own labor.

But why does this inequality in *kinds of property* imply inequality of *authority?* According to Macpherson:

> Once the land is all taken up, the fundamental right not to be subject to the jurisdiction of another is so unequal as between owners and non-owners that it is different in kind, not in degree: those without property are, Locke recognizes, dependent for their very livelihood on those with property, and are unable to alter their own circumstances. The initial equality of natural rights, which consisted in no man having jurisdiction over another cannot last after the differentiation of property. To put it another way, the man without property in things loses that full proprietorship of his own person which was the basis of equal natural rights. (Macpherson, p. 231)

Macpherson's conclusion, then, is that the emergence of capitalist property relations is tantamount to a shift from equality of jurisdiction to inequality of jurisdiction. It is not simply that owners live better than nonowners. Rather, the material inequality of propertied and propertyless creates a condition of dependence that undermines the original equality of jurisdiction within the state of nature. Materially dependent on the propertied, the propertyless lack the freedom that is required for participation in the original agreement. And the fact that they do not participate implies their subordination in the state.

There are at least three problems with this view. First, I think that it is a mistake to construe *natural* equality and freedom in a quasihistori-

cal way, as an original equality and freedom that obtains prior to the
differentiation into classes, and is superceded by that differentiation.
And in the discussion below (pp. 312–314), I will present an alternative
construal of equal freedom.

Second, Macpherson's account conflicts with Locke's emphasis on
the fundamental distinction between property and authority. One of
the basic themes of the *Treatises,* and one of the two central lines of
criticism of Filmer in the *First Treatise,* is the separation between property and authority.[9] Sharply criticizing the feudal identification of property and authority, Locke argues that property ownership does not
even require the existence of authority, much less confer it; and that
authority is not owned by those who exercise it, but is entrusted to
authorities subject to specified conditions.[10] There is one passage that
draws this distinction in a way that bears most directly on Macpherson's account. It is in the fourth chapter of the *First Treatise,* a chapter
devoted to criticizing Filmer's explanation of political power in terms
of property ownership, ultimately in fact in terms of Adam's ownership
of the entire earth. Having completed his case against the thesis that
Adam *was* the proprietor of the earth, Locke next argues that *even if
he were* the proprietor, still it would not follow that he had any political
authority:

> The most specious thing to be said is, that he that is Proprietor of the
> whole world, may deny all the rest of mankind food, and so at his pleasure
> starve them, if they will not acknowledge his sovereignty, and obey his
> will. . . . God the Lord and Father of all has given no one of his children
> such a property in his peculiar portion of things of this world but that he
> has given his needy brother a right to the surplusage of his goods; so that
> it cannot justly be denied him, when his pressing wants call for it. And
> therefore *no man could ever have a just power over the life of another,
> by right of property in land or possessions* [emphasis added]; since
> 'twould always be a sin in any man of estate, to let his brother perish for
> want of affording him relief out of his plenty . . . ; and a man can no more
> justly make use of another's necessity, to force him to become his vassal,
> by withholding that relief . . . than he that has more strength can seize
> upon a weaker, master him to his obedience and with a dagger at his
> throat offer him death or slavery. (1.41–42)

Thus the use of property advantages to compel submission to authority
is an unjust use of that property. It is a direct threat to preservation;

such threats being uses of force, they cannot justify the resulting sub-mission (see above, p. 304). Locke now completes the case:

> Should anyone make so perverse a use of God's blessings poured upon him with a liberal hand [that is, threaten starvation to those who don't acknowledge sovereignty]; should anyone be cruel and uncharitable to that extremity, *yet all this would not prove that propriety in land, even in this case, gave any authority over the persons of men, but only that compact might;* since the authority of the rich proprietor and the subjec-tion of the needy beggar began not from the possession of the land, but *the consent of the poor man, who preferred being his subject to starving.* And the man he thus submits to, can pretend no more power over him, then he has consented to, upon compact. (1.43)

So it is wrong to make a person an offer that he or she cannot refuse. But even if the offer were legitimate, the acceptance of the offer would still be required to bind the agent. If Macpherson were right, however, Locke's "needy beggar" would not be capable of giving consent, and would therefore be legitimately excluded from the contractual justifi-cation of political authority. Macpherson thus identifies and has Locke identifying the condition of economic-class subjection with a condition of political subjection. But it is precisely this identification that Locke denies in the passage about the beggar. Even in circumstances in which consent is virtually a foregone conclusion, consent and not the material dependence that motivates it is the basis for political authority. It is, therefore, wrong to attribute to Locke the view that the differentiation of property holdings transforms the state of nature from a state of equal *jurisdiction* to a state of unequal *jurisdiction.* But, as we shall see shortly, equality of jurisdiction is the only equality that matters to Locke.

This criticism highlights a third problem: because he has Locke iden-tifying property and authority, Macpherson fails to solve a central prob-lem that he claims to solve.

> The view of Locke's state as in effect a joint-stock company whose share-holders were the men of property has won considerable acceptance. . . . But there is one great difficulty in this view. Who were the members of Locke's civil society? If they were only the men of property, how could Locke make civil society oblige everyone? How could the social contract be an adequate basis of political obligation for all men? Yet undoubtedly

the purpose of the social contract was to find a basis for all-inclusive political obligation. Here is an outstanding difficulty. (Macpherson, p. 195)

Macpherson maintains that his interpretation resolves this "great difficulty":

> The problem inherent in the joint-stock interpretation of Locke's state is now no problem, for we have seen how Locke could consider the state to consist both of property-owners only and of the whole population. He would have no difficulty, therefore, in thinking of the state as a joint-stock company of owners whose majority decision binds not only themselves but also their employees. The laboring class . . . cannot take part in the operations of the company at the same level as the owners. Nevertheless, the laboring class is *so necessary to the operations of the company as to be considered an organic part of it.* (Macpherson, p. 251, emphasis added)

This is no solution at all, and the phrase "organic part" indicates just what is wrong. Macpherson's question was: How could the propertyless have an obligation to comply with the laws of a property owner's state? His answer is that they are an "organic part" of the order, a component required for the proper functioning of the whole. But the central point of Locke's political conception—and the main thrust of his criticisms of Filmer—is that an account of political right must be based on the idea of *voluntary parts,* not *organic parts.* "Nature" he says "gives paternal power to parents for the benefit of their children," while "voluntary agreement gives . . . political power to governors for the benefit of their subjects" (2.173). Had Locke been satisfied with organic justifications of political authority, he would not have written the *Treatises.* So Macpherson's outstanding difficulty remains outstanding.

Before proposing a solution, I must discharge one final obligation. The criticisms I have made strike me as straightforward and in a way obvious. And I think that when one makes straightforward and obvious criticisms of a work that is as serious as Macpherson's, one owes an account of how the problems might have been overlooked. The reason, I believe, is provided by what I described as the intuitive motivations for Macpherson's account, and I provided those motivations then with a view to discharging this obligation now. The hypothesis is that Macpherson simply thought it obvious that if the propertyless were included in the social contract, then it could not issue in a property owner's state. Believing this, he tried to find a plausibly Lockean argument for excluding the propertyless from the social contract. But the background view is incorrect. And to believe it is to neglect a central point about contracts, social or otherwise. The outcomes of rational agreements depend on the relative positions of the bargainers outside the contract. They depend not just on whether the parties are equal in *some* respects, but on the respects in which they are and are not equal.[11] Attentiveness to this point will indicate a solution to the "outstanding difficulty" that does not require attributing to Locke a belief in differential rationality or differential rights.

III. Equal Freedom and the Social Contract

In order to assess the compatibility of Lockean foundations with Lockean institutions, I want to proceed in three steps. First, I will characterize a Lockean contract situation. Then I will indicate several conditions that must be met by a solution to that collective choice problem. And, finally, I will consider whether a property owner's state plausibly satisfies those three conditions.[12]

Equality, Freedom, and Rationality

The first problem is to embed the Lockean conception of freedom, equality, and rationality in, to use Rawls's term, an "initial choice situation." The way that I set up the choice problem may seem less strained if I preface that setup with a word on states of nature and contractual arguments.

A state of nature is the situation that agents are in when there is no common authority over them. In classical contract theories such states play a variety of roles, two of which are important for my purposes here. First, a state of nature is one of the alternatives faced by the parties to the social contract, a second alternative being the existence of a state. The familiar argument is that the insecurity and uncertainty of the state-free condition gives everyone a reason for expecting their basic interests to be better satisfied in a state (or at least in a state of a certain kind) than in a state of nature. Second, the state of nature is the situation in which individuals make a social contract that justifies the existence of the state. Thus it is suggested that because each rationally prefers the existence of a state to the state of nature, people in a state of nature would contract into a state.

But the thesis that individuals in a state of nature would agree to form a state seems unnecessary for a social contract argument to have its justifying force. Familiar problems of collective action could stand in the way of getting together or reaching an agreement in a state of nature, even if it were true both that the state is collectively preferable to the state of nature and that it would be agreed to by free, equal, and rational individuals if they did come together to see if they could reach an agreement. We should separate the question of what would be agreed to by free, equal, and rational individuals who are aware of how bad the state of nature would be from what they would agree to if they were in the state of nature. The problems about coordination and communication raised by agreements within the state of nature are not immediately relevant to problems of justification, because they are not of immediate relevance to the question of rational and free consent.

So what I want to do is to characterize an initial choice situation that is not the state of nature but that does explicitly incorporate Locke's notions of *freedom, equality,* and *rationality,* and thus serves the purposes of justification.

Equality

Locke provides the following account of natural equality:

> Though I have said above, chap. 2, that all men are by nature equal, I cannot be supposed to understand all sorts of equality: age or virtue may give men a just precedency: excellency of parts or merit may place others above the common level: birth may subject some and alliance or benefits others, to pay an observance to those to whom nature, gratitude or other respects may have made it due; and yet all this consists with the equality, which all men are in, *in respect of jurisdiction or dominion one over another,* which was the equality I there spoke of, as proper to the business in hand, being that equal right that every man hath to his natural freedom, without being subjected to the will or authority of any other man. (2.54)

Natural equality is, then, simply equality in respect of the natural right to freedom. The problem of characterizing the notion of equality for the purposes of the social contract reduces therefore to the problem of explicating the natural freedom that it qualifies.

Freedom

Human beings, on Locke's view, are naturally in a state of liberty, not license. We are not in a state of license because we are bound by obligations deriving from the fundamental law of nature, and these natural obligations limit natural liberty (2.6). These natural obligations notwithstanding, Locke does think that human beings are naturally free, which he understands to imply something less than moral license and more than the trivial thesis that there are *some* circumstances in which natural obligations do not dictate the choice of a course of action. In fact, he means to highlight a quite specific limit to the natural obligations, a limit that distinguishes his view from Filmer's.

On Filmer's patriarchal theory, political obligations derive from the obligations of children to parents, and therefore derive from the fact of being born. So no human being could exist without having political obligations. Filmer's "great position," Locke says, was that "men are not naturally free. This is the foundation on which his absolute monarchy stands. . . . To prove this grand position of his, he tells us 'Men are born in subjection to their parents,' and therefore *cannot* be free" (1.6, emphasis added). Contrary to Filmer's "great position," Locke held that human beings are naturally free *because* such natural human obligations as those of children to parents are not political obligations nor do they imply the existence of political obligations (1.6; 2.6).[13] In short, to be free by nature *is* to have no natural *political obligations*. As a consequence, the justification of political association must be directed to individuals who *can* conceive of themselves, and who, for the purposes of the justification of the state, *do* conceive of themselves as not being members of or having the rights and duties of members of a state. As Locke puts it, if Filmer's "foundation [i.e., no natural freedom] fails, all his fabric falls with it, and governments must be left again to the old way of being made by contrivance, and the consent of men . . . making use of their reason to unite together into society" (1.6).

For present purposes, we need not consider Locke's reasons for thinking that we are naturally free. What matters here is only that the thesis that human beings are naturally free can plausibly be explicated in terms of the principle that the justification of political authority is consent. More specifically, Locke's notion of natural freedom supports the views that: (1) political authority requires a consensual justification; (2) the parties to the contract are, as in all post-Hobbesian theories, individuals rather than groups or communities, since it is individuals and not groups that are by nature free; (3) all individuals who are naturally free get an equal vote, since individuals are equally free; and (4) the agreement must be unanimous. The agreement must be unanimous because individuals are naturally free from *all* prior political ties, including the putative political authority of the people or any sort of community. But if individuals are not bound by any such prior ties, then there is no justification for, e.g., a rule of majority decision making in the initial agreement, since such a decision rule would embody an antecedent obligation to comply with the decisions of the group.

Rationality

While they are important, the requirements of equality and freedom do not by themselves constrain the outcome of the contract. To get an agreement the parties to the contract must also have interests. With interests attributed, we can interpret the third main notion, rationality. To suppose that individuals are rational is to suppose that in making an agreement they do so in order to advance these interests. Locke supposes that individuals have a set of basic interests in "life, liberty, health, and indolency of body; and the possession of outward things, such as money, lands, houses, furniture, and the like."[14] Assuming these "civil" interests, a rational agreement is one that each person expects will improve his or her prospects with respect to life, liberty, and goods, for people enter society "only with an intention in every one the better to preserve himself his liberty and property; (for no rational creature can be supposed to change his condition with an intention to be worse)" (2.131). Thus, each rational individual seeks an agreement that will increase his or her *own level* of civil interest satisfaction.[15]

But the rational interests of different individuals are not fully symmetrical. As Macpherson rightly emphasizes, there are natural differentials in property rights, "men [having] agreed to disproportionate and unequal possession of the earth. . . . This partage of things, in an inequality of private possessions, men have made practicable out of the bounds of society, and without compact, only by putting a value on gold and silver and tacitly agreeing in the use of money" (2.50). I will register this asymmetry in the description of the Lockean choice situation by supposing that the parties enter into the agreement as owners of different amounts and sorts of property. There is, so to speak, no "veil of ignorance" over property holdings. To simplify the argument, we can think of the parties as either land owners or landless laborers, who know their status in the property system, and who assess alternative arrangements in light of these holdings.

The parties to the agreement *are* equal. But they are equal solely with respect to the natural right to freedom, the only sort of equality "proper to the business in hand" (2.54). And they are free, for the facts that enter into the contract do not by themselves imply that any individuals—even the needy beggars—are subject to political obligations. Locke's freedom and equality are fully captured in the *form* of the choice situation by the requirement of unanimous agreement. The *content* of the agreement reflects the civil interests, and the different property holdings that individuals bring to the agreement. The question that they will consider is: What arrangements will advantage each of us, given our different starting points?

Three Conditions on an Agreement

The way that I have set up the problem suggests (as I will show) that an agreement must satisfy three conditions. Using the terminology of the theory of cooperative games, I will call these conditions: "individual rationality," "group rationality," and "coalitional rationality." In considering the appropriateness of these three requirements, it is important to keep in mind that the choice situation is *not* a state of nature. As a result we can abstract from problems of *communication* and *enforcement* of agreements. We are supposing in effect that communication is costless and that the parties will make a binding agreement. Without these assumptions, the cooperative approach to the solution would be misguided.[16]

The first condition is *individual rationality*. An agreement satisfies this condition just in case each individual expects to be at least as well off as a result of the agreement as he or she would be if he or she were in the state of nature while all other parties lived in a social order regulated by the terms of the agreement. That an agreement must satisfy this requirement follows directly from the assumption that the parties in the choice situation are rational, together with the requirement of unanimity (see above, pp. 313–314). Everyone must expect to be at least as well off as a result of the agreement, because otherwise they would not make the agreement. And, since I have linked the notion of rationality to civil interests, and am supposing that individuals have definite property rights independently from the social contract—that you *can* take it with you—it is possible to be a bit more precise about these standards of comparison. Each must expect to be at least as well off in terms of life, liberty, and goods as a result of the agreement as they would be in the state of nature with their property. In short, improvements are measured in specific goods, and are relative to the background structure of property. The property owners must be as well off as they would be in the state of nature with their property, the propertyless at least as well off as they would be in the state of nature with their property.

While the individual rationality condition implies that the political order must pareto dominate the state of nature, the second condition—*group rationality*—requires that there be no social state that pareto dominates the state agreed to. That is, there must be no state that makes at least some people better off and none worse off than they would be in the state that is agreed to. This condition is motivated by the construction of the Lockean choice situation in view of the fact that the sole motivation of those entering the contract is the desire to improve *their own level* of civil interest satisfaction. No one, therefore, has any reason to object to a state that improves the situation of others, even if their own conditions are held fixed.[17]

The third condition is *coalitional rationality*. This condition requires that there be no subset of the population that would do better by withdrawing (or seceding) than by agreeing to enter a proposed agreement. Here again, we are supposing that groups can withdraw with their property. So for an agreement to be coalitionally rational it must not be the case that, for example, the entire propertied group would be better off by taking all their property and forming their own state, or that the entire propertyless group would be better off by taking their labor out and forming their own state.

This third condition may seem less motivated than the first two, for at least two reasons. First, there are the obstacles (familiar from discussions of the prisoner's dilemma and other collective irrationality problems) to coalition formation even when the formation of a coalition would produce common benefits. But this first point poses no real objection given the way I have described the initial choice situation. The requirement of coalitional rationality is appropriate in the current context in view of the assumptions of costless communication and enforceable agreements. Given these conditions, and the relational interests of individuals, if a coalition could do better, then it would form and would do better. Thus the choice situation requires that each group must be able to say: given our interests and the current distribution of property, we could not do better in some alternative arrangement.

The second objection to this condition is that its use presupposes that it is legitimate for the members of a society—even the members of a just society—to withdraw from that society. And this might be thought inconsistent with Locke's views about the illegitimacy of such withdrawal, at least by those who have given their express consent to social arrangements (2.121). This objection fails because it misconstrues the aim of the present argument. The aim here is to determine which types of state, if any, are just. In order to answer this question, we ask: What sorts of state could be agreed to, given the civil interests and the current distribution of property? If the answer is that, for example, current arrangements could not be agreed to because they are not coalitionally rational, then they are unjust, and consent to an unjust system is not binding. If they could be agreed to, then express consent is permanently binding. But to consider whether or not the existing form of state is coalitionally rational, we need not suppose that it would *in fact be legitimate* to withdraw from a state to which one has given express consent.

Agreeing to a Property Owner's State

With these three conditions in hand, let us now turn to the question of the agreement to a property owner's state. Are there circumstances in which such a state plausibly satisfies the three conditions? In addressing this question, I will suppose that there are four alternatives facing the contractors: (a) live in a state of nature; (b) form a property owner's state; (c) form a single democratic state composed of both propertied and propertyless; and (d) form separate states for propertied and propertyless, with the propertyless forming a democratic state.[18] This restriction on alternatives is in certain respects artificial. To show that the property owner's state would be agreed to—rather than, for example, a system of universal suffrage with plural votes for property owners—would require a more complete account of possibilities and circumstances.[19] But the restriction I have imposed on the set of alternatives permits a more straightforward account of the structure of Locke's argument, and shows how a property owner's state could be chosen over a democratic state even if the propertyless are included in the agreement. It thus suffices for my concerns here. What I want to show, then, is *not* that the property owner's state is always the solution, but only that there are plausible conditions in which it would be selected over alternatives (a), (c), and (d).

Since it is easy to see why the properties would prefer a state controlled by property owners to all the alternatives, I will focus primarily on the assessment of these alternatives in terms of the three conditions by the propertyless, with special attention to their assessment of the property owner's state.

Consider first the requirement of individual rationality. Recall that the property owner's state is a constitutional state, with "one rule for rich and poor, for the favorite at court and the countryman at plough" (2.142). So the propertyless could expect greater protection than in the state of nature of their life, their liberty, and such goods as they have. And because of the absence of legal barriers to interclass mobility, they include in their expectations some slight probability of gaining property and political rights. It is therefore reasonable to think that the property owner's state satisfies the condition of individual rationality.

To clarify the point I want to anticipate an issue that properly falls under the condition of group rationality. It seems reasonable that a democratic state including both propertied and propertyless would be more likely to adopt redistributive measures favoring the propertyless than that such measures would be adopted in the property owner's state. Abstracting from the consequences of such redistribution for economic growth, this difference in likelihood is sufficient for opposition of rational interests of the propertied and propertyless: the propertied prefer the property owner's state to the democratic state because it is less likely to redistribute; the propertyless prefer the democratic state to the property owner's state because it is more likely to redistribute. This comparison is important. But it is not relevant to the condition of individual rationality. This condition requires only that there be expected civil interest improvement with respect to the state of nature (as always, holding the property system fixed). The fact that the propertyless would prefer being in a democratic state along with the propertied to being in a state run by the propertied does not imply that it would be irrational for them to agree to the property owner's state. We need to see whether the democratic state with the properties is a real alternative.

Consider next the condition of coalitional rationality. Here the relevant comparison by the propertyless is between the property owner's state and the democratic state formed by the propertyless alone. Rational agreement to the property owner's state requires that the property-less *as a group* prefer the property owner's state to their own democratic state. And here again it is plausible to think that *under some circumstances,* and given that the only interests at stake are the civil interests, the propertyless would expect to do better by entering as junior partners in coalition with the propertied than to withdraw and form their own state. There are at least two reasons for this expectation. First, a state composed of the propertyless would be poor, therefore relatively weak, and as a consequence less able to defend itself against external attack. Second, in view of the minimal resources that they control, even the poor members of a rich state might expect a higher level of material well-being than they could expect by living in a poorer state. Locke certainly supposed this. He pointed out that "a king of a large and fruitful territory there [in America], feeds, lodges, and is clad worse than a day-laborer in England" (2.41).

Finally, consider the condition of group rationality. It is plainly not the case that there is an alternative preferred by *everyone* to the property owner's state, since the propertied prefer that state to all other alternatives. While the propertied and propertyless have opposing preferences on the property owner's state and democratic state (for the reasons indicated earlier, p. 319), the condition of group rationality is nevertheless satisfied.

So the property owner's state does satisfy the three conditions. Everyone prefers it to the state of nature, there is no alternative that everyone prefers to it, and it is not the case that some subset of the population would prefer withdrawal with their property to the property owner's state. But does this distinguish the property owner's state from the democratic state? For it is also plausibly true of the democratic state that it is preferred by all to the state of nature, that there is no alternative that is collectively preferred to it, and that the propertied would prefer the democratic state to forming separate states.

But there is something that distinguishes the two, namely the relative power of the propertied, and associated with that difference a complication in their strategy. Suppose that the propertied threaten that they will not enter into a state with the propertyless unless the state is a property owner's state. While they would in fact prefer being in a democratic state to being in a state of nature or in separate states, and everyone knows their preferences—recall that the fraud condition disallows agreements that depend on ignorance about the beliefs of others—they are willing to take the chance of having to carry out their

threat. That is, they prefer the strategy of insisting on a property owner's state to the strategy of agreeing to a democratic state. For, by virtue
of their property, they are stronger than the propertyless. Having
greater resources, they can secure protection; being fewer in number,
it is easier for them to coordinate. Everyone knows these relative
strengths, and therefore knows that the propertyless will give in.

It might be objected that such an agreement provides no justification
for the property owner's state, since it involves a "threat" by the propertied to the preservation of the propertyless, and as I indicated earlier,
consent under threat of force is no consent at all. But this objection
fails. For as I also said earlier, there is no obligation to improve the
circumstances of others over what it would be in the state of nature.
"The only way whereby any one divests himself of his natural liberty,
and puts on the bonds of civil society, is by agreeing with other men.
. . . This any number of men may do, because it injures not the freedom
of the rest; they are left as they were in the liberty of the state of nature" (2.95). In the case under consideration the propertied *offer* a
mutually beneficial arrangement to the propertyless. If there is nothing
illegitimate about refusing to join together at all, surely there is nothing
illegitimate about expressing a willingness to cooperate on mutually
beneficial terms—given the different starting points—and then to refuse to cooperate at all if those mutually advantageous terms are rejected.

Simple and Democratic Orders: A Lockean History[20]

The property owner's state is, then, consistent with Lockean foundations. But it is not the only form of state that is consistent with those
foundations. The agreement supposes that there are propertied and
propertyless, and that, for example, the propertyless cannot do better
in their own democratic state than in a property owner's state. And
it is consistent with Locke's theory of property that neither of these
conditions obtain. To clarify and elaborate this point, and to preempt
a natural misinterpretation of the argument about the property owner's
state, I want now to use the general Lockean framework that I sketched
above in order to show how, under different background conditions—
that is, different property systems and the different rational interests
associated with those systems—different forms of state might be
agreed to. Here I will consider two alternatives, one that Locke himself
discusses, and one that is more contemporary.

In the *Second Treatise* Locke briefly discusses the nature of social cooperation before the introduction of money. Since people in the pre-money situation could only legitimately own what they could use, there were significant limits on legitimate inequality. Locke offers the following piece of political sociology about these circumstances: "The equality of a simple poor way of living confining their desires within the narrow bounds of each man's small property made few controversies and so no need of many laws to decide them, or variety of officers to superintend the process, or look after the execution of justice, where there were but few trespasses, and few offenders" (2.107). In this "golden age (before vain ambition, and *amor sceleratus habendi*, evil concupiscence, had corrupted men's minds into a mistake of true power and honor)" (2.111), the chief concern of societies was external aggression, and not internal conflict.[21] Under these conditions of substantial material equality, Locke thought it was reasonable for individuals to agree to a state in which all political authority is held by one person—a first among equals—and placed there primarily for the sake of military leadership. In this simple society, then, the social contract does result in differences of political rights. But those differences do not correspond to differences in property rights.

The second case is an agreement to a democratic state (say, a capitalist democracy). How could this happen? Recall that in agreeing to the property owner's state, the propertyless judge that they would be worse off by forming their own state than by agreeing to political subordination in a property owner's state (that is, the condition of coalitional rationality was satisfied). But now suppose a point is reached (let us call this point "the late nineteenth century") at which (a) withdrawal by the propertyless is judged preferable to a property owner's state; and (b) it remains true that membership in a democratic state alongside property owners is materially more advantageous than a democratic state formed just by those without property. The change in expectations might result from changes in both the material resources and organizational capacities of the propertyless, changes that might, for example, be prompted by the growth of large-scale industry within the framework of the property owner's state. In the late nineteenth century, the property owners would still prefer the property owner's state to the democratic state. But they also prefer the democratic state with the propertyless to the withdrawal of the propertyless. Now the propertyless can threaten to withdraw unless there is an extension of suffrage rights. Under these circumstances, the democratic state would be chosen over the property owner's state.

I have introduced these brief examples to illustrate that, on my account, the core commitment of Lockean contractualism is not to a particular form of state. A state controlled by the propertied is consistent with Lockean foundations, even if the propertyless are included in the agreement. Together with the two examples just considered, that consistency underscores that the central commitment is to a way of construing the members of the state and a way to characterize the kind of justification for their political system that members might give to one another. The members are, in the first instance, individuals with specified positions in the property system and with differing rational interests that reflect their divergent positions. And the justifications that they provide must treat these positions and interests as fundamental.

IV. Conclusions: Locke and Rousseau

I have tried to indicate what is specific to the notions of freedom, equality, and rationality that figure in Locke's political conception by considering the relationship between the property system and the political order—and particularly by underscoring the fact that the property system serves as part of the background of the agreement in which those notions are embedded, rather than as part of the subject matter of the agreement. The rational interests of the different classes reflect their positions in the property system, and the equal freedom of the members of a social order premises a division between property system and the political order.

By treating the property system as part of the subject matter of the social contract, rather than as part of its background—treating it as social and conventional, not as natural—Rousseau initiated a departure from this Lockean structure of argument. For Rousseau, all features of the social order are subject to public deliberation among equals concerning the requirements of the common good. But if the account I have suggested here is right, that break in the understanding of the relationship between the property system and the political order provides a way of understanding the differences between Lockean and Rousseauean conceptions of freedom, equality, and rationality as well. If the members of the social order do not view themselves and one another as, in the first instance, holders of determinate places in the property system, then they cannot think of their rationality as, in the first instance, a matter of pursuing particular interests that are distinct in known ways from the interests of other members of the order. And without premising the distinction between the property system and the political order, their equal freedom cannot be interpreted simply in terms of a requirement of consent to *political* authority. It must instead be construed in terms of a capacity to enter into public deliberation generally. This view of persons is in one way more abstract than the Lockean view, and yet it suggests the possibility of deeper social bonds. But whether it or the Lockean view is correct depends on how we decide to live our lives.

Notes

I would like to thank Paul Horwich, John Rawls, and the Editors of *Philosophy & Public Affairs* for comments on an earlier draft, Robert Brenner for discussions of a number of issues in the article, and audiences at University of Maryland Law School, Bates College, the University of Massachusetts, the University of Connecticut, McGill University, and Stanford University for raising questions that have helped to clarify the main argument of the essay. Work on the final versions of this article was supported by a grant from the National Endowment for the Humanities.

1. References to Locke's *Two Treatises of Government,* ed. Peter Laslett (Cambridge: Cambridge University Press, 1960) are abbreviated as follows: "1.123" refers to the *First Treatise,* paragraph 123, "2.18" to the *Second Treatise,* paragraph 18.

2. "Parliamentary debates and pamphlet controversies involving the law or the constitution were almost invariably carried on either wholly or partially in terms of an appeal to the past made in this way [i.e., with reference to the ancient constitution]; famous antiquaries were treated as authorities of recognized political wisdom; and nearly every thinker noted for his contribution to political theory in its usual sense—Hunton, Milton, Lilburne, Hobbes, Harrington, Filmer, Nevile, Sidney: only Locke appears to be an exception among notable writers—devoted part of his pages to discussing the antiquity of the constitution." J.G.A. Pocock, *The Ancient Constitution and the Feudal Law* (New York: W. W. Norton, 1957), p. 46; also chap. 9.

3. See 2.140, 2.158, and the reading of these passages in Martin Seliger, *The Liberal Politics of John Locke* (London: George Allen and Unwin, 1968), pp. 283 ff. Cf. also John Dunn, *The Political Thought of John Locke* (Cambridge: Cambridge University Press, 1969), p. 236; and C. B. Macpherson, *The Political Theory of Possessive Individualism* (Oxford: Oxford University Press, 1962), pp. 195, 251ff.

4. See Seliger, *Liberal Politics,* pp. 164–65, 292.

5. I am much more confident that Locke would want to rule out such

agreements than that he would want to do so by building a common knowledge requirement into the notion of a rational agreement. An alternative route would be via the natural duty of "truth and keeping of faith" (2.14). Nothing in my argument depends on the particulars of the solution to this issue.

6. For important (though quite disparate) criticisms see works by Dunn, Seliger, and Tully cited above in footnote 3; Peter Laslett, "Introduction," in Locke, *Two Treatises of Government* (Cambridge: Cambridge University Press, 1960); Alan Ryan, "Locke and the Dictatorship of the Bourgeoisie," *Political Studies* 13, no. 2 (June 1965): 219–30; and Neal Wood, *John Locke and Agrarian Capitalism* (Berkeley: University of California Press, 1984), esp. pp. 7–9, 15–19. My argument in this article is independent of certain important elements of these criticisms. I do not, for example, wish to dispute Dunn's thesis concerning the importance of the natural law in Locke's conception.

7. For recent discussion of capitalism in seventeenth-century England, see Robert Brenner's discussion of agrarian capitalism in *The Brenner Debate,* ed. T. H. Aston and C.H.E. Philpin (Cambridge: Cambridge University Press, 1985), chaps. 1, 10. For the view that Locke is a critic of wage labor, see Tully, *Discourse on Property,* pp. 136ff. Tully claims that people confuse Locke's endorsement of master-servant relations with an endorsement of wage labor. But, Tully argues, being a servant is voluntary, and therefore acceptable to Locke, insofar as "the choice not to become a servant is available to him [the servant]" (p. 137). By contrast, wage labor is involuntary, and therefore unacceptable to Locke, because the wage laborer must work for a capitalist, and can only choose which one to work for. But this understanding of the voluntariness of the master-servant relation is not supported by Locke's remarks on masters and servants, which are directed primarily to contrasting the position of servants with the position of slaves (esp. 2.85–86). A more plausible reading is that the servant's position is voluntary just in case it satisfies three conditions: that there be a *choice of employers,* that the master-servant contract be *limited in time,* and that the terms and conditions of employment be stated explicitly in the contract itself. The agreement between master and servant, Locke says, "gives the master but a temporary power over him, and no greater, than what is contained in the contract between 'em" (2.85). These conditions are sufficient to distinguish the servant from the slave (and from the "vassals" that Locke mentions at 1.42). But they are also perfectly consistent with wage labor. For a parallel treatment of Tully, see Wood, *John Locke,* pp. 85–92.

8. The evidence for Locke's belief in differential rationality is, I think, very unpersuasive. See Macpherson, pp. 232–38.

9. The other central line of criticism concerns the distinction between family and state (1.2). Both lines reflect the deepest difference between Filmer and Locke, that Filmer denies and Locke endorses the view that human beings are naturally free (1.6).

10. On the unity of property and authority in English feudalism, as well as the dynamics of their separation, see S.F.C. Milsom, *Historical Foundations of the Common Law,* 2d ed. (Toronto: Butterworth, 1981); and J.M.W. Bean, *The Decline of English Feudalism: 1215–1540* (Manchester: Manchester University Press, 1968).

11. A simple illustration of this dependence is provided by the Zeuthen-Nash-Harsanyi solution for two-person bargaining games. Those who are better off prior to the game gain the majority of benefits from the game. For discussion, see R. Duncan Luce and Howard Raiffa, *Games and Decisions* (New York: Wiley and Sons, 1957), pp. 124–36.

12. In what follows I draw on Rawls's schematization of social contracts in *A Theory of Justice* (Cambridge, MA: Harvard University Press, 1971), chaps. 20–25.

13. For recent discussion of the historical shifts in the nature of the family reflected in the disagreements between Locke and Filmer about the relationship between family and state, see Lawrence Stone, *The Family, Sex and Marriage in England 1500–1800* (New York: Harper and Row, 1979).

14. Locke, *A Letter Concerning Toleration,* ed. James Tully (Indianapolis: Hackett, 1983), p. 26. See also 2.2, 2.6, 2.11, 2.27–28.

15. To avoid misinterpretation, I should add that I am also assuming that the natural obligations imposed by the natural law—to preserve oneself, and not to harm others in respect of their life, liberty, and property—constrain the choice. In a more complete account of Locke's view, I would incorporate the natural obligations within the conception of rationality, since the motivation for compliance with those laws is to avoid eternal suffering. For discussion of the natural laws and the motivations for compliance with those laws, see *An Essay Concerning Human Understanding* (London: J. M. Dent, 1961), Bk. II, chap. 28, pars. 6, 8.

16. For interesting applications of cooperative game theory to normative issues, see John Roemer, *A General Theory of Exploitation and Class* (Cambridge, MA: Harvard University Press, 1982).

17. This condition could be weakened to the requirement that there be no social state that is better for everyone. Nothing in the argument will turn on this difference.

18. The original contract, as Locke construes it, does not in fact determine the type of regime, but rather forms a people—a collection of individuals governed by the decisions of a majority—who in turn establish the constitution. Thus, I am collapsing the two steps into one. For an excellent discussion of the motivations for Locke's two-stage theory, see Julian Franklin, *John Locke and the Theory of Sovereignty* (Cambridge: Cambridge University Press, 1978), esp. chap. 4. My argument would be more complicated by adhering to the two-step structure, but the conclusion would be the same. What would be required is a unanimous agreement to permit the form of regime to be determined by a majority decision of the property owners, and for constituent power to return to that group in the face of a dissolution of government. On the consequences of dissolution, see the interesting passage from the radical Whig John Wildman cited in Franklin, p. 119.

19. In an earlier draft of this article, I suggested that my argument shows that the property owner's state satisfies the three conditions, and is therefore in the core. I would like to thank John Ferejohn for emphasizing that I should avoid conveying that impression and should emphasize the restrictions on the set of alternatives.

20. It is commonly said that Locke is an ahistorical thinker. But that is misleading. He did believe that certain abstract, nonhistorical principles apply across different historical conditions. But it is possible that it was Locke's awareness of the importance of shifting historical circumstances, rather than an inattention to such circumstances, that led him away from the more superficially historical modes of argument deployed by those constitutionalists who rested their case on the nature of the ancient constitution. Here I agree with David Resnick, "Locke and the Rejection of the Ancient Constitution," *Political Theory* 12, no. 1 (February 1984): 97–114.

21. For further discussion, see Ronald Meek, *Social Science and the Ignoble Savage* (Cambridge: Cambridge University Press, 1976), chap. 1.

9

A Possible Explanation of Rousseau's General Will[1]

Patrick Riley

A "general will" is a philosophical and psychological contradiction in terms; will is a conception understandable, if at all, only in terms of individual actions. The problem cannot be glossed over by attempting to reduce the general will—as did T. H. Green—to a "common ego," or to an analogical forerunner of Kant's pure practical reason.[2] Why, then, did Rousseau make so unviable an idea the center of his political theory,[3] and why has that idea continued to receive serious attention?

The general will has continued to be taken seriously because it is an attempted (though not explicit) amalgam of two extremely important traditions of political thought, which may be called, roughly, ancient "cohesiveness" and modern "voluntarism." Political thought since the seventeenth century has been characterized, among other things, by voluntarism, by an emphasis on the assent of individuals as the standard of political legitimacy.[4] One certainly finds this in many of the most important thinkers between Hobbes and Kant; and even Hegel, while scarcely an "atomistic individualist" or a contractarian, explicitly argued that while "in the states of antiquity the subjective end simply coincided with the state's will," in modern times "we make claims for private judgment, private willing, and private conscience." When a political decision is to be made, Hegel continued, "an 'I will' must be pronounced by man himself." This "I will," he thought, must have an "appropriate objective existence" in the person of a monarch; "in a well-organized monarchy, the objective aspect belongs to law alone, and the monarch's part is merely to set to the law the subjective 'I will'."[5] If even Hegel allows this voluntarist turn in his own non-contractarian theory, it goes without saying that all of social contract theory can be seen as the supreme example of voluntaristic ideas. No theory, then, escaped the enthronement of will—quite literally, in Hegel's case—at some point in the political scheme. Why voluntarism, political legitimacy through authorization by individual wills, came to hold such an important place in Western thought, requires a book to itself, a history of political will.[6] What is probable is that ancient quasi-aesthetic theories of the best regime and the proper end of man gave way, with the introduction of Christianity, to thinking about politics after the model of "good acts": just as good acts required both knowledge of the good and the will to do good, politics now required moral assent, the implication of the individual in politics through his own volition. The freedom to conform voluntarily to absolute standards had always been important in Christian doctrine; the Reformation doubtless strengthened the element of individual choice in moral thinking, while downplaying the role of moral authority. And it was natural enough that the Protestant view of individual moral autonomy and responsibility should spill over from metaphysics into politics, forming the intellectual basis of contract theory. The mere excellence of a social institution would no longer be enough; it would now require rational assent. However voluntarism and contract theory arose, what is certain is that ideas of the "good" state increasingly gave way to ideas of the merely "legitimate" state.[7] And this legitimacy, after the seventeenth century, was often taken to rest on will.

But while voluntarism took care of legitimacy, it could say nothing about the intrinsic goodness of what is willed. It is, of course, possible to assert that whatever is willed is right simply because it is willed.[8] But this was not enough for Rousseau; and it was precisely here that he made a stand for a particular kind of will. He wanted will to take a particular form; he wanted voluntarism to legitimize what he conceived to be the unity and cohesiveness—the generality—of ancient polity, particularly of Sparta and Rome. Indeed his political ideal was the ancient polity, now willed by moderns who were as concerned with reasons for obligations as with perfect forms of government. Against the alleged atomism of earlier contract theory, Rousseau wanted the generality—the non-individualism, or rather the pre-individualism—of antiquity to be legitimized by consent. Here of course he got himself into the paradox of insisting on the willing of the essentially non-voluntaristic politics characteristic of antiquity. He got himself, that is, into a philosophical paradox of willed non-voluntarism; but if this paradoxical concept, the general will, a will which is the corporate "will" of a whole society, a will to stop being willful, cannot be philosophically defended, it can at least be unravelled with interesting implications for all voluntaristic and perfectionist theories—not to mention democratic theories, which are always hard-pressed to fuse what is wanted with what is intrinsically good. And this treatment helps to clear up some of the usually insoluble paradoxes in Rousseau, and to make his thought clearer, if not less problematical.

I

Jean-Jacques Rousseau was a severe critic of modern political life—of its lack of a common morality and virtue, of its lack of patriotism and civic religion, of its indulgence in "base" philosophy and morally uninstructive arts.[9] At the same time, he was a great admirer of the more highly unified political systems of antiquity, in which, as he thought, morality, civic religion, patriotism, and a simple way of life had made men "one," wholly socialized and truly political.[10] And he thought that modern political life divided man against himself, leaving him, with all his merely private and anti-social interests, half in and half out of political society, enjoying neither the amoral independence of nature nor the moral elevation afforded by true socialization.[11]

Why Rousseau thought the unified ancient political systems preferable to modern ones is not too hard to understand. He conceived the difference between natural man and political man in very sharp terms; while for most contract theory political life was merely non-natural (and this largely to do away with arguments for natural political authority), for Rousseau it was positively unnatural, or anti-natural, a complete transformation of the natural man. The political man must be deprived of his natural powers and given others, "which are foreign to him and which he cannot use without the help of others"; politics reaches a peak of perfection when natural powers are completely dead and extinguished, and man is given a "partial and corporate existence."[12] The defect of modern politics, in Rousseau's view, was that it was insufficiently political; it compromised between the utter artificiality and communality of political life and the naturalness and independence of pre-political life, and in so doing caused the greatest misfortunes of modern man: self-division, conflict between private will and the common good, a sense of being neither in one condition nor another.

"What makes human misery," Rousseau said in *Le Bonheur Public*, "is the contradiction which exists between our situation and our desires, between our duties and our inclinations, between nature and social institutions, between man and citizen."[13] To make man one, to make him as happy as he can be, "give him entirely to the state, or leave him entirely to himself . . . but if you divide his heart, you will rip him apart; and do not imagine that the state can be happy, when all its members suffer."[14]

Above all, the imperfect socialization of modern man, in Rousseau's view, allowed private persons and corporate interests to control other private persons, leading to extreme inequality and personal dependence; only generality of laws based on an idea of common good, he thought, could abolish all private dependence, which was for him, perhaps, the supreme social evil. What he wanted was that socialized men might be "perfectly independent of all the rest, and extremely dependent on the city,"[15] for only the power of the state, and the generality of its laws, "constitutes the liberty of its members."[16]

Ancient polities such as Sparta, Rousseau thought, with their simplicity, morality (or politics) of the common good, civic religion, moral use of fine and military arts, and lack of extreme individualism and private interest, had been political societies in the proper sense: in them man was "part of a larger whole" from which he "in a sense receives his life and being."[17] Modern "prejudices," "base philosophy," and "passions of petty self-interest," on the other hand, assure that "we moderns can no longer find in ourselves anything of that spiritual vigor which was inspired in the ancients by everything they did" *(Gouvernement de Pologne)*.[18] And this spiritual vigor may be taken to mean the avoidance (through identity with a "greater whole") of "that dangerous disposition which gives rise to all our vices,"[19] self-love. Political education in an extremely unified state will "lead us out of ourselves" before the human ego "has acquired that contemptible activity which absorbs all virtue and constitutes the life and being of little minds" *(Économie Politique)*.[20] It follows that the best social institutions "are those best able to denature man, to take away his absolute existence and to give him a relative one, and to carry the *moi* into the common unity" *(Émile)*.[21] These social institutions, in ideal ancient polities, were always for Rousseau the creation of a greater legislator, a Numa or a Moses: they did not develop and perfect themselves in political experience, but were "handed down" by the law-giver.[22]

But if Rousseau thought highly unified ancient polity, and its political morality of common good, superior to modern fragmented politics, and its political morality of self-interest, at the same time he shared with modern individualist thought the conviction that all political life was conventional and could be made obligatory only through individual consent. He very definitely thought that he had based political obligation and rightful political authority on convention: "civil association is the most voluntary act in the world; since every individual is born free and his own master, no one is able, on any pretext whatsoever, to subject him without his consent."[23] Indeed, the first four chapters of the *Contrat Social* are devoted to refutations of erroneous theories of obligation and right (paternal authority, the "right of the strongest," and obligation derived from slavery). "Since no man," Rousseau concluded, "has natural authority over his fellow men, and since might in no sense makes right, convention remains as the basis of all legitimate authority among men."[24]

And yet Rousseau was also clear that contract theory provides, in itself, little more than a mere theory of political obligation. In the *Lettres de la Montagne* (VI), speaking of contract and consent, he said that a state is made one by the union of its members; that this union is the consequence of obligation; and that obligation can follow only from convention. He admitted that the foundation of obligation had divided political theorists: "according to some, it is force; according to others, paternal authority; according to others, the will of God."[25] All theorists, he said, establish their own principle of obligation and attack that of others. "I myself have not done otherwise," Rousseau declared, "and, following the soundest element of those who have discussed these matters, I have settled on, as the foundation of the body politic, the contract of its members." And he concluded by asking, "what more certain foundation can obligation among men have, than the free agreement of him who obliges himself?"[26]

One may suspect that for Rousseau, contract theory was more a way of destroying wrong theories of obligation and authority, than of creating a comprehensive theory of what is politically right. While for Hobbes and Locke the theory of obligation by consent is of central importance, for Rousseau it is not a complete political theory. Any political system "which confines itself to mere obedience will find difficulty in getting itself obeyed. If it is good to know how to deal with men as they are, it is much better to make them what there is need that they should be" (*Économie Politique*).[27] That, in a word, was Rousseau's criticism of all contract theory: it dealt too much with the form of obligation, with will as it is, and not enough with what one ought to be obligated *to,* and with will as it might be.

His criticism of Hobbes is based on this point. Hobbes had, indeed, established rightful political authority on consent, rejecting paternal authority and obligation based on either natural or divine law; he had made law (and therefore morality) the command of an artificial "representative person" to whom subjects were "formerly obliged" through transfer of natural rights (save self-defense) by consent.[28] But Hobbes had done nothing to cure the essential wrongness (in Rousseau's view) of modern politics; private interest was rampant, and indeed paramount, in Hobbes's system (could one not decide whether or not to risk one's life for the Hobbesian state?). The essential error of Hobbes, Rousseau thought, was to have read back into the state of nature all the human vices which half-socialization had created, and thus to see culturally-produced depravities as "natural" and Hobbesian absolutism, rather than the creation of a feeling of a common good, as the remedy for these depravities. "The error of Hobbes and of the philosophers," Rousseau declared, "is to confound natural man with the men they have before their eyes, and to carry into one system a being who can subsist only in another" *(L'État de Guerre).*[29] Rousseau, who thought that a perfectly socialized state (like Sparta) could elevate men, and turn them from "stupid and limited animals" into moral and intelligent beings,[30] must have thought Hobbesian politics incomplete, one "which confines itself to mere obedience," one which did not attempt to make men "what there is need that they should be," but which, through a system of mere mutual forbearance,[31] did not undertake any improvement in political life. "Let it be asked," said Rousseau, "why morality is corrupted in proportion as minds are enlightened";[32] Hobbes might well have an enlightened view of obligation (to the extent that he based it on consent), but he did nothing about the moral corruption caused by "private interest" and "individual will."

Rousseau, then, held in his mind, at once, both the idea that the closely unified political systems of antiquity (as he idealized them) were the most perfect kinds of polity, and the notion that all political society is the conventional creation of individual wills through a social contract. Holding both these ideas created problems, for while the need for consent to fundamental principles of political society, for creation of a mere political construct through "will and artifice," are doctrines characteristic of what Michael Oakeshott has called the "idiom of individuality,"[33] the ancient conception of a highly unified and collective politics was dependent not only on a morality of the common good quite foreign to any insistence on individual will as the creator of society and as the basis of obligation (and Rousseau sometimes recognized this, particularly in the *Économie Politique)*, but was also dependent on a view of political life as the highest, most all-embracing end of man, and was, moreover, considered both natural, and prior, ontologically if not chronologically, to the independent existence of self-sufficient men. Given the ancient view of the morality of the common good and the supreme importance and naturalness of political life, ancient thought had not had to create theories of political obligation (which are needed only when the duty to obey is in doubt): politics being the highest end of man, obligation was not a real problem, and the task of the great legislator was not to show why men ought to obey, but merely in what way—under which kind of regime—they should do so. Legislation was the task of giving the most perfect form to an intrinsically valuable activity.

Rousseau, not being a systematic philosopher (as he often pointed out), never really reconciled the tensions between his theory of obligation, and his model of political perfection. If one wants to make Rousseau more consistent than he cared to be, one must admit that his ancient ideal model, as the creation, not of a contractual relation of individual wills, but of a great legislator working with political education and a common good morality, is not "obligatory" on citizens, is not founded in right. It is true that Rousseau sometimes spoke as though ancient systems were constructed by mutual individual consent; but he did not usually speak in those terms. Even though, for him, all political society, ancient or modern, is artificial in the sense that it is not the original condition of man, contract theory comprehends an additional element of artifice, namely the notion that a society must be created by the will of all its members. Rousseau rarely spoke as though ancient polity had been artificial in this sense; he usually said that ancient systems were created, not by contract, but by the genius of legislators like Moses and Lycurgus. Moses, for example, "had the audacity to create a body politic" out of "a swarm of wretched fugitives"; he "gave them customs and usages."[34] Lycurgus "undertook to give institutions" to Sparta; he "imposed on them an iron yoke" *(Gouvernement de Pologne)*.[35] It is, really, only in the *Contrat Social* that Rousseau makes much reference to consent or contract in ancient politics; the usual emphasis (as in the *Économie Politique* and *Gouvernement de Po-*

logne) is on great men, political education, and the absence of a highly
developed individual will.[36]

One can say, moreover, if one wants to juxtapose parts of Rousseau's
thought to each other, that he made fundamental errors in analyzing
the unified spirit of ancient politics, by recognizing the desirable *effects*
of a morality of the common good, without recognizing that the very
absence of a notion of individual will as supreme had made that morality (and thereby that unity) possible. But, after all these things have
been pointed out, it remains to be said that Rousseau was consistently
clear that modern calamities caused by self-interest must be avoided,
and that the political systems created by ancient legislators were better
than any modern ones. Although it did not always occur to Rousseau
that both the merely self-interested will which he hated, and the will
necessary for consent to conventional society, were part of the same
idiom of modern political thought, and perhaps inseparable, he always
thought that mere will, as such, could never create a proper political
society. For him, then (whatever the confusions over naturalness, will,
or the presence or absence of either or both in any political idiom),
the problem of political theory, above all in the *Contrat Social,* became
that of reconciling the requirements of consent (which obligates) and
perfect socialization (which makes men "one"); men must somehow
choose the politically perfect, somehow will that complete socialization
which will preclude self-division. Will, though the basis of consent, cannot be left as it is in traditional contract theory, with no proper object.
If it is true that it is the source of obligation, it is also true that merely
self-interested will is the cause of everything Rousseau hated in modern
civilization.[37] And perfect political forms, whatever Rousseau might
have said about their being "given," must now (in the *Contrat Social*)
be willed.

Setting all the contradictions and vacillations aside, then, there are
two important elements in the two views that Rousseau held simultaneously: first, that the importance of ancient polity had to do with its
unity and its common morality, and not with its relation, or lack of it,
to contract theory; second, that individual consent (whatever this
might do to the "legitimacy" of Sparta) is needed for obligation, which
is needed because the state is conventional. It is impossible to make
every element of Rousseau both consistent and true to the political
principle that he tried to establish: that will is not enough, that perfect
polity alone is not enough, that will must be united to perfection, and
that perfection must be the standard of what is willed. And this, per-

haps, is the source of that odd idea, *general will:* a fusion of the generality (unity, communality) of antiquity with the will (consent, contract) of modernity. What makes Rousseau, without doubt, the most utopian of all great political theorists, is his insistence that even a perfect political system be willed by all subject to it. "Undoubtedly," he said, "there is a universal justice derived from reason alone; but this justice, to be admitted among us, must be mutual . . . conventions and laws are necessary, therefore, to unite rights with duties, and to accomplish the purposes of justice."[38] Though "that which is good and conformable to order is such by the nature of things, independent of human conventions,"[39] those conventions are yet required.

Rousseau's political thought is a noble attempt to unite the best elements of contract theory, of individual consent, with his perfect, unified ancient models, which, being founded on a morality of common good, had no private wills to "reconcile" to the common interest (which was natural), and thus no need of consent, no need of contract. It is this (perhaps unconscious and certainly unsystematic) attempt to fuse two modes of political thought, to have common good *and* individual will, which gives Rousseau's political thought that strange cast which some have thought contradictory, a vacillation between "individualism" and "collectivism," but which was not merely that. The problem for Rousseau was more specific and more subtle: how one can obey only his own free will, the source of obligation, in society; how it is possible to purify this will of mere private interest and selfishness, which create inequality, destroy virtue, and divide man against himself; how it is possible to insure that this individual will will want only what the common good—preferably a common good like that of ancient politics—requires. It is really a problem of retaining will, but of making it more than mere will, so that society will have a common good and a general interest, *as if it enjoyed a morality of the common good*—a morality which Rousseau sometimes recognized as the real foundation of ancient unity.

Looked at from this point of view, all of the paradoxes and "problems" in Rousseau's theory become comprehensible: why will must be retained, and why it must be made "general"; how general laws will promote the common good, but why not law, but legislative will, is final; why a great legislator can suggest perfect political forms, and why he cannot merely impose them. Above all, it is clear that this point of view helps to explain the greatest paradox in all of Rousseau—that is, the paradox created by the fact that, in the original contractual situation, the motives needed by individuals to relinquish particular will and self-interest, and to embrace a "general" will and the common good, cannot exist at the time the compact is made, and can only be the *result* of the socialization and common morality that society alone can create.[40] It is certain that if either an ideal of social perfection (Sparta), or a nation of conventional society created by mere will, were enough for Rousseau, he never would have insisted on a combination of will and perfect socialization, on a general will. There would, in fact, be no paradox at all, if perfection were only a formal question, if the state were founded on a morality of the common good and obligation were not a central problem. A great legislator, like Moses or Lycurgus, could create the best forms, and obedience would be only a question of correspondence to a system naturally and rationally right. But Rousseau said that a new-born people must, in order to will good laws, be able to "appreciate sound political principles";[41] these cannot be merely given to them, but must be willed. Why is it that "the social consciousness to be created by the new institutions would have to preside over the establishment of those same institutions,"[42] unless, somehow, the people must understand and will the system? There would be no paradox of cause and effect (the central problem of sound politics) in Rousseau if men did not have both to will, and to will a perfection which presupposes (on Rousseau's own terms) a transcendence of mere will, and the attainment of all the advantages of a morality of the common good, without actually having that morality, which would destroy obligation.

It remains to show that the attempted fusion of individual will and common-good morality is comprehended in the notion of the general will.

II

Rousseau begins the *Contrat Social,* not with the conception of general will, but with a fairly traditional contractarian view of the origin of society. Men being naturally (if not by nature)[43] perfectly independent and society made necessary only by the introduction of property (and the consequences of this introduction), men unite by contract to preserve themselves and their property. In this conventional society, there is an area of common interest, "for if the opposition of private interests made the establishment of societies necessary, it is the agreement of these same interests that made it possible."[44] It is "what these several interests have in common," says Rousseau, "that constitutes the social bond." It is only on the "basis of this common interest that society must be governed."[45]

Rousseau does not talk in these rationalistic, contractarian terms for very long. Soon enough it turns out that society's "common interest" is not merely what a lot of private interests have in common: society, when it is perfect, is a complete transformation of these private interests; it is only when "each citizen is nothing, and can do nothing, without all the rest," that society "may be said to have reached the highest attainable peak of perfection."[46] It is only, in other words (keeping in mind which societies had attained peaks of perfection), when society is much like highly unified ancient society, that "perfection" is reached; it is only "in so far as several men conjoined consider themselves as a single body"[47] that a general will can operate.

This transformed society must be governed on the basis of common interest (which has become something more than traditional common "interest"); only general laws, the creation of a general will (sovereignty), can govern the common interest.[48] Laws must be perfectly general, because the general will which makes them "loses its natural rectitude when directed toward any individual and determinate object."[49] The sovereign (the people when "active," when willing fundamental law) must, of course, make such law: "the people subject to the laws should be their author; only those who are forming an association have the right to determine the conditions of that society."[50] But, if fundamental law is the creation of a general will, how does such a will come about? It cannot be the sum of individual wills, for "the particular will tends by its nature to partiality,"[51] and this, clearly, has been the source of modern "calamities." Law must be willed by those subject to it, for will is the source of obligation. Yet mere wills can never yield generality, and law must be perfectly general, which can happen only "when the whole people legislates for the whole people."[52] If general laws alone, composed with a view to the common good, were enough, there would be no problem; but even the most general laws must be willed. How can a self-interested multitude "by itself execute so great and difficult a project as a system of legislation?"[53] How can a genuine general will, which will create general "conditions" for society, arise?

It is on this point that Rousseau is weak, uncharacteristically weak; he is always able to say what a general will must *exclude*, but he cannot say what it *is*. And this should come as no surprise. For, strictly speaking, the idea of general will is an impossibility; the ideas of generality, and of will, are mutually exclusive. Will, whatever its crudity as a psychological construct, is characteristically a concept of individuality, of particularity, and it is only metaphorically that one can speak of will as "general." No act of philosophic imagination can conjure up anything but a personal will. What can be imagined (and what, in any case, Rousseau admired in ancient society), is not really a "general" will, but a political morality of common good, in which individual will is, to be sure, not suppressed, but simply does not appear in contradistinction to, or with claims or rights against, society. What gave ancient polity (particularly in theory) its unity was not the concurrence of many wills on central points of common interest; rather a moral idiom in which extreme socialization was natural, and in which there was little notion of "will and artifice," gave rise to this unity.

There are a number of revealing passages in which Rousseau observes that something like a political morality of common good, rather than a general will, is necessary for the unity and communality which he desires—for example, at the end of Book II of the *Contrat Social,* where he discusses "the most important of all" laws, "which preserves the people in the spirit of its original institutions," that is, "manners, morals, customs and, above all, public opinion . . . a factor with which the great legislator is secretly concerned when he seems to be thinking only of particular regulations."[54] Here Rousseau does not, of course, speak of consent or will, but of a kind of political education which will promote a common good.

And he gave other indications that he knew that unity was the consequence of thinking about political relations in terms of a common good, rather than in terms of "cancelling out" of private wills "all the mutually destructive pluses and minuses," so that a "general will remains as the sum of the differences."[55] Indeed, in the *Économie Politique* he said that if men "were early accustomed to regard their individuality only in its relation to the body of the state, and to be aware, so to speak, of their own existence merely as a part of that of the state, they might at length come to identify themselves in some degree with this greater whole. . . ."[56] If children are educated in state laws which promote only a common good and a common morality, "they will learn to cherish one another mutually as brothers, to will nothing contrary to the will of society."[57] There are similar passages in the *Gouvernement de Pologne,* and in the *Projet pour la Corse,* in which the idea of a morality of the common good, reinforced by political education and legislation, is set forth, with little or no reference to consent or to will.[58]

But, much of the time, and particularly in the *Contrat Social,* Rousseau speaks not in the idiom of the common good, but of a tension between particular will and general will, and of *reconciling* these wills.[59] Indeed, the whole concept of political virtue is entirely tied up with this reconciliation of wills, as Rousseau demonstrates in the *Économie Politique.* There he says that the "first and most important rule of legitimate or popular government" is "to follow in everything the general will," but that, in order to follow the general will it must be known, and clearly distinguished from individual or particular will, and that "this distinction is always very difficult to make, and only the most sublime virtue can afford sufficient illumination for it."[60] A few pages later, he says that "if you would have the general will accomplished, bring all particular wills into conformity with it; in other words, as virtue is nothing more than the conformity of the particular wills with the general will, establish the reign of virtue."[61] Is it not clear that the argument is circular?—that conformity of particular to general will creates virtue, and that virtue is necessary to bring particular will into conformity with general will? This circularity is not due to the fact that Rousseau had no clear conception of virtue; on the contrary, ancient politics were models of virtue, as he described them.[62] The circularity is caused by trying to make virtue *as* unity, *as* communality, dependent on reconciliation of particular to general will, whereas in fact (and as Rousseau recognizes on adjoining pages of the same treatise), virtue as conformity to a common good morality is the creation of great legislation and political education. Vacillation on the true source of ancient unity and communality (reconciliation of wills, or absence of will), is the cause of the circularity of the concept of virtue in Rousseau; moreover, this circularity reflects the same kind of cause-effect paradox as that referred to at the end of part I. In both cases, Rousseau knows perfectly well what he admires: the virtue of ancient society, and the perfection of laws in ancient society. It is only when, in both cases, he tries to describe the possibility of these attributes in terms of reconciled will that he falls down. Nor is this surprising; for, as has been noted, he did, sometimes, recognize that the absence of the very notion that caused all his problems—will as supreme—had constituted the greatness of antiquity. All the paradoxes, circularities and vacillations in Rousseau are caused by the attempted fusion of moral-political idioms which are incompatible on fundamental points.

A clear illustration of just this point is Rousseau's treatment of Brutus in the *Histoire des Moeurs;* in that fragment Rousseau, observing that "it will always be great and difficult to submit the dearest affections of nature to country and virtue,"[63] cites Brutus' execution of his treasonous sons as an example of this "submission," not ever mentioning that this was no case of "submitting" particular will to a general will, but (more likely) a case of a common-good morality (coupled with the rights of the Roman *pater familias*) at work. Yet in other works written at about the same time, he makes no reference to submission of will in Roman society, and talks only of legislation and political education.[64]

Nonetheless (and despite these vacillations), it is easy to see why a fusion of political idioms was attempted. For even though perfect socialization was Rousseau's ultimate ideal, consent and will, as the source of obligation, were too important, to be summarily discarded. Thus the general will, though an impossibility, was a necessity.

"Actually," said Rousseau, "each individual may, as a man, have a private will contrary to, or divergent from, the general will he has as a citizen" *(Contrat Social).*[65] This could not, of course, be the case in a state with a common-good morality reinforced by legislation and education (the system sketched in the *Économie Politique*). The passage cited from the *Contrat Social* shows that in that work, the most "contractarian" of Rousseau's writings, and the closest thing he had to a systematic political theory, neither mere will nor perfection wins out alone. For in the *Contrat Social,* there is the possibility that a private person (already a concept of modern individualism) may regard "the artificial person of the state as a fictitious being," and that this "may make him envisage his debt to the common cause as a gratuitous contribution."[66] It seems clear that if Rousseau were *not* trying (however unsystematically) to reconcile will and perfect socialization, these problems could not exist: the new state could not be considered a fictitious being (for it would educate men to think something different); one would not think of his political role as a "contribution" (because one would be naturally part of a greater whole); and there would be no conflict between man and citizen (because one would be naturally part of a greater whole); and there would be no conflict between man and citizen (because the distinction would not exist). Is not the paradox that a man must be "forced to be free"[67] if his particular will does not conform to the general will an indication that Rousseau tried to gain the advantages of a common-good morality (particularly in the *Contrat*

Social) through reconciliation of wills, and this only because will is necessary to obligation?

There is, finally, in Rousseau's most systematic political work (the *Contrat Social),* no postulation of a political morality of the common good as the source of the much-desired unity. Rather, there is a constant attempt to bring particular will into conformity with general will through the efforts of a "great legislator." What the great legislator, in his wisdom, knows to be good, supplies the absence of a common-good morality. Now, the difference between the great legislator of ancient politics and Rousseau's ideal legislator, corresponds exactly to the difference between giving a presupposed unity (without strong will) a perfect form (antiquity), and making people *will* perfect forms (modernity). "All" in the contractual period "stand equally in need of guidance."[68] Individuals "must be obliged to bring their wills into conformity with their reason," that is, they must will that which is, in itself, rationally best. The combination of individual consent and the legislator's guidance "will effect a union of understanding and will within the social body."[69] And what is rationally best (to avoid that self-division caused by half-socialization) is the perfectly united and communal polity of antiquity. The legislator, who effects the bringing of will into conformity with reason (not by force, but through persuasion and religious devices), supplies the defect of common-good morality, and simply gets each individual to will something like the laws which *would have* resulted from such a morality. What Rousseau ultimately has, then, is not a "general will" (which is inconceivable), but a "will to the general," which is conceivable if one recalls that political perfection requires both truly general laws and consent to them. Rousseau did not, could not, abolish will—but he prescribed the form that it must take, and this form is clearly derived from the generality and unity of ancient polity (as Rousseau saw it)—but without a morality of common good, which would have destroyed obligation.

Moreover, not only the form of laws (generality) is derived from ancient models; the *conditions* under which good laws (and indeed good states) are possible, are little more than idealizations of ancient political circumstances. A people is "fit for legislation," according to Rousseau, if it has no old laws, if it is free from threats of invasion and can resist its neighbors, if it is small enough that its "individual members can all know one another," if it can get along without other peoples, if it is "neither very rich nor very poor," and can be self-sufficient, and if it is one which "combines the firmness of an old people with the docility of a new one."[70] Clearly most of these conditions of the possibility for good polity are abstracted from Rousseau's idealized version of ancient city-states, particularly Sparta. Not only the form of a good political system, then, but also the empirical conditions which could make such a system possible, are derived from Rousseau's models of perfection.

What has been said thus far may be summarized in this way: 1) a perfect state (that is, a perfectly socialized, united and communal state) would have perfectly general laws (that is, laws dealing only with Rousseau's vision of a common good); 2) but laws, especially the most general laws, must be willed by everyone subject to those laws, in order to be obligatory—and they must be made obligatory, for society is merely conventional; 3) therefore, will must take the form of general laws; 4) but will tends to the particular, and law, though the creation of will, must somehow be general; 5) moreover, for particular wills to appreciate the necessity of general laws, effect would have to become cause; 6) therefore, a great legislator, whose instruction can supply the defect of a morality of the common good—the only morality which would *naturally* produce general laws—is necessary; 7) but this legislator is impossibly rare, and, in addition, he cannot create laws, however general and good, for sovereignty is inalienable; 8) thus the legislator must have recourse to religion, and use it to gain the consent of individuals to the general will; 9) but now "consent" is something less than real consent, since an irrational device has been used; 10) finally, the whole system is saved for individual will by the fact that "a people always has a right to change its laws, even the best,"[71] that legislative *will*, rather than law itself, is supreme, and that the entire social system can be abolished by will, for "there is not, and cannot be, any sort of fundamental law binding on the body of the people, not even the social contract."[72]

The theory of Rousseau, then, ultimately reduces itself to two elements: the need for a great legislator to create a "general will," and the extreme limitations put on this legislator by the fact that this general will, though (of course) general, is still will, and must be will. Both elements are the consequence of attempting to unite all the requirements of will with all the advantages of perfect socialization. The legislator may formulate and propose general laws which will produce perfect socialization, and he can get them "willed" through religious devices; but the sovereign cannot be permanently bound, even by perfect laws, and can change these laws and even dissolve society. Thus neither perfection nor will has all the claims in Rousseau; but will can finally be, even if only in a destructive way, triumphant, for if a people "is pleased to do itself harm, who has a right to prevent it from doing so?"[73]

It is not meant, by analyzing Rousseau in this way, that he was always perfectly consistent in desiring that particular wills should consent to that which an ancient morality of common good would require; indeed, he vacillated on several points, notably in his treatment of civil religion, in which he allowed any tolerant sect to exist, so long as it did not claim exclusive truth or refuse to subscribe to the basic articles of civic religious policy.[74] Above all, though, Rousseau insisted that each socialized man should somehow "obey no one but himself," and thought he had found a solution to this problem in making the conditions of society (laws) perfectly general and equally applicable to all, so that, the conditions being equal for all, and willed by all, "it is in the interest of no one to make [social requirements] burdensome to the rest,"[75] and that, since the society cannot wish to hurt all its members by enacting bad general laws, society need offer its members no guarantees.[76] But this system is essentially modified by the fact that a will to general laws absolutely cannot be attained with mere wills as they are (the cause-effect problem again), but only through the influence of a great legislator; by Rousseau's assertion that there is no real limit to the extent of undertakings possible between the sovereign and its members;[77] by the idea that the sovereign is the sole judge of how many "powers" of individuals must be socialized;[78] and by the notion that an ideal society should be very highly socialized indeed. It is modified above all by part IV, chapter II of the *Contrat Social,* which shows, perhaps more clearly than anything in Rousseau, that consent is no longer to be a question of mere volition, and that the general will is something like a modified common-good morality.

> The constant will of all the members of the state is the general will; that is what makes them citizens and free. When a law is proposed in the assembly of the people, what the voters are being asked is not precisely whether they do or do not approve of the proposal, but whether or not it is in conformity with the general will, which is their own. Each, when casting his vote, gives his opinion on this question; and the declaration of the general will is found by counting the ballots. Thus when an opinion contrary to my own prevails, this proves nothing more than that I was mistaken, and that what I thought to be the general will was not.[79]

The meaning of this (usually confusing) passage can be understood if "common good" be substituted for "general will"; then it can be seen how general will is *constant* will, and how citizens are not being asked whether they approve a proposal, but whether it is in conformity with a common good.

With all of these modifications in mind, it is clear that, while Rousseau's theory of society and law really is, as he insisted, an attempt to preserve liberty, that liberty is conceived in an odd way: it is "obedience to self-imposed law"[80] (which must, of course, be general law). Liberty, then, comes down to freeing the individual of all private dependence by making him "very dependent on the city" and its general and equally-applied laws. But, though liberty is obedience to self-imposed law, proper law cannot be created without modification of will by a great legislator, and thus the very idea of liberty is, like other elements of Rousseau, a fusion of the idioms of individual will and of highly unified society. It is because of these modifications that Rousseau's political theory cannot be so easily assimilated to traditional constitutionalism, or to Kant's theory of law, as some have imagined.[81] For legislative will, and not law itself, is supreme in Rousseau. Nor can Rousseau be easily assimilated to the German "romantic" tradition of the early nineteenth century, because he would never have replaced general *will* with the historical evolution of national *spirits;* he was clear that history, in itself, cannot "justify" anything.[82] This non-assimilability to other traditions proves that those who view Rousseau as a unique and isolated figure are probably correct; he was, in his own words, one of those few "moderns who had an ancient soul."[83]

III

The only object of this study has been to elucidate the concept of the general will, and to clear up some of the paradoxes in the *Contrat Social,* by analyzing what Rousseau thought about will and contract, on the one hand, and about perfect political systems, on the other. It has not been a central object to attack Rousseau as unsystematic, to reproach him for not adequately reconciling two modes of political thought, or to "improve" his ideas by making them more consistent. No series of conceptual ambiguities can detract anything from Rousseau's status as the greatest of political psychologists and the most eloquent critic of the psychological destruction wrought by inequality. Nonetheless, it is evident that there is an insurmountable conceptual problem in Rousseau's political thought, and it is this: voluntarist theories are usually composed of two parts, a theory of will as a moral agency, and a theoretical standard of right to which will ought to conform (arbitrary willfulness usually being rejected as a standard of right). In Locke or in Kant, the standard of right to which will must conform (natural law in the first case, universal rational law in the second) does not contradict voluntarism (once one gets around the problem of reconciling free will and absolute standards: in itself a problem which defeated a Leibniz and reduced Kant to hypotheses). But in Rousseau the standard to which will must conform (ancient perfection, or its equivalent) is itself non-voluntaristic; and therefore will and the standard to which it must conform are contradictory. The standard which gives will its object is the very negation of voluntarism. And it is for this reason that Rousseau's political system is somewhat paradoxical. The idea of general will, the paradox of cause and effect in the contractual situation, the circularity of the concept of virtue—all these are due to an attempt to fuse the advantages of a politics founded on will, and of one founded on reason and perfection. One must, in Rousseau, will the kind of society in which one lives, because "to deprive your will of all freedom is to deprive your actions of all morality,"[84] and this deprivation destroys the obligation one has to obey. Yet mere will can yield only particularity and inequality, and will never produce rational perfection. To retain the moral attributes of will, but to do away with will's particularity and selfishness—that is the problem of Rousseau's political thought. It is a problem which reflects the difficulty which Rousseau found in making free-will and rational authority co-exist in his moral and political thinking. Freedom of the will is as important to the morality of actions for Rousseau as for any traditional voluntarist; but he was suspicious of the very faculty, the only faculty, which could moralize. And that is why he urged, in the *Économie Politique,* that "the most absolute authority is that which penetrates into a man's inmost being, and concerns itself no less with his will than with his actions."[85] Can the will be both morally autonomous and subject to the rationalizing influence of authority? That was the point which Rousseau never settled altogether. Even Émile, the best-educated of men, chooses to continue to accept the guidance of his teacher.[86] How much more, then, do ordinary men need the guidance of a great legislator when they embark on the setting up of a system which will not only aid and defend, but also *moralize* them! The relation of volition to authority is one of the most difficult and one of the most inscrutable problems in Rousseau; the general will is dependent on "a union of will and understanding within the social body,"[87] but that understanding, which is provided by authority, weakens the idea of will as an autonomous authorizing faculty.

To project the question on a grander scale, one can see in Rousseau's political thought an intuitive attempt to reconcile the two greatest traditions of Western political philosophy, that of "will and artifice" and that of "reason and nature" (Oakeshott). For general will is surely rationalized will. And yet it is not self-rationalized will in a Kantian sense, but will rationalized by the standards and conditions of idealized ancient polity.

Whatever Rousseau's means, in undertaking a fusion of two great modes of political thinking, and however unsuccessful the attempt to make general will a viable conception, one must always, while analyzing and even criticizing the result, grant the grandeur and importance of the effort. For if one could succeed in having the best of both idioms, one would have a political philosophy which would synthesize almost everything valued in the history of Western political thought.

Notes

For the convenience of American readers, reference has been made whenever possible to a standard English translation of Rousseau. All translations from French editions are my own.

1. This title was adopted not out of modesty, but simply because this article makes certain assumptions which are not universally agreed on. Most importantly, it holds that Rousseau understood "will" not only as a psychological attribute but also as a moral faculty; that there is an implicit metaphysical dimension in Rousseau without which a concept such as "willing" would be incomplete. By treating the concept of volition in psychological rather than in metaphysical terms, however, Mrs. J. N. Shklar, in her persuasive *Men and Citizens: A Study of Rousseau's Social Theory* (Cambridge University Press, 1969) is able to make the general will both internally consistent and closely related to Rousseau's individual psychology. That is, by treating individual will as a defense-mechanism, and the general will as a collective defense-mechanism (used largely as a weapon against inequality, whose effects for Shklar are mainly psychologically destructive), she is able to make the general will conceptually plausible. This reading, however, seems to involve a weakening of those (admittedly few) passages in which Rousseau speaks, in a traditional way, of volition as a moral faculty whose endorsement is the source of all moral legitimacy, e.g., "to deprive your will of all freedom is to deprive your actions of all morality" *(Contrat Social,* chapter IV). This idea is clearly the foundation of Rousseau's attack on paternalism and on the equation of right and force. It

is certainly possible to conceive the "general will one has as a citizen" in a psychological and metaphorical sense, if one imagines this "generality" in terms of factors wholly congruent with psychology: education, public spectacles and games, the authority of the legislator. But this can never show how a will in anything *but* a psychological sense can be general, simply because the education and authority congruent with psychology are *not* congruent with a concept of free will and of moral choice. A psychological treatment of volition does in fact hold out the best prospect of a consistent treatment of Rousseau; but it also involves a weakening of the voluntarist and contractarian elements of his philosophy.

2. Green, T. H., *Lectures on the Principles of Political Obligation* (Longmans, Green and Co., London, 1941), pp. 82ff.

3. Barth, Hans, "Volonté Générale et Volonté Particulière chez J.-J. Rousseau," in *Rousseau et la Philosophie Politique*, Annales de Philosophie Politique No. 5 (Presses Universitaires de France, Paris, 1965), pp. 44ff.

4. Chapman, John, "Political Theory: Logical Structure and Enduring Types," in *L'Idée de Philosophie Politique*, Annales de Philosophie Politique No. 6 (Presses Universitaires de France, Paris, 1965), pp. 65–69.

5. Hegel, G. W. F., *Philosophy of Right*, translated T. M. Knox, Oxford University Press, London, 1942, pp. 280, 288–289.

6. Plamenatz, John, "Equality of Opportunity," in *Aspects of Human Equality*, edited L. Bryson, (Harper and Bros., New York, 1957), pp. 79–107.

7. Jouvenel, Bertrand de, *Sovereignty*, translated by J. Huntington (University of Chicago Press, Chicago, 1957), various passages.

8. Leibniz accused Hobbes and Pufendorf of adhering to this view. "To say *stat pro ratione voluntas*, my will takes the place of reason," Leibniz observed, "is properly the motto of a tyrant." He traced this line of thought back to Thrasymachus in the *Republic*, and urged that Hobbes, "who is noted for his paradoxes, wanted to maintain nearly the same thing as Thrasymachus." See Leibniz, G. W., *Meditation sur la Notion Commune de la Justice*, edited G. Mollat, Verlag J. H. Robolsky, Leipzig, 1885, pp. 56ff.

9. See particularly Rousseau, J.-J., *Discourse on the Arts and Sciences*, translated G. D. H. Cole (E. P. Dutton and Co., New York, 1950), pp. 172–174; Rousseau, J.-J., *Gouvernement de Pologne* in *Political Writings*, edited C. E. Vaughan (Basil Blackwell, Oxford, 1962), Vol. II, pp. 430, 437–438; Rousseau, J.-J., *Disease on Inequality*, translated G. D. H. Cole (E. P. Dutton and Co., New York, 1950), pp. 247ff., 266ff.; Rousseau, J.-J., *Lêttre à M. d'Alembert*, critical edition of M. Fuchs (Librairie Droz, Geneva, 1948) (entire).

10. See particularly Rousseau, *Gouvernement de Pologne*, op. cit., chapters II and III; Rousseau, *Discourse on the Arts and Sciences*, op. cit., pp. 153–158; Rousseau, J.-J., *Economie Politique* in *Political Writings*, edited Vaughan, op. cit., vol. I, pp. 253–254; Rousseau, J.-J., *Rome et Sparte*, in *Political Writings*, edited Vaughan, op. cit., vol. I, pp. 314–318; Shklar, J. N., "Rousseau's Two Models: Sparta and the Age of Gold," *Political Science Quarterly* 81 (March 1966), 25–51.

11. Rousseau, J.-J., *Le Bonheur Public*, in *Political Writings*, edited Vaughan, op. cit., vol. I, pp. 325–326.

12. Rousseau, J.-J., *Le Contrat Social,* translated F. Watkins, in *Political Writings* (Thomas Nelson and Sons, Edinburgh, 1953), p. 42 (hereafter cited as CS).

13. Rousseau, *Le Bonheur Public,* op. cit., p. 326.

14. *Ibid.*

15. Rousseau, CS, op. cit., p. 58.

16. *Ibid.*

17. *Ibid.,* p. 42.

18. Rousseau, J.-J., *Gouvernement de Pologne,* translated F. Watkins, in *Political Writings,* op. cit., pp. 166–167 (hereafter cited as *Pologne).*

19. Rousseau, J.-J., *Économie Politique,* translated G. D. H. Cole (E. P. Dutton and Co., New York, 1950), p. 308 (hereafter cited as *Éc. Pol.).*

20. *Ibid.*

21. Rousseau, J.-J., *Émile* (excerpt), in *Political Writings,* edited Vaughan, vol. II, p. 145.

22. Rousseau, *Pologne,* pp. 163–165.

23. Rousseau, CS, p. 117.

24. *Ibid.,* p. 8.

25. Rousseau, J.-J., *Lettres de la Montagne,* in *Political Writings,* edited Vaughan, vol. II, pp. 199–200.

26. *Ibid.*

27. Rousseau, *Éc. Pol.,* p. 297.

28. Oakeshott, Michael, *Rationalism in Politics,* (Methuen and Co., London, 1962), pp. 258ff.; Oakeshott, Michael, Introduction to Hobbes' *Leviathan* (Basil Blackwell, Oxford, 1957), pp. xxxv–l.

29. Rousseau, J.-J., *L'État de Guerre,* in *Political Writings,* edited Vaughan, vol. I, p. 306.

30. Rousseau, CS, p. 20.

31. Oakeshott, *Rationalism in Politics,* p. 261.

32. Rousseau, *L'État de Guerre,* p. 307.

33. Oakeshott, *Rationalism in Politics,* pp. 249–251.

34. Rousseau, *Pologne,* pp. 163–165.

35. *Ibid.*

36. Rousseau, *Éc. Pol.,* pp. 293–311.

37. *Ibid.,* pp. 307–309.

38. Rousseau, CS, pp. 37–38.

39. *Ibid.,* p. 37.

40. *Ibid.,* p. 44. Cf. Rousseau, J.-J., *Des Lois,* in *Political Writings,* edited Vaughan, vol. I, p. 331.

41. *Ibid.* (CS).

42. *Ibid.*

43. Since, for Rousseau, the pre-social man is a "stupid and limited animal," and becomes a moral and intelligent being only in society, there is a sense in which man's highest nature (rather than original nature) *is* social. Cf. Rousseau, J.-J., *Lêttre à M. Philopolis,* in *Political Writings,* edited by Vaughan, vol. I, p. 223.

44. Rousseau, CS, p. 25.

45. *Ibid.*

46. *Ibid.*, p. 42.

47. *Ibid.*, p. 113.

48. *Ibid.*, pp. 26, 29–30, 38–40.

49. *Ibid.*, p. 32.

50. *Ibid.*, p. 40.

51. *Ibid.*, p. 25.

52. *Ibid.*, p. 38.

53. *Ibid.*, p. 40.

54. *Ibid.*, p. 58.

55. *Ibid.*, p. 29.

56. Rousseau, *Éc. Pol.*, pp. 307–308.

57. *Ibid.*, p. 309.

58. Rousseau, *Pologne*, chapters II–IV; Rousseau, J.-J., *Projet pour la Corse*, translated F. Watkins, in *Political Writings*, p. 300.

59. Rousseau, CS, pp. 40–41.

60. Rousseau, *Éc. Pol.*, p. 293.

61. *Ibid.*, p. 298.

62. Rousseau, *Pologne*, chapters II–III; Rousseau, *Rome et Sparte*, in *Political Writings*, edited Vaughan, vol. I, pp. 314–320.

63. Rousseau, J.-J., *Histoire des Moeurs*, in *Political Writings*, edited Vaughan, vol. I, p. 337.

64. Rousseau, *Éc. Pol.*, pp. 302–310.

65. Rousseau, CS, pp. 18–19.

66. *Ibid.*, p. 19.

67. *Ibid.*

68. *Ibid.*, p. 40.

69. *Ibid.*

70. *Ibid.*, pp. 53–54.

71. *Ibid.*, p. 57.

72. *Ibid.*, pp. 17–18.

73. *Ibid.*, p. 57.

74. *Ibid.*, pp. 152–155.

75. *Ibid.*, p. 15.

76. *Ibid.*, p. 18.

77. *Ibid.*, p. 33.

78. *Ibid.*, p. 31.

79. *Ibid.*, pp. 117–118.

80. *Ibid.*, p. 20.

81. Cassirer, Ernst, *Rousseau, Kant and Goethe*, translated Gutmann, Kristeller and Randall (Harper Torchbacks, New York, 1963), pp. 30ff.

82. Rousseau, J.-J., *Première Version du Contrat Social*, in *Political Writings*, edited Vaughan, vol. I, p. 462.

83. Rousseau, J.-J., *Jugement sur la Polysynodie*, in *Political Writings*, edited Vaughan, vol. I, p. 421.

84. Rousseau, CS, p. 9.

85. Rousseau, *Éc. Pol.*, p. 297.

86. Rousseau, J.-J., *Emile*, translated B. Foxley (Everyman's Library, J. M. Dent and Sons, London 1911), p. 444.

87. Rousseau, CS, p. 41.

10

Reflections on Rousseau: Autonomy and Democracy

Joshua Cohen

I. Rousseau's Contract Theory

Rousseau's *Social Contract* defends "principles of political right" and explores the operations of institutions in light of those principles. In his discussion of Rousseau in *Will and Political Legitimacy* (chap. 4), Patrick Riley criticizes the defense of principles. He argues that there are tensions between the "voluntarism" endorsed in Rousseau's contractarian theory of legitimacy and the "morality of the common good" that Rousseau embraces in describing his political ideal, and he maintains that the general will is a failed attempt to overcome these tensions.[1] Riley's own explication of Rousseau's views about the social contract and the general will are vague and unsatisfactory. In order, therefore, to evaluate Riley's criticisms, I first sketch an account of the main elements of Rousseau's view, and then use this sketch to assess the alleged tensions.

Autonomy and Social Interdependence

Rousseau's defense of principles of right in the *Social Contract* assumes conditions of social interdependence.[2] Abstracting from certain matters of detail, he supposes in particular that: (1) individuals each have basic needs and interests that they aim to satisfy; (2) the satisfaction of these needs and interests depends on the actions of others. In particular, if each acts solely with the aim of advancing his or her own interests (the "will of all"), all do less well than if their actions are coordinated; (3) agents have the capacity to recognize and do recognize their dependence on the actions of others (that is, they recognize that mutually beneficial coordination is possible); and (4) individuals have views—typically conflicting views—about the claims that they can legitimately make on one another (*SC* I.6.ii, I.7.vi–viii, II.1.i, II.3.ii; IV.1.vi; *GM* I.2; *D2*, pp. 154–59).

The aim of the *Social Contract* is to identify norms of social cooperation that are reasonable in view of conditions (1)–(4) together with two central features of human beings: first, that human beings have an equal capacity for and interest in *freedom;* and second, that we are *motivated by self-love.*[3] "The fundamental problem," as he puts it, is to "Find a form of association that [1] *defends and protects the person and goods of each associate* with all the common force, and by means of which [2] each one, uniting with all, nevertheless *obeys only himself and remains as free as before*" (*SC,* I.6.iv, emphases and bracketed numbers are mine). The problem is to characterize a form of social interdependence that permits each to secure the benefits of association—the protection of person and goods, the development and exercise of capacities, the broadening of ideas and feelings (*SC* I.8.i)—without sacrificing the freedom that defines our nature.

This fundamental problem is "solved by the social contract" (*SC* I.6.iv), that is, by answering the question: What kind of association would be rationally agreed to by socially interdependent individuals who are moved by self-love and, above all, by an interest in securing their freedom?

Rousseau's contractual problem has, he believes, a determinate solution (*SC,* I.6.v), namely, a society in which each member *"puts his person and all his power in common under the supreme direction of the general will"* (*SC* I.6.ix)[4] In such a society, authority rests ultimately in a shared understanding of the common good. More exactly, for a general will to provide supreme direction, the social order must satisfy four main conditions.[5] First, members (that is, citizens) have separate, particular interests (*SC* I.7.vii), and take those interests as providing reasons for action.[6] Second, citizens *share* and it is *common knowledge* that they share a conception of their common interests (of the "common good") though they may have different beliefs about what will advance those common interests.[7] Although no determinate conception of the common good follows from Rousseau's social contract, it does impose some general constraints on what will count as a genuine conception, including a requirement that the interests of each member (in security of person and goods, and in liberty) be advanced (*SC* II.1.i, II.11, and below p. 293).[8] Third, citizens take the fact that an institution or law advances common interests as itself providing *a* reason for supporting that institution or law, and recognize that they ought to act on reasons of the common good when they have reasonable assurance that others will so act. Fourth, social institutions generally conform to and citizens have reasonable confidence that the institutions conform to their shared conception of the common good.

Rousseau's argument that the general will is the solution to the social contract is very compressed (*SC* I.6.vi–viii). But it has two main elements, corresponding to the considerations of self-love and freedom that figure in the description of the contract. The fact that the social order ought to advance common interests corresponds to the fact that the contract is a unanimous agreement among rational individuals who are moved by self-love. And the fact that the members of the order share the conception of the common good that the social order ought to advance corresponds to the interest in remaining "as free as before." By sharing the conception, they achieve the autonomy that comes from acting on principles they recognize as their own, from "obedience to the law one has prescribed for oneself" (*SC* I.8.iii). For citizens to have, that is, the general will as a rule is for them to have "their own will as a rule," and so "it [the social contract] leaves them as free as before" (*OC* III [*LM*], p. 807; *SC* I.8.iii, II.4.viii; *E,* p. 461; *OC* III *(PF),* pp. 483–84).

This account of the contract, the general will, and the connections between the two is, of course, only the barest sketch. But it suffices for present purposes insofar as it highlights the role of social interdependence and autonomy, and provides some intuitive content for the main notions in Rousseau's theory. Having thus fixed an interpretation of certain central features of Rousseau's view—what I will refer to as a "social autonomy" interpretation—we can now consider Riley's objections.

Rousseau's Dilemma?

According to Riley, "Rousseau's system is somewhat paradoxical." The source of the paradoxes, he says, is the fact that "the standard to which will must conform—ancient perfection or its equivalent—is itself nonvoluntaristic; therefore, will and the standard to which it must conform are contradictory. The standard that gives will its object is the very negation of voluntarism" (p. 121). This description of the tension between Rousseau's "voluntarism" and his embrace of what Riley calls a "common good morality" resists straightforward construal. At least two importantly different accounts of the alleged tension are supported by Riley's discussion.

The first account of the tensions is that Rousseau shifts between a social and an individualistic *explanation of the acquisition of moral notions*. The social explanation assumes that people live in a society and holds that the acquisition of norms occurs through a process of socialization in which they learn the norms of the society; the individualistic explanation does not make that assumption and holds that acquisition takes place through an initial agreement.

> Despite the fact that he sometimes treats moral notions *as if they simply arose in a developmental process during the course of socialization,* Rousseau often *falls back on a kind of moral a priorism, particularly when speaking of contract and obligation,* in which the wills of free men are taken to be the causes of duties and of legitimate authority. (p. 102, emphases added; see also pp. 16, 123, 202)

It is certainly true that Rousseau offers an account of the acquisition of moral notions "during the course of socialization." And it is true as well that he endorses "a kind of moral a priorism" in his contractual justification of the general will. But it is not correct to say that Rousseau "falls back" from the one to the other, since the theory of socialization and the social contract respond to two different questions. The social contract addresses the question: What are the correct social norms? It is not an account of the acquisition of those norms. The account of socialization addresses the question: How do people develop an understanding of, and motivation to act on, the correct principles of right (that is, acquire a general will)? His response to this question draws on his psychology and theory of institutions. In part his answer is that socialization in a democratic order leads to the formation of a general will. While the social contract shows that autonomy requires a general will, the psychological theory suggests that socialization is the way that a general will, and therefore autonomy, is socially engendered.

Rousseau's views about acquisition and justification are not wholly disconnected. They are linked by the notion of reciprocity which figures in the contractual argument for the general will (*SC* I.6.viii, II.6.ii), in motivation formation (*E,* pp. 213–14), and in the social experience in a democratic order which leads to the formation of a general will. The social contract idealizes, so to speak, what political participation realizes (see below, pp. 293–294). But these connections notwithstanding, the *point* of the contract and of the account of socialization are different whereas Riley seems to confuse them.

The removal of this confusion does not, however, eliminate the problem that Riley is concerned about. It leaves a second construal of the tension between voluntarism and common good morality that does not turn on the putative use of the social contract as an explanation of acquisition. Thus Riley refers to what he calls the "greatest paradox in all of Rousseau: the paradox created by the fact that in the original contractual situation the motives needed by individuals to relinquish particular will and self-interest and to embrace a general will and the common good cannot exist at the time the compact is made but can only be the result of the socialization and common morality that society alone can create" (p. 110).

The suggestion is that Rousseau faces a dilemma in his contractual justification of the general will. If the parties to the social contract are *not socialized,* then they will not agree to a social order regulated by a general will. For if they are not socialized, then they are self-interested. And if they are purely self-interested, then they cannot rationally agree to be motivated by non-self-interested reasons. If, however, the parties to the contract *are socialized,* then they already have a "common good morality." But since that morality is "the very negation of voluntarism" (p. 121), if citizens have a common good morality, then they would themselves reject the voluntarist conception of morality embodied in the social contract. Therefore, the contract either fails to justify the general will or it has no justificatory power at all. There is no single point of view, however, from which both a contractual justification and the common good morality embodied in the general will might consistently be endorsed.

This dilemma raises interesting questions about Rousseau's view. But the questions it raises pose genuine difficulties only if we reject the social autonomy interpretation and instead construe Rousseau as endorsing what I will call "self-effacing Hobbesianism."[9] In the discussion that follows, I will first outline this interpretation, then indicate that, while self-effacing Hobbesianism may be coherent, it is not a view that Rousseau could accept, and finally suggest that Riley's dilemma concerning the consistency of Rousseau's contractual justification and common good morality can be resolved within the social autonomy interpretation.

According to self-effacing Hobbesianism, individuals are initially motivated solely by their own long-term interests in protecting their person and goods (hereafter I will refer to these as their "self-interests"). There comes a point at which they recognize that mutually beneficial coordination is possible, and that it is in their own long-term self-interest to cooperate on mutually beneficial terms if they can rely on the cooperation of others. They recognize as well that there are two obstacles to mutually beneficial coordination. First, there are a variety of mutually beneficial arrangements, none of which provides a focal point for their cooperation. An explicit stipulation of terms of order overcomes the first problem. Second, they need to ensure the stability of the resulting arrangements. But they see that their agreement is not self-enforcing both because there will be temptations to violate the agreement arising from motivations other than long-term self-interests and because they need assurance that others will keep the agreement.

Assessing various solutions to their dilemma, the contractors decide that a Hobbesian sovereign will likely be insufficient to motivate general compliance and to produce a stable order. For even with an absolute sovereign, obedience depends on self-interested calculation, and they judge that calculators are not reliable cooperators (*SC* I.3.i). The contractors conclude that only a society with a general will can ensure the stable satisfaction of the long-term self-interests, and so agree that they ought to have a general will. Aware, however, that one cannot just *decide* to have a general will, they agree to institutions that they expect will, over time, transform individuals in society from self-interested individualists into citizens whose primary allegiance is to the common good—thus producing a "remarkable change in man, by substituting justice for instinct in his behavior and giving his actions the morality they previously lacked" (*SC,* I.8.i).

Self-effacing Hobbesianism responds to Riley's dilemma as initially stated, since it shows that self-interested individuals *could* rationally "embrace" a general will, even if their first embrace consists only in the recognition that they ought to have a general will that takes precedence over their particular interests. But there is a variant of the dilemma that is not resolved, as a continuation of the historical story shows.

Once "the remarkable change in man" occurs, the members of society no longer regard themselves as, at bottom, self-interested. While they continue to have separate interests, their chief allegiance is to the common good, and their chief reason for complying with the rules of the association is that those rules advance the common good. Since they continue to have self-interests, some justification for their form of association is provided by the fact that it *would* be rational, in view of those self-interests alone, to bootstrap their way into the general will. But the fact that purely self-interested individuals would agree to the association cannot be their chief reason for complying with it, since they are not such individuals. Thus, if individuals regard self-interested reasons as fundamental, then they can agree that they *ought* to have a supreme general will but they do not *have* one. If they have one, then the self-interested contract does not provide *them* with the basic justification for having it. There is, then, no single point of view which embraces both the contractual justification and the general will.[10]

The absence of such a point of view is not by itself, however, an objection to a theory. A social contract theory could in principle be self-effacing. But I do not think that Rousseau held such a theory. He gives no evidence of believing that a contractual argument cannot provide a justification for having a general will to those with such a will. He appears instead to endorse a non-self-effacing interpretation of the social contract, and in fact to believe that public recognition that the social order would be agreed to contributes to the stability [solidité] of that order (*OC* III [*LM*], pp. 806–807; *SC* II.6.ii). If Rousseau requires that the contractual justification be non-self-effacing, and if the only way to make sense of Rousseau's combination of social contract theory and common good morality is to interpret him as endorsing self-effacing Hobbesianism, then a variant of Riley's dilemma raises a serious problem.

But the self-effacing Hobbesianism interpretation is not correct. While it captures certain strands of Rousseau's view, it rests on a misunderstanding of Rousseau's fundamental problem. That problem is not: What sort of society would rational, asocial, and purely self-interested individuals agree to? And Rousseau's view is not that such individuals would agree that they ought to regulate their actions by non-self-interested reasons. His question is: What form of association would *socially interdependent individuals* agree to if they were interested in protecting their person and goods and *in being free?*[11] Rousseauean contractors do have interests in person and goods, and those interests are advanced by a society directed by a general will. But the protection of those interests is not the only or the primary aim of the participants in the social contract, and in particular not the sole source of the "common good morality" that issues from that contract. Its source, as I indicated earlier (p. 279), is also in the freedom that socially interdependent individuals aim to preserve. By contrast with self-effacing Hobbesianism, then, the social autonomy interpretation emphasizes both that social interdependence sets the problem which the social contract addresses, and that there is, so to speak, an anticipation of the general will—something universal—present within the contractual situation itself, and therefore a basis for that will in the nature of human beings.

To see how the social autonomy interpretation meets Riley's dilemma, I want to sketch a version of that dilemma that might be thought to arise even with the rejection of self-effacing Hobbesianism, and then suggest why it in fact does not arise. The dilemma here can again be stated as a conflict between the standpoint of contractor and the standpoint of citizen. As contractors, individuals regard themselves as free. From this standpoint, an allegiance to the common good is simply one possible allegiance among others, and lacks any special authority. Volunteers in service to the common good, persons who regard themselves as contractors cannot have the attachment to the common good that is required on Rousseau's conception of the general will. Thus from the point of view of the contractor, the contract does not justify the general will.

Citizens, on the other hand, identify with the common good. They do not regard themselves most fundamentally as free choosers of ends, but as members of a state, and their choices are always made against the background of an identification with that state. And so the question of what would be chosen when this identity is abstracted from is of no interest from the perspective of the citizen (if the question has any content at all). Trying to answer it, like trying to write a book on *Chess Without the King: Opening Strategies,* shows that reflection has gone on holiday.[12] To treat the social contract as providing reasons for having a general will they would have to regard the freedom that figures in the contract as more fundamental than the substantive ends that they have as citizens. So regarding themselves would, however, undermine their allegiance to those ends. For once they recognize their freedom, they would also come to regard their social order as simply one among the many alternative choices they might make about how to live. So here again, there is no single point of view from which both the contractual justification and the common good morality might both be embraced.

This is an important problem, and my brief remarks here are intended to indicate how a more complete response might proceed, and not to provide that response. In these remarks I will assume that the general will *is* the solution to the problem of collective choice presented by Rousseau's social contract (see pp. 188–89, above). This may seem to beg the question presented by this second version of the dilemma. But that appearance is misleading. The question: Why have a general will? cannot be answered simply by showing that people constrained to make a social contract would agree to the general will. For even if they would, one still needs to say what reason there might be for individuals to comply with the terms of an agreement that they would make if they had to reach an agreement.[13]

First, then, consider the dilemma from the perspective of the individual with an interest in freedom but who does not have a general will. In this consideration, recall that Rousseau's defense of the general will premises the existence of social interdependence. It is not addressed to individuals who are not members of a society, with a view to persuading them that social cooperation is preferable to no cooperation. In assuming that there is social interdependence, he assumes that people have desires that can only be satisfied socially, developed capacities that can only be expressed socially, and ethical views. Nor does Rousseau hold that it is reasonable for a single person to have and to act on a general will under circumstances in which there is no assurance that others will do the same (*SC* II.6.ii; *GM* I.2).

Imagine, then, a person who has reasonable assurance that others will act to advance the common good, who recognizes that existing institutions do advance common interests, and who is aware (as we are now supposing) that the general will would be agreed to by the members of the society. The person is faced with two alternatives. The first is to have and to act on a general will, knowing that that will is the outcome of the social contract; the second is to conform to the requirements of the institutions only instrumentally, that is, only when such conformity advances their particular interests. Is there any reason to choose the former over the latter?

Rousseau supposes that a person who is self-consciously free desires to act in a way that manifests that freedom (to be "as free as they were before"). In view of that desire, the instrumental attitude is not satisfactory. For such a person wants more than an availability of alternatives within a system of laws and institutions that they view as a set of constraints imposed by others on their action. Rather, they want to be able to regard those institutional "constraints" as themselves conforming to their own judgments of what is right. Instead of taking the instrumental attitude which regards the social framework as constraining, the free person wants to affirm the framework of rules itself; they want to "have their own will as a rule" (*OC* III [*LM*], p. 807). But under circumstances in which there is a widely shared general will to which institutions do on the whole conform, to affirm the arrangements—to have one's own will as a rule—is just to have a general will. The relationship between the interest in freedom and the general will is, it should be emphasized, not of the same kind as the relationship between long-term self-interest and the general will suggested by self-effacing Hobbesianism. Having a supreme general will is a *means* for advancing long-term self-interests (even if it can only serve as such a means for someone who does not see it instrumentally). Having a general will is not, by contrast, a means to autonomy; under the conditions described above, it is, Rousseau claims, what autonomy consists in.

This indicates the lines along with a response to the first horn of the dilemma—the problem from the standpoint of the contractor—could be pursued. What of the second? Is it true that actually having a general will or a common good morality precludes regarding oneself at the same time as autonomous—that, as Riley puts it, a common good morality is the "very negation of voluntarism."

Riley's claim can be taken in either of two ways, corresponding to two interpretations of "common good morality." On the first, to endorse a common good morality is to endorse the communitarian relativist *theory* of morality on which there is no distinction between the moral rightness of an action for an agent and that action's advancing the common good of the community to which the agent belongs. This gives force to the claim that a common good morality is the very negation of voluntarism. But the fact that Rousseau endorses a non-self-effacing contractual justification of social norms shows that he did not believe the communitarian relativist theory of morality and did not endorse the view that an identification with the common good must be unreflective.

On the second construal, to have a common good morality is not to endorse a *theory* of morality but to embrace the *substantive moral conception* that one ought to act to advance the common good. But having put communitarian relativism to the side, it is no longer clear why a common good morality is inconsistent with the voluntarist theory embodied in the social autonomy interpretation of Rousseau's contract. There would be such inconsistency if considerations of autonomy could not support a general will. In the ways that I suggested earlier, however, reasons of autonomy can provide reasons for having a general will. So the second aspect of the dilemma can be handled by responding more fully to the first.

Much more would need to be said to provide such a full response, and to judge, finally, whether the social autonomy interpretation provides the basis for a full answer to Riley's dilemma about voluntarism and a common good morality, or whether it is really true that self-conscious freedom dissolves the general will. In considering that problem here, I have tried to defend Rousseau's views only in the limited sense of emphasizing that they are not straightforwardly *incoherent* in the ways that Riley suggests, and indicating some of the resources that Rousseau has for responding to his problem. Keeping in mind the importance of both autonomy and social interdependence in framing the fundamental problem addressed by the social contract, as well as the structure of the general will, Rousseau's solution to the fundamental problem may seem less an incoherent attempt to found an undifferentiated community on an abstract form of "voluntarism," and more a reasonable attempt to justify a social ideal in terms that might be of interest to those living both inside and outside of that ideal. . . .

Notes

1. Patrick Riley, *Will and Political Legitimacy* (Cambridge, MA: Harvard University Press, 1982). Discussions of Rousseau by Hegel and the British Hegelians also suggest such a tension. See G.W.F. Hegel, *The Philosophy of Right*, trans. T. M. Knox (Oxford: Oxford University Press, 1952), paragraphs 29, 258; *Lectures on the History of Philosophy*, volume 3, trans. E. S. Haldane and Frances Simpson (London: Routledge & Kegan Paul, 1892); T. H. Green, *Lectures on the Principles of Political Obligation* (Ann Arbor: University of Michigan Press, 1967), sec. 77; Bernard Bosanquet, *The Philosophical Theory of the State* (London: MacMillan and Company, 1899), pp. 84–102; Brand Blanshard, *Reason and Goodness* (London: Allen and Unwin, 1961), chap. 14, esp. pp. 402–403.

2. Rousseau's works are cited in the text as follows: *SC* I.6.i: *On the Social Contract*, ed. Roger D. Masters, trans. Judith R. Masters (New York: St. Martin's Press, 1978), Book I, chapter 6, paragraph 1; *GM* I.2: *Geneva Manuscript*, ed. Roger D. Masters, trans. Judith R. Masters (New York: St. Martin's Press, 1978),

Joshua Cohen

Book I, chapter 2; *PE: Political Economy*, ed. Roger D. Masters, trans. Judith
R. Masters (New York: St. Martin's Press, 1978); *D2: The Discourse on Inequality* in *The First and Second Discourses*, trans. Roger D. Masters and Judith R.
Masters (New York: St. Martin's Press, 1964); *E: Emile*, trans. Allan Bloom (New
York: Basic Books, 1979); *P: The Government of Poland*, trans. Willmoore Kendall (Indianapolis: Bobbs-Merrill, 1972); *C: Constitutional Project for Corsica*
in *Rousseau: Political Writings*, trans. Frederick Watkins (London: Nelson,
1953); *OC* III *(LM): Lettres écrites de la montagne* in *Oeuvres Complètes*, eds.
Bernard Gagnebin and Marcel Raymond, vol. 3 (Paris: Gallimard, Bibliothèque
de la Pléiade, 1959–1969); *OC* III *(PF): Fragments Politiques* in ibid.; *LD: Letter
to M. D'Alembert on the Theatre*, trans. Allan Bloom (Ithaca: Cornell University
Press, 1968).

    3. On freedom as an aspect of human nature, see *D2*, pp. 114, 167–68; *SC*
I.4.vi; *E*, p. 280. Chapter 7 of James Miller, *Rousseau: Dreamer of Democracy*
(New Haven: Yale University Press, 1984) provides an insightful treatment of
this central issue.

    4. In this formulation of the clauses of the contract, Rousseau does not say
that the general will provides *the* direction (or the *sole* direction) of a person
and his powers, but the *supreme* direction. Neglect of this distinction leads
naturally to the view that Rousseau endorsed a particularly extravagant form of
communitarianism on which the general will provides the sole direction. See,
for example, Cassirer, *The Question of Jean-Jacques Rousseau*, trans. Peter Gay
(Bloomington: Indiana University Press, 1963), p. 52.

    5. There are some fifty-five separate passages in the *SC* that at least men-
tion the general will. (I would like to thank Marilyn Webster for help in compiling a list of these passages.) The interpretation here comes from trying to piece
them together with one another and with passages in *GM*, *PE*, and elsewhere.

    6. Nannerl Keohane, *Philosophy and the State in France: The Renaissance
to the Enlightenment* (Princeton: Princeton University Press, 1980), p. 445; Judith Shklar, *Men and Citizens: A Study in Rousseau's Social Theory*, 2d ed.
(Cambridge: Cambridge University Press, 1985), pp. 185–86.

    7. Hilail Gildin (*Rousseau's Social Contract* [Chicago: University of Chi-
cago Press, 1983], pp. 54–56) and Keohane (pp. 439–42, 448) correctly emphasize that Rousseau's talk about the common good should be explicated in
terms of the interests of the individual members of an association. See *SC* II.i.i
Using the example of a pure public good, Gildin underscores as well that to
interpret the common good in terms of the common interests of individuals is
not to identify the general will with the will of all. A public good meets a common interest, but it would not be voluntarily provided by individuals acting on
their private interests. To put the point very schematically: the general will
wills the cooperative solution to a positive-sum game whose noncooperative
solution—the will of all—is Pareto suboptimal. For further discussion, see
Brian Barry, "The Public Interest," *Proceedings of the Aristotelian Society* 38
(1964): 9–14; W. G. Runciman and Amartya Sen, "Games, Justice, and the General Will," *Mind* 74 (1965): 554–62; David Braybrooke, "The General Will De-
mystified," unpublished; and W. T. Jones, "Rousseau's General Will, the Pareto
Principle, and the Problem of Consent," Caltech Social Science Working Paper,
no. 412 (December 1981).

8. On the requirement that the good of each be advanced, see *PE,* pp. 220–21; *OC* III *(PF),* p. 511; *OC* IV, p. 1126. Because the general will wills the common good, and the common good is understood in nonutilitarian terms, Rousseau holds that the institutional problem is to ensure that deliberations and decisions reflect the general will, not to protect citizens from that will (*SC* I.7.v, II.4).

9. On self-effacing theories, see Derek Parfit, *Reasons and Persons* (Oxford: Oxford University Press, 1984), secs. 9 and 17.

10. For discussion of problems faced by Hobbesian contractualism when it is understood as a public justification of terms of social cooperation, see David Gauthier, "The Social Contract as Ideology," *Philosophy & Public Affairs* 6, no. 2 (Winter 1977): 130–64.

11. Miller's emphasis on freedom (pp. 61–62, chap. 7) is close to the right track here, although he downplays the role of "particular" interests in protection of the person and goods. The problem, as Keohane underscores, is to find a way to combine both aspects of the self in the argument (Keohane, pp. 442–49, 461–63).

12. See Philippa Foot, "Morality as a System of Hypothetical Imperatives," in *Virtues and Vices and Other Essays in Moral Philosophy* (Berkeley: University of California Press, 1978), pp. 157–73; Bernard Williams, "Persons, Character, and Morality," in *Moral Luck* (Cambridge: Cambridge University Press, 1981), pp. 1–19; Michael Sandel, *Liberalism and the Limits of Justice* (Cambridge: Cambridge University Press, 1982); and Michael Walzer, *Spheres of Justice* (New York: Basic Books, 1983).

13. For discussion, see Rawls, *A Theory of Justice* (Cambridge, MA: Harvard University Press, 1971), pp. 257, 565, 570–72. Also, T. M. Scanlon, "Contractualism and Utilitarianism," in *Utilitarianism and Beyond,* eds. Amartya Sen and Bernard Williams (Cambridge: Cambridge University Press, 1982), pp. 116–19; and Bernard Williams, *Ethics and the Limits of Philosophy* (Cambridge, MA: Harvard University Press, 1985), pp. 64–70. I am following Rawls's distinction (p. 257) between construing the problem of the content of freedom as a collective choice problem and construing it as a problem for a "single self," and focusing here on the latter.

11

Rousseau, the Problem of Sovereignty and the Limits of Political Obligation

John Charvet

In one of his well-known utterances Rousseau says that the problem of the social contract is to show how a subject of communal law can nevertheless be said to obey only himself and remain as free as he was before.[1] The latter freedom consisted in his being his own master in a state of nature. Rousseau's answer to the problem is, of course, that the individual obeys only himself if he is ruled in the community by its general will, which is his own will. But as we know the general will is not necessarily the actual will of the community. Since the general will legitimatized constitution specifies a supreme popular legislative assembly operating a majority decision procedure, we can say that the constitutional sovereign—the final decision-making will—is the majority will of the people's legislative assembly.[2] This majority will may not, on occasion, will the general will. Since the general will is said to be sovereign, and indeed to possess absolute sovereignty, it must be sovereignty in a different sense from that in which the majority will is constitutional sovereign. Rousseau says that when the majority is not willing in accordance with the general will, freedom no longer exists.[3] This follows from his claim that the freedom of the subject of communal law depends on his subjection only to the general will.

Since the general will must be a "superior" sovereign to that of the majority will, whatever that could mean, it would seem that a citizen should be able to appeal from a decision of the majority to the general will. However, his account of the contract includes the standard contractarian argument, to be found in Hobbes and Locke and others, that a necessary condition of political society is the surrender by each contractor of the right of private judgement that he possessed in the state of nature.[4] Leviathan, or the community, or the general will substitutes for the multiplicity of private judgements on the good a binding public judgement. Rousseau endorses the absolute sovereignty of this public reason in common with Hobbes, and in effect Locke *malgré lui*,[5] precisely because he accepts their view that the maintenance of an authoritative public judgement is incompatible with the retention by the individual of the right to judge the justice of the laws. Of course, what they must mean by the right of private judgement here is the right of the individual to make a moral judgement that is authoritative for him in determining how he is morally permitted or required to act. The theory of absolute sovereignty holds that political association is possible only on condition that the "state" decides these matters for all. So if the envisaged appeal of the individual citizen from the majority will to the general will involves the reclaiming of his right of private judgement, it should not be permissible.

Yet, the surrender of private judgement on Rousseau's account is to the general will, not to the majority will. However, the general will is defined for the most part as the ideal will of the community for its common good—what each person would will as his good when he thinks, together with the others, of his good as community member, and not as separate individual. In this sense the sovereign "has no need to give guarantees to the subjects, because it is impossible for a body to wish to hurt all of its members . . . The Sovereign by the mere fact that it is, is always all that it ought to be."[6] But as such an ideal will the general will cannot be the actual will of a constitutional sovereign. For such a sovereign is necessarily a particular person or body of persons whose will may not be in conformity with the ideal. Rousseau's constitutional sovereign, as he is fully aware, may be corrupted. So it would seem that Rousseau ought to say that a citizen who believes that the majority will is corrupt may appeal to the general will. But what would such an appeal amount to? Since the general will is essentially ideal, there is, and can be no official body in the community that can declare it. If the majority will cannot, neither could any other. Yet if the appeal of the aggrieved citizen is to the general will as the ideal will of the community, he would appear to be claiming the right of private judgement against duly constituted public authority.

That Rousseau does not see the difficulty must be because he systematically identifies the sovereign general will as the ideal will of persons as community members with the actual constitutional sovereign.

For example, in describing the limits of Sovereign power he states that each contractor alienates to the community only that part of his liberty and possessions which the community needs, but that it is for the sovereign to make this judgement.[7] Presumably such a sovereign will cannot be morally criticized by the subject without his claiming an unacceptable right of private judgement. Yet this sovereign must be an actual constitutional sovereign, since his decision must produce a definite law. At the same time it is clear that Rousseau believes that the sovereign he is describing as making this judgement is the general will, and hence necessarily all that it ought to be. Furthermore, it would appear obvious that no one could seriously hold that the solution to the problem of private judgement in a state of nature involves the surrender of that judgement to a purely ideal will, since each person would still have to interpret the ideal for himself, and no move from the state of nature would have been achieved. The only possible solution is the creation of an actual constitutional sovereign with authority to bind everyone, thereby substituting his public judgement for the separate private judgements of the subjects. So Rousseau must believe that his ideal general will is at the same time actualized in the will of the constitutional sovereign. Yet *this* sovereign, as we know, may be corrupted.

We should perhaps attend to the fact that Rousseau is very much concerned in his political theory with the social and political conditions under which a majority decision of the legislative assembly can be expected to coincide with what the ideal general will would legislate. These conditions involve, on the one hand, the independence of each citizen of all the others in respect of his private life and interests, so that each is dependent on the others only politically in his public life as citizen, and on the other hand their equality (more or less). These stipulations are designed to ensure that when each citizen votes for a *general* law in the legislature, and so must express his particular interest in a general form, the interest that he generalizes will be one he shares with his equal and independent fellow citizens. It will be a common interest, and so will satisfy the requirements for a general will. We could, therefore, understand Rousseau to be saying that, provided my constitution is followed, the actual sovereign will be the same as the ideal sovereign, and so there will be no problem of private judgement. If the actual sovereign is corrupted, then freedom is impossible, and legitimate rule and political obligation disappear, so there is no point in raising the question of a subject's appeal from an unjust majority will. The problem is, nevertheless, that the subject must have exercised his private judgement in judging that the majority will is corrupt and hence illegitimate, and this is incompatible with the supposed conditions of political association, which Rousseau accepts.

I now want to consider this problem from a broader contractarian perspective. The problem of sovereignty for Hobbes and Locke, as I said, is also to substitute a unified public reason for the multiplicity of private reasons that exist in the state of nature. This problem does not arise, even for Hobbes, from the lack of common and knowable rules for preserving men in multitudes. Such rules exist; they are the laws of nature, and everyone can see that he has an interest in interacting with others on their basis. The difficulty is that, while everyone has good reason to follow the natural laws, which are both in each person's interest (if generally followed) *and* commanded by God; in fact each also has good reason to distrust the others' willingness to adhere in a state of nature, and under such insecure conditions the laws of nature permit, or indeed command, a person to give priority to his self-preservation over that of others. Hence in pursuing his self-preservation at the expense of others, he will not be acting contrary to the law of nature; he will be following its first law to preserve himself, and Hobbes's famous phrase regarding each person's right to everything is merely the most extreme expression of that situation.[8]

The solution to the predicament of the state of nature obviously involves the creation of a system of collective security through which persons can come to trust each other to follow the secondary laws of nature which enjoin equal respect for each other's liberty, and thus to act in ways which permit of everyone's preservation. But the achievement of this solution requires the surrender of each person's private judgement to the collective authority of the state. This authority unifies the multiplicity of private wills in one public will. In Hobbes's formula the sovereign represents the will of each subject, whose will is thus contained in the sovereign's will,[9] but I take the basic idea of this formula to be present also in Locke's and Rousseau's theories. It is the idea of the subject's commitment through the contract to pursue his self-preservation collectively, together with the others, through a common will designated as the sovereign who speaks for them all. The surrender of private judgement involves the contractor's undertaking no longer to pursue his self-preservation as an *individual* enterprise on the basis of which he has a right to put his self-preservation first in any conflict with another. Instead he commits himself to adopt a common standpoint on each person's self-preservation, including his own, which requires the non-prioritizing of anyone's right, and hence the acknowledgement of their equal rights. The sovereign's will must express this common standpoint, and hence be directed at the common good.

What, then, if the sovereign monarch or assembly fails to act from the common standpoint in pursuit of the subjects' common good? The sovereign is supposed to pursue the common good by following the laws of nature, or rather by giving the general principles of the natural law a determinate content appropriate to the particular situation of the collection of persons whose common will the sovereign expresses. The relation between the natural law and the common will is this: the secondary rules of natural law, which enjoin equal liberty and so on, if they are generally accepted and followed constitute the conditions under which *all* can be preserved, or rather under which each stands the best chance of being preserved. So the secondary rules express the standpoint of community or collective self-preservation. The primary rule, which commands everyone to preserve himself and to give himself the priority if he judges his preservation to be under threat, expresses the standpoint on the good of separate individuality.[10] Contractarian political theory, then, holds that persons cannot successfully follow the secondary rules of the law of nature and adopt the common standpoint on their good without creating a concrete sovereign, who will take decisions binding on everyone, and hence unify their wills in his will. The reason for this is primarily that if an individual acts on his own in adopting the common standpoint, he can have no security that others will reciprocate, and hence there will be a good chance that he will not be preserved. So the problem is not that the secondary laws of nature do not constitute a common standpoint on the good, for they are essentially rules for preserving men in multitudes. It is rather that in the absence of an effective coercive power persons cannot trust each other to pursue their good from that standpoint. There is, however, an additional theme to be found in that contractarian theory which emphasizes the indeterminacy of persons' rights in the state of nature, so that, even with good will and mutual trust, there would still be a need for a concrete collective authority to give determinacy to the general principles of equal liberty.[11]

The common standpoint on the good that is inherent in the secondary rules of natural law is essentially an ideal one. It is the standpoint of morally motivated persons who commit themselves to pursue their self-preservation only in so far as it is compatible with the equal rights of others. If an individual in the state of nature is directing himself by such a law, then he will be acting from a *general* standpoint on the good, yet he will be doing so by exercising his *individual* judgement in determining what the law requires of him and others. Since he has good reason to distrust others in a state of nature, he cannot reasonably act from the common standpoint in such a state. If he does so act, and the others do not reciprocate, he will not be preserved. Hence by the first law of nature he should not commit himself to act from the common standpoint outside a political society. The latter acting through the coercive power of its concrete sovereign brings about the conditions in which each can reasonably undertake to govern himself by a moral general will. However, political society involves a further act of surrender of individual judgement. The contractor must give up his individual self-direction by the natural law for the sake of a collective self-determination in accordance with that law through the judgement and will of the sovereign. The first act of surrender consists in the abandonment of the individual standpoint on the good, that is characteristic of the first law of nature, for the common standpoint of the secondary rules of natural law, while the second surrender is that of individual interpretation of the latter for the collective interpretation expressed through the sovereign. Although one can and must distinguish the two surrenders, the standard "Hobbesian" argument for the necessity of political society holds that they must be made simultaneously, for according to that argument it is reasonable to commit oneself to act from the moral standpoint only as a member of a political society possessing sovereign power.

We can now return to the question of what is to be done should the sovereign act contrary to the common standpoint on the good which constitutes the rational core of his sovereignty? What if he acts contrary to the natural law basis of his authority? According to the Hobbesian theory of absolute sovereignty, *nothing* can be done. For if we are morally allowed to appeal against the sovereign's will to the natural law principles which should be its foundation, then we would be claiming back the right of individual interpretation of the law of nature which has to be surrendered as the condition of political association. Furthermore, we cannot simply place ourselves in an individually determined moral position, for by reconstituting the state of nature relations between persons we immediately destroy the circumstances in which it is reasonable for us to commit ourselves to act from a moral will. We would be back with the first law of nature and the state of war.

It would seem that Hobbes must be right on this issue. We cannot claim a *moral* right to disobey the sovereign, not because the sovereign cannot be immoral, but because the existence of sovereign power is a necessary condition for the reasonableness of our adoption of the moral standpoint. Since there is no viable moral position outside the political community, we could have nowhere to stand from which we could be morally entitled to reject the sovereign's commands. The apparent ability of one or a few individuals to take up such a stance to the sovereign will depend on the willingness of the great majority to continue to obey. The supposedly moral few will in effect be moral free riders on the law abidingness of the remainder, and may be thought to deserve thoroughly the punishment the sovereign hands out to them.

Can we learn anything on this matter from Rousseau's conception of the sovereignty of the general will? If we understand the general will to involve the sovereignty of the common standpoint on the good, and hence the first surrender of the individual standpoint, then it expresses only the supremacy of the moral point of view over that of private interest or in other words the abandonment of the right of the individual to give priority to his self-preservation over that of others—the move, in Rousseau's terms, from the maxim of natural goodness, which tells us to pursue our good with the least possible harm to others, to the sublime maxim of rational justice which affirms the principle of equality.[12] However, in this sense the general will would be nothing other than the will to live with others from the standpoint of natural law, and Rousseau clearly adopts the "Hobbesian" argument on our obligations under natural law. He believes that there is a natural law, that it is ultimately derived from God and discoverable by our reason and to which we are obliged in conscience. But we are not required to follow it in a state of nature because to do so would expose the just to exploitation and destruction by the unjust, and everyone is entitled to preserve himself.[13] So the moral life for Rousseau as it is for Hobbes, is dependent on our forming a political community which can solve the security problem and give specificity to our duties. In other words we have to make the first and second surrenders of the individual standpoint at the same time, and the sovereignty of the general will understood as that of the moral standpoint is worthless unless it is actualized in the concrete will of a sovereign power.

Perhaps then the much maligned "Hobbesian" position on absolute sovereignty must be accepted after all. It seems clear at any rate that Rousseau must accept it. Nevertheless, we should recall what I claimed earlier regarding Rousseau's strategy for securing the conformity of the will of the actual sovereign to the underlying moral structure or ideal general will of the communal personality. We need arrangements which ensure the independence and equality of the citizens from a private point of view and their mutual dependence only at a public-political level, for then a majority will, having to be expressed in the general form of law, will be likely to satisfy the requirements of moral equality and so be a valid utterance of the general will. These arrangements can be understood as the constitution of the political community. They form a basic structure of laws and institutions that are just because they are ones which everyone would agree to in the founding contract made from a position of freedom and equality. So long as this constitution is preserved, then the decisions of the constitutional authorities will be good because the actual conditions in which the decisions are made by a majority, even though they give the majority power over the minority, will approximate to the ideal conditions of just association as defined through the founding contract. Yet, once again, nothing can guarantee that the popular assembly will not be corrupted, and the majority vote for a partial interest rather than the common interest.

However, once we have the idea of a just constitutional structure as providing the basic lineaments of the moral personality of political community, then the members can surely appeal from a decision of the sovereign to the constitution. But they must be able to appeal to someone—to a court that has responsibility to act as a guardian of the constitution. Otherwise, a person in rejecting the authority of a particular law will be reasserting his right to interpret the moral standpoint for himself, and as we have seen there can be no actual moral space for such a right to occupy. Of course, Rousseau does not make any provisions for a constitutional court, and in any case one may say that the introduction of such a body would involve only the postponement of the moral crisis that the community faces when the sovereign is believed to be acting contrary to the constitution. For the court itself may be corrupted or be subject to unjust political power, and surely the individual citizen will be capable of making that moral judgement, if he is in a position in the first place to bring a case before the constitutional court.

We need to examine more carefully the nature of the judgement by a citizen of the injustice, and hence moral invalidity, of a constitutionally legitimate decision. Undoubtedly, the citizen can, as a matter of fact, correctly or incorrectly judge that such and such a decision was corrupt. The issue is whether that judgement is a *moral* one in the sense in which the moral nature of the judgement involves the acknowledgement of a duty on persons to act on its basis. In that sense, if the citizen judges a law to be unjust he, *ipso facto,* claims that he is not morally obliged to obey it, and indeed is morally obliged to disobey. The moral nature of the judgement makes the judgement authoritative for him with regard to his actions, and thereby supersedes the authority of the sovereign over them. However, since there cannot be from the "Hobbesian" position, to which Rousseau subscribes, a duty to disobey the sovereign power, for that would suppose one had a duty to follow the secondary rules of natural law in a state of nature, the individual's critical judgement of the moral quality of the sovereign's will cannot be a moral one. It must be understood as a non-moral, objective judgement that the sovereign's actions are not in accordance with the moral standpoint and are morally worthless. The possibility of such a judgement presupposes that the moral standpoint possesses an objective, structural content, so that anyone can ascertain whether an action conforms to it or not without necessarily taking up the moral standpoint itself. The latter would involve the commitment to interact with others from its perspective, and no one has reason to do that except through the moral personality of the state and its sovereign power.

Let us suppose, then, that we are faced with an unjust sovereign who acts contrary to the constitutional basis of his authority, and we have no constitutional means of redress. What is our morally uncorrupted citizen to do? He can, of course, correctly judge that the sovereign is unjust from a moral point of view. But in doing so he will be taking up a standpoint independent of sovereign power, and hence independent of the moral point of view itself. In effect, he will have placed himself in a state of nature again in relation to the unjust sovereign, but also in relation to his fellow citizens. In a state of nature he can perfectly well see that the commands of the unjust "sovereign" are not conducive to civil peace, and hence to the possibility of moral life, and this fact relieves him of all *moral* obligation to obey them. But it does not mean that he has any moral obligation *not* to obey them, or to do what he can to defeat them. In the state of nature the first law of nature reasserts itself, and entitles a person to give priority to his own self-preservation over that of others. Hence he may be well advised from a prudential point of view to obey the unjust "sovereign," since this will not be a state of nature in which all have equal power. The freedom and equality that is necessarily characteristic of any state of nature is in the first place the equal freedom of all from any moral authority, so that no one is *morally* obliged to obey another. It is a morally free world. Yet the uncorrupt person, while morally free to do whatever is necessary to preserve himself knows also that his best chance of self-preservation in the long run, and that of his descendants, is to re-create a morally based state power. Hence he should (prudentially) seek to join himself with any others, whose judgements have likewise remained uncorrupted, in such an enterprise. This may involve him in withdrawing from his unjust state to throw in his lot with its enemies, should these exist. In that case he would be joining himself to a morally constituted state in an undertaking, that aims to create or preserve an international society of states, which itself conforms to the moral point of view.

The "Hobbesian" argument tells us that it is in our interest to endeavour to unite with others in a political association based on the secondary laws of nature. This must be seen as a prudential, and not a moral, interest. Hence it cannot explain how our prudential obligation to associate on the basis of the moral standpoint can be transformed into a moral obligation. For if the sole motivational support for political association is self-interest, and the adoption of the moral point of view necessarily requires the individual to subordinate his pursuit of his self-preservation to the constraints of equal laws, then he will never have abandoned the individual standpoint in the first place. Whenever the moral requirements conflict with self-interest, the individual cannot but by nature of his non-moral motivation pursue his individual self-preservation at the expense of the moral laws.

Now both Hobbes and Rousseau acknowledge the inadequacy of the purely prudential point of view on the reasons for following the natural law. They recognize that there is something called justice, and both think of justice as stemming from God and obliging us on a basis other than that of our natural self-interest.[14] So perhaps we should see them as saying that once the security problem of the state of nature is solved through the creation of a state structure in accordance with our prudential interest, then we are morally obliged to follow just laws by virtue of our obligation in conscience to observe God's laws. However, this appeal to a moral obligation to obey the secondary laws of nature, that is owed ultimately to God, would appear to make the moral obligation independent of our self-interested reasons for forming a political association on moral terms. If so, it would be fatal to the Hobbesian–Rousseauan position. For then we would have a moral obligation to follow the secondary laws of nature in a state of nature. This is what Locke asserts to be the case. But one obviously cannot say that a person has an unconditional obligation to obey the secondary laws of nature, and at the same time that under conditions of insecurity a person is entitled to give his own preservation priority over that of others. For the latter entitlement makes the moral obligation conditional on the settlement of the security problem, and thus on political association. One cannot be both unconditionally and only conditionally under moral obligation.

Is it, then, that God has made us in such a way that we naturally seek our own preservation and, having made us intelligent, has enabled us to see that we can best preserve ourselves through political association based on the secondary laws of nature; while at the same time God has *commanded* us to preserve ourselves and hence to create political association on moral terms? Although our prudential interest in moral community cannot make us moral enough to support what we nevertheless recognize to be in our interests, our obligation to obey God's commands does the trick by giving us a reason distinct from that of our natural self-interest to commit ourselves to the moral life, but only conditionally on the solution of the security problem. In other words we would have to treat God as commanding us to be moral only conditionally. We would have an unconditional obligation to God to make ourselves conditionally just. This may be Hobbes's view of the matter, but it is hardly Rousseau's. For Rousseau it is our conscience which reveals the obligatory nature of justice to us, and I cannot see that he is aware that justice, to be compatible with his political theory, should command us only conditionally.[15]

Is not the position attributed above to Hobbes similar to the one that Kant adopts in his political theory? On Kant's view there is only one obligation of justice in the state of nature, and that is to join with others in leaving that state and entering a political society.[16] This would be an unconditional obligation to bring about the political conditions under which we can fulfil our other obligations under natural law. However, a moral obligation to leave the state of nature would be different form a purely prudential obligation to the same effect, only if the former obliged us to seek to bring about a political union even at risk to our self-preservation. Since the general spirit of this proposal is to make our obligations of justice conditional on political union, it is surely unacceptable to retain an obligation that binds us unconditionally to acts which may be detrimental to our self-preservation. But if we interpret the obligation as requiring nothing more than what our prudential reason prescribes, then it is difficult to see that it adds anything to that reason, and thus to the solution of the motivational problem that arises from it.

It is the appeal to a moral or natural law which obliges independently of self-interest, whether the law is God-based or not, that destroys the coherence of the classical seventeenth- and eighteenth-century contractarian theories of political sovereignty and obligation. Such an independent moral obligation would, of course, provide the moral space for a citizen's morally inspired disobedience to an unjust sovereign that is lacking in the "Hobbesian" position. But the appeal undermines the contractarian theory of political association. Contemporary contractarianism in the manner of Rawls and Scanlon would seem to provide an answer to this difficulty.[17] For the principles of justice are purportedly derived from the contract itself through the idea of an agreement on terms of social cooperation under ideal conditions. Yet it is doubtful whether they do avoid a commitment to the equivalent of an independently valid and obliging moral law. Certainly Rawls fails to do this. For although the principles of justice are supposed to be derived from the contract, in fact the original position is structured so as to satisfy our prior moral intuitions as to what is fair. In effect we stipulate that there is an equal bargaining power between the parties represented by the veil of ignorance, and thus ensure that they will agree on the foundational principle of equality. But if we know that equal rights over the social primary good is what is fair independently of the contract, we are back with a natural law which would appear to be binding on us whether or not we have settled the security problem. As for Scanlon, his account of the contract depends on the notion of the "reasonable" in the formula "what no-one can reasonably reject" in an initial position in which the contracting parties are committed to cooperating on terms which they can justify to others. However, we are not told enough about the meaning of the reasonable to know how to interpret the Scanlonian contract. Despite the inadequacies of Rawls's and Scanlon's own theories, I still believe that their project to derive the principles of justice through the notion of a contract, subject to certain appropriate changes, is viable.[18]

Notes

1. J. J. Rousseau, *The Social Contract*, translated by M. Cranston, Penguin Books, Harmondsworth, 1968, p. 60.

2. Rousseau, however, requires qualified majority voting on more important decisions. Rousseau, *The Social Contract*, p. 154.

3. *Ibid.*, p. 154.

4. *Ibid.*, pp. 60–1; T. Hobbes, *Leviathan*, Basil Blackwell, Oxford, 1955, p. 112; J. Locke, *Two Treatises of Government*, Cambridge University Press, Cambridge, 1964, p. 342.

5. Locke is standardly supposed to permit a subject to appeal against his government to God, or in other words to Natural Law. He does in fact make a famous statement to this effect. But this would be to permit the *individual* to retain his state of nature right of private judgement of that law, and is incompatible with the passage quoted in note 4 which refers to the necessary surrender of his private judgement in the creation of political society. Locke for the most part refers not to the individual's rights against the government, but the *people's* right, and his conclusion emphatically states that the "power that every individual gave the society, when he entered into it, can never revert to the individuals again, as long as society lasts, but will always remain in the community; because without this, there can be no Community." *Two Treatises of Government,* pp. 445–6.

6. *The Social Contract*, p. 63.

7. *Ibid.*, pp. 74–75.

8. Actually the first branch of the first law says seek peace, and only the second branch tells us "by all means we can to defend ourselves." *Leviathan,* p. 85.

9. *Ibid.*, p. 107.

10. It may be questioned whether Locke embraces such a primary rule. Indeed he does in the following passage: "Everyone as he is bound to preserve himself, and not to quit his station wilfully; so by the like reason when his own preservation comes not in competition ought he, as much as he can, preserve the rest of mankind." *Two Treatises of Government,* p. 289.

11. *Leviathan,* p. 110; *The Social Contract,* p. 66. See also I. Kant, *The Metaphysical Elements of Justice,* Library of Liberal Arts, Bobbs-Merrill, Indianapolis, 1965, p. 76.

12. J. J. Rousseau, *A Discourse on Inequality,* translated by M. Cranston, Penguin Books, Harmondsworth, 1984, p. 101.

13. *The Social Contract,* pp. 80–1.

14. *Leviathan,* p. 94; see also pp. 104–5. *The Social Contract,* pp. 80–1. See also J. J. Rousseau, *Emile or On Education,* translated by Allan Bloom, Basic Books, New York, 1979, pp. 289–94.

15. *Ibid.*, p. 289.

16. *The Metaphysical Elements of Justice,* pp. 71–2.

17. J. Rawls, *A Theory of Justice,* Clarendon Press, Oxford, 1972; T. Scanlon,

"Contractualism and Utilitarianism," in A. Sen and B. Williams (eds.), *Utilitarianism and Beyond,* Cambridge University Press, Cambridge, 1982.

18. For a discussion of these changes, see J. Charvet, "Contractarianism and International Relations," in D. Boucher and P. Kelly (eds.), *The Social Contract from Hobbes to Rawls,* Routledge, London, 1994.

12

The General Will

Arthur Ripstein

Rousseau's political thought is sometimes considered a part of the contractarian tradition, if not its centerpiece. After all, the title of his best-
known work is the *Social Contract*. There is some reason to assimilate
Rousseau to the contractarian tradition; his appeal to a pre-social condition is of a piece with Lockean and Hobbesian concerns with explaining the possibility of *acquired* obligations.

But there is another, deeper, strain in Rousseau's thought, a strain
that resists easy assimilation to contractarianism. This is the issue
broached by two of Rousseau's best known, and most cryptic, concepts. The first of these is the general will; the second is the notion of
forcing someone to be free. These concepts address not merely the
acquisition of new obligations, but the very possibility of obligations.
They operate at a higher level of abstraction than normal contractarian
concerns. This has surprising, though perhaps welcome, implications
for a reading of the *Social Contract*: Rousseau is not particularly interested in the question of exactly which political structures and obligations the general will will issue. Rather, his concern is with the manner
in which any sort of structures are able to generate both obligations
and the possibility of freedom. While Hobbes is interested in the
causal powers of institutions to motivate, and Locke in the possibility
of legitimate institutions, Rousseau's concern is with the possibility of
institutions at all. Rousseau wants to know how an aggregate of persons
can become a creator of rights and obligations, able to coerce its members on grounds of freedom. " 'Finding a form of association that defends and protects with all the common force the person and goods of
each associate, by means of which each united with all, obeys none but

himself, and remains as free as before.' This is the fundamental problem whose solution is given by the *Social Contract.*"[1]

For Hobbes, institutions are judged and justified against the background of prior interests. For Locke, they are judged in relation to prior "natural" rights. For Rousseau, neither judgment nor justification can be prior; both must take place in a community.

> But the social order is a sacred right which serves as a basis for all others.
> However, it is not a natural right; it thus must be founded on covenants.
> The question is what those covenants are. (I. i) (M. p.47)

The question, then, is: how could something serve as the basis of right, if there are no "natural" standards of justification? In particular, how can covenants create rights?

In explaining Rousseau's view, I will develop an analogy between political community and the sort of "community" that is made up of the speakers of a natural language. Certain important distinctions are more clear in linguistic than in political communities. Like political communities, linguistic communities are made up of individuals who share an intuitive grasp of the principles governing their activity. Within limits, the members of a linguistic community also hold each other to those principles by correcting mistakes when they arise. But the parallel only goes so far: I shall not claim that linguistic communities generate obligations and freedom in the ways that Rousseau claims that political communities do.

I. The Will and the General Will

The central concept of *The Social Contract* is the "general will." Rousseau never explicitly defines the general will, and the task of making sense of it is made harder still by the fact that he does not provide a clear account of what he takes individual willing to be.[2] Yet it seems as though he wants to use the individual will as a model of the general will. His choice of the word "will" (*volonté*) suggests this, as does the notion of making the general will "one's own," substituting it for my private will in matters that affect the collectivity.

I. 1. Individual Wills

Let us begin, then, by briefly considering several sorts of intentions, or "wills."[3] The most obvious sort of intention is desire for some external object or state of affairs. We might call these "individual desires." Individual desires reveal themselves in their consequences. Their importance is manifested by the prevalence of teleological explanations of human action. Thus opening a window is a way of satisfying a desire for fresh air. Animals plainly have desires of this sort: the cat wants to catch the bird, the dog wants to be taken for a walk. Each acts to achieve some end, and the action is successful if the end is achieved. Prior to Contract and Society, *homo sapiens* can have only this sort of desire.

Individual desires may take social goods for their objects. Like desires for natural goods, desires for competitive social goods are always directed towards some end-state. Desires for the well-being of others share the same structure: if I want you to get a good night's sleep, I must tiptoe around the house to bring about the desired result.

Individual desires can come into conflict, both within the individual and between individuals. The latter sort of conflict does not depend on supposing anything like mutual antipathy; two people meaning well for each other might interfere with each other's projects in spite of themselves.

I.2 We-Intentions

A more interesting and immediately relevant case comes when interests must be shared in order to be realized. In such cases, co-operators, or potential co-operators, share intentions about what they as a group will do. Following Sellars, I will call such intentions to co-operate "we-intentions."[4] I will represent them as having the form:

Would that we, members of group C, do X.

Two sorts of we-intentions must be distinguished. I shall call the first sort "shared ends." Thus, for example:

Would that we, John, Paul, and Ringo, move the piano.

Like individual desires, shared ends aim at bringing about some result: in our example, the desire is satisfied if the piano is moved.

Shared ends may be consciously avowed, but they needn't be. Someone might unwittingly join in an ongoing activity, and actively help to accomplish it, yet not realize she is doing so. They are important in the completion of a wide variety of tasks. Rousseau recognizes their importance for the social contract:

> As men cannot create new forces, but only combine and control those which already exist, there is no other way in which they can preserve themselves than by forming an aggregation of their powers strong enough to overcome any resistance, putting themselves under a single motive and acting in concert. Such a sum of forces can only arise from the union of separate men. (I. vi) (M., p. 53)

If individuals had no ends in common they would not even form aggregates, let alone communities. But the mere sharing of ends is not sufficient to generate a community. Quite the opposite; all kinds of accidental collections of people share co-operative goals. Thomas Schelling once instructed a hundred subjects to meet an unidentified person in New York on a given date. They were given no other information, except that the unknown person was given the same information; the time and place were not determined. Schelling reports that over eighty of the people assembled under the clock at Grand Central Station at noon.[5] Here we have a clear example of the members of a group sharing a goal, and co-ordinating their behavior accordingly. Indeed, they even have the higher-order goal of sharing their goal with each other. Yet they do not form a community. Part of the reason is temporal; Schelling's group will dissolve as soon as its task is completed. But the deeper reason is clear: Schelling's aggregate places no obligations on its members.

Even the sharing of large-scale and long-term goals is not sufficient to create a community. Such shared ends are closer to what Rousseau calls "the will of all." Of themselves, they are not sufficiently stable to comprise a general will:

> For while it is not impossible for a private will to accord with the general will on some point, it is at least impossible for such an accord to be regular and enduring; for the private will inclines by its nature towards partiality, and the general will towards equality. (II. i) (M., p. 59)

The general will cannot be made up of the coincidence of private wills because private wills cannot be depended on to coincide.

I.3 Articles of the General Will

Consider now another sort of we-intention, brought out by contrast with a shared end. Imagine two similar, but importantly different proposals that Émile might make to Sophie:

> Let us buy two cars and a house in the suburbs, and send our children to good schools.

and

> Let us be lovers, we'll marry our fortunes together.

The difference is that whereas the first suggests a series of specific future projects, each with its own end-state, the latter does not. Rather, it sets the conditions for unspecified possible future interactions. For obvious reasons, I will call this sort of we-intentions "articles of the general will."

A linguistic parallel may help here. Contrast:

> Would that we, speakers of English, all yell "pimento."

with

> Would that we, speakers of English, permit inferences of the form *modus tollens*.[6]

The difference between these examples is not merely one of generality, but of structure. The first specifies a single interaction; the latter both sets the conditions of unspecified future interactions and includes a further condition of mutual enforcement.

All articles of the general will have the form:

> Would that we, the members of the community, each allow/forbid each other to do X.

Each such article includes three clauses: (i) the intention that I do x, (ii) the intention that I hold others to doing x, and (iii) the intention that others hold me to doing x. The third clause is central to Rousseau's thought. Every article of the general will includes what Rousseau calls the "tacit engagement":

> Would that we, willing though weak, held each other to our general will.

We can now proceed to political examples. Consider two prominent in Rousseau's day:

> Would that we, . . . allow no person to own another.

> Would that we, . . . allow each person to keep the product of his own labor.[7]

In each case, the content of "own" is left unspecified. If the principles are to have any force, the members of the community must agree about their interpretation. That agreement does not need be explicit any more than agreement about the grammatical and inferential rules of a language needs to be. Rather, the members of the community share a general will if they all agree in their judgments about what counts as a violation of the general will, even if they cannot fully articulate any principles underlying those judgments.

Rousseau's claim is that a community consists in a group of people in agreement both about the conditions of their interaction and their intention to hold and be held by each other to that agreement. To be the objects of that sort of agreement, the articles of the general will must be impartial; all must will the same thing. It must apply to all, each person able to judge how it applies to particular cases, including his or her own.

II. Applications

If the general will is understood as setting the conditions of future interaction among the members of a community, a number of Rousseau's more puzzling remarks fall into place.

II.1. The General Will and the Will of All

Rousseau contrasts the general will and the will of all as follows:

> There is often a great difference between the will of all and the general will; the latter studies only the common interest, while the former considers private interest, and is only the sum of individual desires. If we take

away from these same wills the pluses and minuses which cancel each
other out, the remaining sum of the difference is the general will. (II. iii)
(M., p. 61)

The will of all is easy enough to make out; we, the members of the
community, might each want a skating rink for our children, and thus
together all want to build it. Even without the arithmetic metaphor, the
general will is less clear. What would be left if everyone's private interest were canceled by any that conflicted with it? If I favor a skating rink,
and you favor a ski-jump, our wills cancel each other, and our children
will be left with nowhere to play. If this sort of disagreement were
to aggregate, our community might be paralyzed; why suppose that
anything of importance would survive cancellation? The problem is not
that long-term sharing of goals is impossible or even unlikely; the community may have a "will of all." But the will of all cannot be definitive of
the community, because it is at the mercy of every change in individual
desires.[8] If the general will governs the conditions of interaction of the
community, it would survive the cancellation of *any* individual desires
by conflicting desires. The general will is the "sum of the differences"
not because it is not canceled, but because it cannot be canceled by
individual desires. Even if we cannot agree about what winter sport
facility to build, we might still agree about how to resolve our disagreements.

II.2 Voting

This reading of the general will has the further virtue of making
sense of Rousseau's cryptic remarks about voting:

> The votes of the greatest number always bind the rest; and this is a conse-
> quence of the contract itself. Yet it may be asked how a man can be free
> and forced to conform to wills which are not his own. How can the oppos-
> ing minority be both free and subject to laws to which they have not
> consented?
>   I answer that the question is badly formulated. The citizen consents to
> all the laws, even those that are passed in spite of him, and even those
> that punish him when he dares to break any one of them. The constant
> will of all the members of the state is the general will; it is through it that
> they are citizens and free. When a law is proposed in the people's assem-
> bly, what is asked of them is not precisely whether they approve of the
> proposition or reject it, *but whether or not it is in conformity with the*

general will which is theirs; each by giving his vote gives his opinion on
this, and the counting of votes yields a declaration of the general will.
When, therefore, the opinion contrary to my own prevails, this proves
only that I have made a mistake, and that what I thought to be the general
will was not. (emphasis added) (IV. ii) (M., p. 110)

Leaving aside for the moment the question of freedom, how could a
group of people disagree about their common ends, or worse yet, their
common principles of association, and still amount to a community? If
the sharing of principles is the basis of community, how is such disagreement even possible? If disagreement is possible, and some can be
mistaken, why suppose that the majority knows best? What kind of
question would a majority be especially well qualified to answer?

Consider our linguistic parallel again: linguistic communities typically have a fair bit of slack; deviant usages and even deviant grammars
are not uncommon. Suppose, though, that for some reason it were to
matter whether, say, "critique" was to be used as a verb. We can imagine a convention of the speakers of the language, or their delegates,
voting on whether it should be so used. If current practice among aca-
demics is any guide to the probable outcome of such a vote, a substantial minority would be outvoted. Though it is perhaps awkward to say
that those in the minority were simply mistaken about whether it was
a verb, it is not all that far from the truth. The convention of speakers
would be *deciding* future usage on the basis of past usage. Past usage
provides inconsistent precedents; the members of the linguistic community must decide which ones to extend into the future. Once that
decision is made, those in the minority are mistaken about what future
usage will be. If everyone votes in good faith, each person does not
express her preference about its future use, out of a desire to minimize
his or her past errors instead, each attempts to articulate his or her
sense of what the community's practice is. In so doing, each is not
merely making a judgement about actual usage; instead each seeks to
articulate what is considered correct usage. Though the linguistic community's shared sense of correctness may diverge from the majority's
actual usage, the majority cannot be mistaken about what the community takes to be correct.

In this example, Rousseauian voting combines elements of *creating*
the general will and *discovering* it. The linguistic general will is created
by the practices of the community, including its conception of correctness. Although that shared conception of correctness does not exist

apart from the community, any member of the community may be mistaken about it on any occasion.

Something similar can be said about the general will of a political community: voting on the general will is necessary in those cases in which the existing general will fails to speak with a single voice. The general will is not a comprehensive and closed system of rules, but a variety of overlapping and sometimes conflicting principles, each of which has some claim to the community's allegiance. As new circumstances arise, these considerations may come into conflict, or fail to speak with a single voice. The members of the community must then decide which has a greater claim on them, both by considering their grounds for accepting them and the consequences of their extension. After considering both sides, each voter articulates his or her sense of the community's practice to judge whether, say, introducing a progressive income tax is in keeping with it. Those in the majority determine what the general will will be; in so doing they decide what the community's future practice will be.

Why leave the decision up to the majority rather than, say, the Académie Française? In the linguistic case, there is no clear answer, perhaps because it doesn't much matter whether a minority, or even a majority of the people are dissatisfied with the result. Also, in the linguistic case there is some temptation to say that the majority may not have fully mastered the nuances of the language.

In a political community, the majority occupies a special position. As mutual enforcers of the general will, the members of the community share the intention to be held by the others to the articles of the general will. If this is to be possible, each must presume the others to be capable of interpreting it in particular cases. This is crucial to Rousseau's account of voting. It explains his insistence that there be no communication between voters: each has sufficient command of the general will to weigh all of the relevant arguments alone.[9] It also accounts for placing the decision in the hands of the majority rather than some more select panel of experts. The entire community is expert in interpreting the general will. When experts disagree, the majority decision reveals what most members of the community had presumed all along. Thus it reveals the content of the agreement that all had accepted. That is why Rousseau says that majority vote is "a consequence of the contract itself." In consenting to the articles of the general will, they also consent to others' interpretations of it.

What of the minority who disagree? Their disagreement concerns the interpretation and extension of the existing articles of the general will. They are mistaken about what the community will hold its members to. As a result, they are also mistaken about the full consequences of the articles of the general will they have already consented to. Thus they are mistaken about what they have consented to all along. Presumably they can also be shown that they were mistaken, by the very process of reasoning that led the majority to reach its decision.

Rousseau's account is most plausible in the case of an overwhelming majority. If each voter supposes him or herself to agree with all of the other voters, but is not certain of the details of what they agree about, those who find themselves outvoted by a majority might plausibly concede that they were mistaken about what they had agreed to. The conviction that one shares a we-intention with others will outweigh suppositions about the detail of its content. In the case of a bare majority, those in the minority might wonder whether they all had been party to the same agreement to begin with. It is far easier to suppose an isolated error is an error.[10]

Finally, it is important to keep in mind the particular circumstances in which the need for a vote will arise. Questions of policy—for example whether to build a particular road or bridge—do not lend themselves to Rousseau's account of voting. Rousseau concedes that a democracy empowered to decide all issues is the ideal government for gods, but doubts that it is suited to mortals attending to public affairs.[11] In such cases, the outvoted minority must accept a policy based on preferences they may not share. There may be something to be said in favor of democratic decisions in cases in which a "will of all" is lacking, but it cannot be plausibly maintained that the minority was mistaken— except in the trivial sense that they were mistaken about the outcome of the vote.[12] Rousseau is not talking about majority approval, but about majority appraisal. The members must decide whether or not some proposal is in keeping with the general will, that is, whether it is in keeping with a perspective that they all suppose themselves to share. It is because that perspective is shared that the votes of the majority outweigh those of the minority.

II.3 Freedom

Now that we have seen the structure of Rousseau's account of political community, it is natural to ask whether that account can bear the weight of political obligation. What normative force is carried by the sort of agreement Rousseau describes? The answer is to be found in Rousseau's cryptic comments about freedom. If the general will can justify forcing someone to be free, it can also create obligations.

Recall the two remarks he makes on this point:

> Whoever refuses to obey the general will shall be constrained to do so by the whole body, which means nothing other than that he shall be forced to be free. (I. vii) (M., p. 55)

> As a result of the contract . . . they have exchanged natural independence for freedom. (II. iv) (M., p. 62)

The general will creates freedom in two ways. Only one of these has a parallel in language. Community makes a certain kind of freedom possible because it makes new modes of interaction possible by providing means for forming reliable expectations about one's fellows. Fixed rules governing the use of land allow one to engage in long term cultivation. This is not a trivial matter; the security provided by a community is the precondition of an important sort of freedom. It is important for Rousseau:

> Although in civil society man loses some of the advantages that belong to the state of nature, he gains far greater ones; his faculties exercised and developed, his mind enlarged, his sentiments ennobled, and his whole spirit elevated. (I. viii) (M., p. 56)

This is still "natural" freedom, the existence of expanded opportunities and the ability to appreciate them, and the absence of constraints on their pursuit. Here the parallel with language is simple and obvious: without shared linguistic practices, the possibilities of communication and expression are curtailed or perhaps even vitiated.[13]

But this is not the only sense in which the general will creates freedom. If we are to make sense of the notion of "forcing to be free," something more robust is called for; agreeing with one's fellows on every issue, or even every procedural issue, is not required in order to benefit from the expanded opportunities provided by association.

To understand Rousseau's positive account of freedom, we must leave the parallel with language behind; it does not extend to the justification of coercion. Isolated, or even systematic grammatical or semantic errors are compatible with reaping the benefits of a stable language. There may be something to be said for correcting mistakes of language, but it is difficult to see how these are matters of freedom. In the political realm, it might be legitimate to constrain wrongdoers for any number of reasons; Rousseau makes the strong claim that in the process their freedom is enhanced.

One promising approach is to suppose that the agent has chosen to conform to the general will, thus justifying coercion as a way of resolving a conflict between two incompatible desires. If a citizen wants both to act on the general will and to do something it forbids, then there is some sense to be made of such a suggestion; the agent is freely acting on one of her desires, in a situation in which she cannot act on both.[14] This seems to be a promising line, for it makes coercion depend on the coerced person's will. But as an account of freedom, it has a serious gap: there must be some reason for resolving the conflict in favor of the general will rather than whichever desire the agent considers more pressing at the time. After all, the general will has a special status. If someone has two conflicting desires, say for both chocolate and vanilla ice cream, when she can have only one, forcing her decision in *some* direction might make her free, but there is no particular direction in which she should be forced. We need some account of what enables the general will to override conflicting desires on grounds of freedom.

Rousseau is explicit about his conception of freedom only once in the *Social Contract,* when he speaks of "moral freedom, which alone makes man the master of himself; for the impulse of appetite alone is slavery, while obedience to a law one prescribes to oneself is freedom" (I. viii) (M., p. 56). Freedom is somehow related to self-rule, but Rousseau does not say exactly how. In *Émile* Rousseau offers a seemingly different account of freedom, equating it with independence from the will of another. We need some account of how a community can allow one self mastery and freedom from appetite without turning into dependence on the will of another.

Commonplace examples make the notion of freedom as overcoming the impulse of appetite plausible: the dieter who succumbs to temptation, and the "ex"-smoker who sneaks a secret puff have abandoned their long term plans for the sake of immediate temptation. They are less free than they would be if they could hold back entirely. Metaphors of "enslavement" complement those of addiction. The reason that such persons are "enslaved," more so than regular smokers and gourmands, is that they have decided to control their various appetites. If that decision is to be more than an empty ritual, it must apply even when temptation gets in the way. Otherwise each is refraining only when they have no inclination to succumb, which is not refraining at all. The failure to stick with their decisions places their behavior outside the control of their wills. The person enslaved by impulse, like the person subject to the will of another, has a will of her own, but is unable to act on it. Although the impulses each is subject to are their own, they are not subject to their will.

So far we have a conception of metaphysical rather than political freedom. The enslaving desire is the momentary impulse; sticking with one's longstanding desire is the means to freedom. This cannot be the entire account for two reasons. First, the sort of violations of the general will that Rousseau is most concerned with involve deliberate and reflective violation. The person who must be forced to be free is not the person who says "I don't know what came over me"; but the person who plans and carries out some crime.[15] The conflict is not between momentary impulse and considered intention, but between considered intention and we-intention. Why should the we-intention prevail? Second, in joining society, one "exchanges natural for moral freedom"; Rousseau owes us some account of why this sort of moral freedom is not available outside of a community. If he can show that, he will have shown how one can be forced to be free.

In forcing the agent to act in conformity with the general will, the community is forcing him to act on his most important choice: to become a member of that community. He has chosen to will impartially with all of the others: to do what each allows the others to do, and to avoid doing what each forbids the others to do. In so choosing, he has also chosen to be held to that will if necessary: just as the dieter's decision would be empty unless she wishes to act on her diet even when she is tempted not to, so the citizen must intend to accept the general will at all times. Otherwise the choice to do as they allow him to is empty. The general will always includes what Rousseau calls the "tacit engagement": "Would that we, willing though weak, held each other to our general will." Coercion is legitimate on grounds of freedom because the agent has *chosen* to be coerced. That is why the general will must win out if it is at odds with any individual desire. Otherwise it has not been willed at all.[16]

We are left with the question of why the choice to be a member of a community is more important than any particular desire. Consider our examples of the dieter or smoker again. Each can plainly continue to intend not to overeat or smoke even while succumbing. The friend who destroys the secret cache of cigarettes or refuses to stop for ice cream can be said to be forcing the weak willed person to be free by holding her to her will. In each of these cases, the choice to refrain from smoking or overeating is a more important choice because it involves a genuine exercise of will, and hence at least holds out the possibility of free action. The desire to quit smoking includes the desire to have it outweigh conflicting desires. Thus it involves a deeper exercise of will then the impulse that it comes into conflict with. That is the sense in which it is a law given to oneself, binding in general rather than just applying in a particular instance.

Just as the desire to quit smoking involves the desire to outweigh conflicting desires, so does the desire to will collectively with the other members of one's community. It carries with it the tacit engagement that one be held to it. If one has given such a law to oneself, its scope ensures that it outweighs any other particular desire. Compared to the general will one has accepted, any particular desire is just a passing fancy. If assent to the general will is to have any consequences at all, it must outweigh all competing desires.[17] Still, accepting the general will as fully binding may be more than most people would agree to. However deep an exercise of will it may be, Rousseau needs some further account of its appeal. It is to that account that we must now turn.

III. The Social Contract and the Social Contract Tradition

Rousseau's account of the ability of institutions and agreements to create obligations illustrates his distance from the social contract tradition of Hobbes, Pufendorf, and Locke. The metaphor of a contract has two strands to it, which can be brought out by considering legal contracts.

First, a contract is an agreement in which all parties consent to the specified arrangements. On the other hand, contracts are normally made among parties taking no interest in one another,[18] on the basis of their estimation of the advantages it will bring. As Locke puts it, parties contract "Only with an intention in every one to better preserve himself, his liberty, and his property—for no rational creature can be supposed to change his condition with an intention to be worse."[19]

Rousseau keeps one element of the legal model by making all of the members of the community parties to the contract. But he rejects the second. In contrast, both Hobbes and Locke reject the first, but adopt the second. Hobbes supposes that no state of nature ever occurred, and so does not think that the agreement to institute a commonwealth ever actually took place. Instead, his discussion of the state of nature is meant to show that people *would* agree to institute a sovereign in such circumstances, and so to show that "sovereignty by acquisition" is legitimate.

Rousseau cannot justify particular arrangements by showing that they would be chosen by agents concerned to advance their own interests because there is no common currency in which to compare the goods provided by agreement with any imaginable alternative: "Although in civil society man loses some of the advantages that belong to the state of nature, he gains far greater ones; his faculties exercised and developed, his mind enlarged, his sentiments ennobled, and his whole spirit elevated" (I. viii) (M., p. 56). Anyone in the imagined state of nature would be foolish to surrender anything in return for a promised enlarging of his mind, ennobling of his sentiments, and elevation of his spirits, for prior to enlargement, ennoblement, and elevation, their rewards would be inconceivable. Nor can we imagine a group coming together and realizing that such advantages could be gained if only they would agree to some set of rules. The ability of the general will to generate obligations does not derive from its origins in individual self-interest; its justificatory force derives from being shared by the members of a community, whatever their reasons for sharing it.[20] The distance between the two approaches reveals itself on two issues central to the tradition Rousseau rejects: the "free rider" problem, and the issue of tacit consent.

III.1 Free Riders

It is important to contrast Rousseau's justification of coercion on grounds of freedom with the superficially similar problem of coercing "free riders" to bear their share of the costs of achieving some shared end. The difference between the two problems illustrates the distance between Rousseau and the social contract tradition. Political life is rife with free-rider problems; I might endorse a progressive tax on income as a way of funding public goods like parks and libraries, yet not wish to pay my share. My fellow-citizens have every reason to coerce me: without my contribution, each of them will need to shoulder an additional burden; without the threat of sanctions, there may be so many free riders that the project cannot be completed.

Rousseau was plainly aware of the free rider problem; in the *Discourse on the Origins of Inequality*[21] he gives an example of a member of a stag hunt who abandon the co-operate venture in order to chase a passing hare. Free riders do not consent to the laws they exempt themselves from; they are what Rousseau calls "foreigners" living among the citizens. The difference is important; non-citizens are like Hobbesian or Lockean contractors in that they obey the laws of the community based on their estimation of the advantages of doing so. Should they no longer find conformity to those laws advantageous, there is no sense in which they intend to conform. Because their intention to conform was entirely instrumental, they gain nothing by way of an exercise of their will by being held to it once the intention has passed. They may be liable to coercion on grounds of equity or efficiency, but not on grounds of freedom.[22]

III.2 Tacit Consent

The limited application of Rousseau's account of freedom has immediate consequences for the issue of tacit consent. Rousseau does not presume that residence in a community implies "tacit consent" to its laws. If the choice to be a member of the community is to be binding and justify coercion, a stringent condition must be met. Rousseau saw the danger in tacit consent models, a danger pointed out most devastatingly by his one-time patron, Hume:

> Should it be said, that, by living under the dominion of a prince, which one might leave, every individual has given his *tacit* consent to his authority, and promised him obedience; it may be answered, that such an implied consent can only have a place, where a man imagines that the matter depends on his choice. . . . Can we seriously say, that a poor peasant or artisan has a free choice to leave his country, when he knows no foreign language or manners, and lives, from day to day, by the small wages which he acquires? We may as well assert, that a man, by remaining in a vessel, freely consents to the dominion of the master, though he was carried on board while asleep, and must leap into the ocean, and perish the moment he leaves her.[23]

Rousseau limits his claims about consenting to the general will to what he calls "free states," for, "elsewhere, family, property, lack of asylum, necessity or violence may keep an inhabitant in the country unwillingly, and then his mere residence no longer implies consent to the contract or to the violation of the contract" (IV. ii,n.) (M., p. 110). These are stringent conditions of *natural* freedom which must be met if it is to be legitimate, on grounds of *civil* freedom, to coerce wrongdoers.

The very factors that Rousseau supposes prevent consent from creating obligations are the grounds that Hobbes and Locke suppose bring people into society. When the conditions are met—staying in the community is not a matter of necessity or even material advantage—the agent has chosen to be a part of the community. To act against this choice is to yield to momentary temptation, and act unfreely. Thus when one violates it, one can be forced back to freedom.[24]

Notes

1. Jean Jacques Rousseau, *du Contrat Social* (Paris: Gallimard Editions Pleiade, 1964), I.vi. All translations are my own; for convenience I have included page references to Judith Masters' translation (New York: St. Martin's Press, 1978) as in (M., p. 53) as well.

2. In *Discours sur l'origine et les fondements de l'inegalité parmi les hommes* (Paris: Gallimard Editions Pleiade, 1964) Rousseau does distinguish two types of desire, *amour de soi,* or self love, and *amour propre,* or pride. Unfortunately for our purposes, he focuses on their origins rather than their role in motivating behavior.

3. I borrow this analytical device from Peter King, "Toward a Theory of the General Will," *History of Philosophy Quarterly,* vol. 4 (1987), pp. 33–51.

4. Wilfrid Sellars, *Science and Metaphysics* (London: Routledge and Kegan Paul, 1966), Ch. 6.

5. Thomas Schelling, *The Strategy of Conflict* (Cambridge, MA: Harvard University Press, 1980), pp. 55–56.

6. The parallel with language may seem imperfect, because the overwhelming majority of we-intentions shared by a linguistic community can seldom be made explicit, and may not even be explicable in principle. In fact, this apparent disanalogy is not a disanalogy at all. As we shall see, the we-intentions of a political community rest on practical, rather than explicit, understanding in a similar way.

7. Marx's call for the abolition of wage labor can be cast in these terms: "Would that we, workers of the World, allow no person to *hire* another."

8. Roger Masters, *The Political Philosophy of Rousseau* (Princeton: Princeton University Press, 1968) misinterprets Rousseau's arithmetic metaphor, and construes the general will as the overlap of individual desires. Hegel seems to have misread Rousseau in a similar way, and made an obvious objection:

He takes the will only in a determinate form as the individual will, and he regards the universal will not as the absolutely rational element in the will, but only as a "general" will which proceeds out of this individual will as out of a conscious will. The result is that he reduces the union of individuals in the state to a contract and therefore to something based on their arbitrary wills, their opinion, and their capriciously given consent.

The Philosophy of Right, translated by T. M. Knox (Oxford: Oxford University Press, 1952). The coalition of individual wills is arbitrary, and their giving of consent capricious, because the area of overlap between individuals has no rationale; it is merely coincidental. Rousseau's conception of the general will is more sophisticated; he maintains that the general will tends towards equality (II.i), not uniformity. His limitation of the general will to institutional arrangements makes this clear.

9. As we have seen, the members of the community must regard one another as competent judges of the content of the general will. Thus there is nothing to be gained by allowing discussion. Discussion also carries risks. Any isolated voter might be moved by extraneous and irrelevant considerations; communication among voters makes it possible for such extraneous factors to compound due to eloquence, personal loyalties, and the like.

10. I fear that this may create as many problems as it solves for Rousseau. The picture that emerges is one on which to be mistaken is to misunderstand; if one can be mistaken about a general will that one has consented to, in what sense is that consent genuine? It seems as though those who are outvoted may find themselves no longer consenting. Does this show that they never really did consent, or that their consent was capriciously given? I confess to seeing no way for Rousseau to claim that in such circumstances they can nonetheless be freely held to it.

11. III.iv. M, p. 85.

12. Immediately following the passage just quoted, Rousseau does distinguish between "laws" and "business matters" and suggests that both may be subject to voting. However, given his insistence that voting involves judgments about conformity with the general will, he must be distinguishing between general and particular rulings. Particular "business matters" require immediate actions, which is why Rousseau supposes a bare majority is sufficient.

13. On the "expressive freedom" created by language, see Robert Brandom "Freedom and Constraint by Norms," *American Philosophical Quarterly,* vol. 16 (1979), pp. 187–96.

14. I owe this suggestion to Peter King, "Toward a Theory of the General Will."

15. There may be some cases in which the general will allows appetites to be kept in control; the kleptomaniac is perhaps liberated by overtly enforced property laws and rehabilitation programs; the drug addict trying to reform is aided by limitations on the availability of drugs. Such examples are still unrepresentative; each is being forced to a freedom that is available, at least in principle, outside of society.

16. What of the obvious objection that the individual might have *changed his mind,* and no longer wishes to be a part of the community? If that change of mind is genuine he can no longer be coerced on grounds of freedom. Whether there are other legitimate grounds of coercion depends on the details of the particular case.

17. What of those renegades who self-consciously choose not to be a part of any community? This is not a possibility that Rousseau takes seriously. Who would choose to belong to no community, and forego all possibility of stable conditions of interaction? Perhaps Rousseau himself; he spent his life scorning the decadence and dishonesty of the societies he found himself in. Rousseau's *Confessions* reveal how far his own life and his own world fell short of the ideals he aspired to for both individuals and communities; perhaps the grounds of legitimate coercion and conformity arise only in communities more voluntary than those Rousseau found himself in.

18. Or, at least insufficient interest to simply carry out their end for the other party's benefit.

19. John Locke, *Second Treatise of Government* (Indianapolis: Bobbs-Merrill, 1952), p. 73.

20. Rousseau's own account of the content of the general will in specific cases involves a legislator who bestows a suitable set of laws and mores on a community. The examples he offers are all classical: Moses, Numa, and Lycurgus. I cannot explore the role of the legislator in detail here; suffice it to say that the legislator does not bestow laws by showing them to be advantageous to the members of the community. Rousseau claims that the legislator studies the community and chooses laws in keeping with their national temperament.

21. See note 2 above.

22. There may be cases in which somebody consents to a different law than is in effect, for example wishing that the law prohibiting slavery or murder prevent others from owning or killing him, but not prevent him from owning or killing others. The person who wishes to be exempt from the law but protected by it is a "foreigner"; one cannot consent to a different general will than the rest of the community, for it is essential that it be shared. Rousseau is sometimes thought of as an intellectual forerunner of modern "totalitarian" regimes; because his account of freedom only applies to those who have consented to the general will, the charge is plainly unfair.

23. David Hume, "Of the Original Contract" in David Hume, *Essays Moral, Political, and Literary* (Indianapolis: Liberty Press, 1985), p. 485. Hume's essay was originally published in 1748, fourteen years prior to the *Social Contract.* Although Rousseau did not read English, his long association with Hume's Parisian followers makes it plausible to suppose that Hume's objection to theories of political consent was familiar to him.

24. I am grateful to Dale Aaron, David Gauthier, Peter King, Calvin Normore, Benjamin Zipursky, and an anonymous referee for comment and discussion. An ancestor of this paper was read at the Canadian Philosophical Association Annual Congress in May, 1986, where Duncan MacIntosh acted as commentator.

Bibliography

1. General

Elshtain, Jean Bethke. *Public Man, Private Woman: Women in Social and Political Thought*, pp. 100–27, 147–70. Princeton: Princeton University Press, 1981.

Gauthier, David. "The Social Contract as Ideology." 1977. Reprinted in *Moral Dealing: Contract, Ethics, and Reason*, pp. 325–54. Ithaca, N.Y.: Cornell University Press, 1990.

Lessnoff, M. H. *Social Contract*. London: Macmillan, 1986.

Rapaczynski, Andrzej. *Nature and Politics: Liberalism in the Philosophies of Hobbes, Locke, and Rousseau*. Ithaca, N.Y.: Cornell University Press, 1987.

Riley, Patrick. *Will and Political Legitimacy: A Critical Exposition of Social Contract Theory in Hobbes, Locke, Rousseau, Kant, and Hegel*. Cambridge, Mass.: Harvard University Press, 1982.

Shanley, Mary Lyndon. "Marriage Contract and Social Contract in Seventeenth-Century English Political Thought." In *The Family in Political Thought*, ed. J. Elshtain, pp. 80–95. Amherst: University of Massachusetts Press, 1982.

2. Hobbes

Brown, K. C., ed. *Hobbes Studies*. Oxford: Basil Blackwell, 1965.

Cranston, M., and R. S. Peters, eds. *Hobbes and Rousseau*. New York: Anchor Books, 1972.

Curley, Edwin. "Introduction to Hobbes' *Leviathan*." In Thomas Hobbes, *Leviathan*, ed. E. Curley, pp. viii–xlvii. Indianapolis: Hackett, 1994.

Gauthier, David. "Hobbes' Social Contract." In *Perspectives on Hobbes*, ed. G. A. J. Rodgers and A. Ryan, pp. 125–52. Oxford: Clarendon Press, 1988.

———. *The Logic of Leviathan: The Moral and Political Theory of Thomas Hobbes*. Oxford: Clarendon Press, 1969.

————. "Thomas Hobbes: Moral Theorist." 1979. Reprinted in *Moral Dealing: Contract, Ethics, and Reason*, pp. 11–23. Ithaca, N.Y.: Cornell University Press, 1990.

————. "Taming Leviathan." *Philosophy & Public Affairs* 16 (Summer 1987): 280–98.

Gert, Bernard. "Introduction." In Thomas Hobbes, *Man and Citizen*, ed. B. Gert, pp. 3–32. Indianapolis: Hackett, 1991.

Hampton, Jean. *Hobbes and the Social Contract Tradition*. Cambridge: Cambridge University Press, 1986.

Kavka, Gregory S. *Hobbesian Moral and Political Philosophy*. Princeton: Princeton University Press, 1986.

King, Preston, ed. *Thomas Hobbes: Critical Assessments*. 4 volumes. London: Routledge, 1992.

Leyden, W. von. *Hobbes and Locke: The Politics of Freedom and Obligation*. New York: St. Martin's, 1982.

Lloyd, S. A. "Contemporary Uses of Hobbes' Political Philosophy." In *Rational Commitment and Social Justice: Essays for Gregory Kavka*, ed. J. Coleman and C. Morris. Cambridge: Cambridge University Press, 1998.

Macpherson, C. B. *The Political Theory of Possessive Individualism: Hobbes to Locke*. Oxford: Clarendon Press, 1962.

Martinich, A. P. *A Hobbes Dictionary*. Oxford: Blackwell, 1995.

————. *Thomas Hobbes*. New York: St. Martin's Press, 1997.

Skinner, Quentin. "Thomas Hobbes and the Proper Signification of Liberty." *Transactions of the Royal Historical Society* 40 (1990): 121–51.

Somerville, Johann P. *Thomas Hobbes: Political Ideas in Historical Context*. New York: St. Martin's Press, 1992.

Sorell, Tom. *Hobbes*. London: Routledge & Kegan Paul, 1986.

————, ed. *The Cambridge Companion to Hobbes*. Cambridge: Cambridge University Press, 1996. (See esp. the essays by Richard Tuck, Alan Ryan, and M. M. Goldsmith.)

Tuck, Richard. *Hobbes*. Oxford: Oxford University Press, 1989.

————. "Hobbes and Locke on Toleration." In *Thomas Hobbes and Political Theory*, ed. Mary G. Dietz, pp. 153–71. Lawrence: University of Kansas, 1990.

————. "Introduction." In Thomas Hobbes, *Leviathan*, revised student edition, ed. R. Tuck. Cambridge: Cambridge University Press, 1996.

3. Locke

Ashcraft, Richard. *Locke's* Two Treatises of Government. London: Allen & Unwin, 1987.

Dunn, John. *Locke*. Oxford: Oxford University Press, 1984.

————. *The Political Thought of John Locke: An Historical Account of the*

Argument of the "Two Treatises of Government." Cambridge: Cambridge University Press, 1969.

——. "What Is Living and What Is Dead in the Political Theory of John Locke?" In *Interpreting Political Responsibility: Essays 1981–1989*, pp. 9–25. Princeton: Princeton University Press, 1990.

Farrell, Daniel M. "Coercion, Consent, and the Justification of Political Power: A New Look at Locke's Consent Claim." *Archiv für Rechts- und Sozialphilosophie* 65, 4 (1979): 521–43.

Grant, Ruth W. *Locke's Liberalism.* Chicago: University of Chicago Press, 1987.

Laslett, Peter. "Introduction." In John Locke, *Two Treatises of Government*, student edition, ed. P. Laslett, pp. 3–122. Cambridge: Cambridge University Press, 1988.

Lloyd Thomas, D. A. *Lockean Government.* London: Routledge, 1995.

Parry, Geraint. *John Locke.* London: Allen & Unwin, 1978.

Simmons, A. John. *The Lockean Theory of Rights.* Princeton: Princeton University Press, 1992.

——. *On the Edge of Anarchy: Locke, Consent, and the Limits of Society.* Princeton: Princeton University Press, 1993.

Snyder, David C. "Locke on Natural Law and Property Rights." *Canadian Journal of Philosophy* 16 (December 1986): 723–50.

Sreenivasan, Gopal. *The Limits of Lockean Rights in Property.* New York: Oxford University Press, 1995.

Tully, James. *A Discourse on Property: John Locke and His Adversaries.* Cambridge: Cambridge University Press, 1980.

——. "The Framework of Natural Rights in Locke's Analysis of Property." 1979. Reprinted in *An Approach to Political Philosophy: Locke in Context*, pp. 96–117. Cambridge: Cambridge University Press, 1993.

——. "Locke." In *The Cambridge History of Political Thought 1450–1700*, ed. J. Burns, pp. 616–52. Cambridge: Cambridge University Press, 1991.

Waldron, Jeremy. *The Right to Private Property.* Oxford: Clarendon Press, 1988. Chapter 6.

4. Rousseau

Barry, Brian. "The Public Interest." *Proceedings of the Aristotelian Society*, supplementary volume 38 (1964): 1–18.

Cohen, Joshua. "The Natural Goodness of Humanity." In *Reclaiming the History of Ethics: Essays for John Rawls*, ed. A. Reath, B. Herman, and C. Korsgaard, pp. 102–39. Cambridge: Cambridge University Press, 1997.

Dent, N. J. H. *Rousseau: An Introduction to his Psychological, Social and Political Theory.* Oxford: Basil Blackwell, 1988.

——. *A Rousseau Dictionary.* Oxford: Blackwell, 1992.

Dérathé, Robert. *Jean-Jacques Rousseau et la science politique de son temps*. Paris: Vrin, 1988 (1950).

Gauthier, David. "The Politics of Redemption." Reprinted in *Moral Dealing: Contract, Ethics, and Reason*, pp. 77–109. Ithaca, N.Y.: Cornell University Press, 1990.

Hall, John C. *Rousseau: An Introduction to His Political Thought*. Cambridge, Mass.: Schenkman, 1973.

Jones, W. T. "Rousseau's General Will and the Problem of Consent." *Journal of the History of Philosophy* 25 (January 1987): 105–30.

King, Peter. "Towards a Theory of the General Will." *History of Philosophy Quarterly* 4 (January 1987): 33–51.

Miller, James. *Rousseau: Dreamer of Democracy*. New Haven: Yale University Press, 1984.

Okin, Susan Moller. *Women In Western Political Thought*. Princeton: Princeton University Press, 1979. Chapters 5–8.

Riley, Patrick, ed. *The Cambridge Companion to Rousseau*. Cambridge: Cambridge University Press, 1999.

Shklar, Judith. *Men and Citizens: A Study in Rousseau's Social Theory*, second ed. Cambridge: Cambridge University Press, 1985.

Wokler, Robert. *Rousseau*. Oxford: Oxford University Press, 1995.

———. "Rousseau's Perfectible Libertarianism." In *The Idea of Freedom*, ed. A. Ryan, pp. 233–52. Oxford: Oxford University Press, 1979.

———. "Rousseau's Two Concepts of Liberty." In *Lives, Liberties, and the Public Good: New Essays in Political Theory for Maurice Cranston*, ed. G. Feaver and F. Rosen, pp. 61–100. London: Macmillan, 1987.

Authors

John Charvet is Reader in Political Science at the London School of Economics. He is the author of *The Social Problem in the Philosophy of Rousseau* and the recently published *The Idea of an Ethical Community*.

Joshua Cohen is Professor of Philosophy and Sloan Professor of Political Science at the Massachusetts Institute of Technology and editor of the *Boston Review*. The author of several influential papers on democratic theory, he is coauthor (with Joel Rogers) of *On Democracy, Inequity and Intervention, Rules of the Game*, and *Associations and Democracy*. He is currently writing a book on democratic theory.

David Gauthier is Distinguished Service Professor of Philosophy at the University of Pittsburgh. He is the author of *The Logic of Leviathan, Morals by Agreement, Moral Dealing: Contract, Ethics, and Reason*, and many essays on Hobbes, Hume, Rousseau, and Kant. He is at present writing a book on Rousseau's thought.

M. M. Goldsmith is Senior Lecturer in Philosophy at Victoria University, Wellington, New Zealand, and the author of *Private Vices, Public Benefits: Bernard Mandeville's Social and Political Thought* and *Hobbes's Science of Politics*.

Jean Hampton was, until her death in 1996, Professor of Philosophy at the University of Arizona. In addition to *Hobbes and the Social Contract Tradition*, she was the coauthor of *Forgiveness and Mercy* (with Jeffrie Murphy), and the author of *Political Philosophy* and *The Authority of Reason*.

Gregory S. Kavka was, before his death in 1994, Professor of Philosophy at the University of California at Irvine. Among his works are *Hobbesian Moral and Political Philosophy* and *Moral Paradoxes of Nuclear Deterrence.*

Christopher W. Morris is Professor of Philosophy at Bowling Green State University in Ohio and the author of *An Essay on the Modern State.*

Patrick Riley is Michael Oakeshott Professor of Political Philosophy at the University of Wisconsin at Madison. His numerous articles and books include *Will and Political Legitimacy, Kant's Political Philosophy, The General Will before Rousseau,* and *Leibniz's Universal Jurisprudence.* He is the editor of the forthcoming *Cambridge Companion to Rousseau.*

Arthur Ripstein is Professor of Philosophy and Law at the University of Toronto. He is the author of *Equality, Responsibility, and the Law,* as well as a number of essays on the history of political philosophy.

A. John Simmons is Commonwealth Professor of Philosophy at the University of Virginia and the author of *Moral Principles and Political Obligations, The Lockean Theory of Rights,* and *On the Edge of Anarchy: Locke, Consent, and the Limits of Society.*